Barbara Henning has composed a ̶v̶a̶l̶e̶n̶t̶i̶n̶e̶ ̶t̶o̶ ̶h̶e̶r̶ ̶m̶o̶t̶h̶e̶r̶, Ferne, whose tragic young life she recreates with loving detail and an eye for family romance. The resulting immediacy gives these American proletarian figures their due, whether in the shadow of war, death or everyday living. This memoir's fundamental power lies in breaking open memory's dam with a heart-language that makes space for what is, after all, our common lot.
Chris Tysh, *Night Scales: A Fable for Klara K*

Barbara Henning is an indomitable writer, thinker, traveler and a stalwart weaver of the threads through the heart centers and margins of her own existence. This is a daughter's complicated love story of a mother and a city and a time before we knew more than we thought to know. A poignant tribute of what haunts the premises in all the fractures and layers in the souls of America. A brilliant—and in a strange way—a most timely intervention.
Anne Waldman, *Trickster Feminism*

Henning crosses realms in an obsessed pursuit to track and recreate the intangible unknowns about her mother's life and early death. In the process, she creates a new kind of documentary novel, layering a mix of documentation, memoir and story, and thereby creating the history of a woman and of a city. We come to know and appreciate Ferne within the jazzy, jittery details of Detroit's wartime and post war life, and within the embrace of a complex family. With a poet's microscopic eye and a collagist's steady hand, Henning's search for answers creates widening rings in a pool with Ferne's premature death the stone at the center.
Kimberly Lyons, *Capella*

Ferne, a Detroit Story, by Barbara Henning, is a stunning recreation of her mother's life. Ferne Hostetter died when the author was eleven years old. The weaving together of family photos, newspaper clippings and extracts from historical sources about the 1920s through the 1950s, gives Henning's book a tremendous power, the magnetic power of lost chances. Dying young is very much circumstantial. But the losses Ferne suffered, reach into family life itself, which was under assault from the Depression, the call-ups of men to fight in World War II and, later, McCarthyism. Henning measures this assault without flinching and as a mark of her optimism, she shows how Ferne's large family manages to negotiate these buffetings. Via her interweaving of source material and invented scenes, Henning creates an empathy for the woman who looks out at us from the book while asserting her dignity, humanity and grace.
Jim Feast, *Long Day, Counting Tomorrow*

Ferne

Ferne

A Detroit Story
by Barbara Henning

SPUYTEN DUYVIL
New York City

Library of Congress Cataloging-in-Publication Data

Names: Henning, Barbara, author.
Title: Ferne : a Detroit story / by Barbara Henning.
Other titles: Ferne, a Detroit story
Description: New York City : Spuyten Duyvil, [2022] |
Identifiers: LCCN 2021048633 | ISBN 9781956005318 (paperback)
Subjects: LCSH: Hostetter, Ferne Elizabeth, 1921-1960 |
    Women--Michigan--Detroit--Biography. | Hostetter family. | Henning
    family. | Henning, Barbara,--Family. | Rheumatic heart
    disease--Patients--Biography. | Mothers and
    daughters--Michigan--Detroit--Biography. | Working
    class--Michigan--Detroit--Social life and customs--20th century. |
    Detroit--Social life and customs--20th century--Pictorial works.
Classification: LCC F574.D453 H67 2022 | DDC 977.4/34--dc23/eng/20211007
LC record available at https://lccn.loc.gov/2021048633

TABLE OF CONTENTS

for Ferne

When the air is dry
and the spores are ripe,
the cases break—

INTRODUCTION

> Just as the body is formed initially in the mother's womb,
> a person's consciousness awakens wrapped in another's consciousness.
> —MIKHAIL BAKHTIN

When I was born on October 26, 1948, in St. Joseph's Hospital in Detroit, Michigan, I was Ferne Elizabeth Hostetter's first child. For nine months my heart beat alongside her heart. I moved when she moved. I listened to the muted sounds of her voice as she talked to my father, her mother and sisters. Then, for eleven years, the dialogue that mattered most to me was with my mother. I listened to her tell stories about her childhood growing up in the city. I listened when she talked with her mother and her closest sister, my Aunt Jeane. My understanding of my existence and my ethics and values started to take shape by listening to my mother.

I remember once sitting at her feet listening while she put pin curls into my hair. She explained that her life might be cut short, she was probably going to die soon and as the oldest child I would have to take her place. On January 4, 1960, she died. I was 11 years old. As I went from being an adolescent to a teen, I kept trying to find her in my dreams and memories, to become like her, perhaps to even become her. Her old stockings with black seams and runs were in the drawer in my father's room. I took them upstairs to my room; they still smelled like her. I wore them to junior high school. I dyed my hair the same henna shade she had colored her hair. I grew up watching her cigarettes fill ashtrays, each one marked with red lipstick. As a young teenager I started smoking. Later I wore her leather fringe jacket—not as a hip, stylish woman of the 40s—but as a hippie in the 70s. When I moved into my first apartment, I painted the kitchen yellow, the same color she had painted her kitchen. When I ironed my boyfriend's shirts, it was as if I was my mother ironing my father's shirts. She was an expert seamstress, making most of our clothes, as well as making and selling drapes to the neighbors. When I left home, I bought an old Singer like hers and tried, somewhat ineptly, to make my own clothes. When I became ill in my 20s, it was as if I were my mother whose heart was failing. The doctor thought I might also have had rheumatic fever, but the skip in my heart later went away. When I gave birth to my daughter, I put on my robe and walked down the hallway. I was my mother giving birth to me. When I was in a love relationship with a man, I would at times mistakenly see him through her eyes (or through an abandoned child's eyes) as someone who wasn't doing a good enough job taking care of me. When I was 38 years old and her death date passed, I was surprised that I was still alive. Even when I became more aware of what I was doing, the emotional imprint was a constant challenge.

As a young woman, Ferne documented her life with photographs, arranging them into 20 small photo *Snaps* books. When I was young, I would pore over these photos. There she was with her Buster Brown haircut and there I was with mine. We children loved going to visit her mother, our grandmother, on Sunday afternoons, becoming part of a gathering of eight children and their families eating, laughing and playing together. In the albums, I could peek back into my mother's childhood right there in that same house. Then we'd drive home to our tract house in a nearby suburb where there were no streetcars and the world was much quieter. When I was 18 years old, I moved into an apartment on the east side of Detroit, right around the corner from where my mother had grown up.

In 1996, when my father died, my family gave me the *Snaps* books. He had locked them away for 35 years, never letting us look at them, the same way he had locked away the pain from the loss of his wife. Little by little, as I scanned the photos for my brother and sisters, I started to imagine and write about Ferne's life. But I needed to know more about Detroit during the time when she was a child and a young woman. As I was going through the albums, I came upon a photograph Ferne had taken August 20, 1939, in the alley outside her house with the notation: "Times paper boys." My grandparents had rented garage space to *The Detroit Times*. The boys would pick up papers there and start their routes. My father had also worked as a paperboy and picked up his papers from their garage.

Times paper boys

August 20, 1939

When I read about the history of the newspaper, I learned that William Randolph Hearst and his son had owned it for almost the same period that my mother had lived, 1920 to 1960. Because there were so many connections, I decided to consult this newspaper to understand what was happening in Detroit during Ferne's lifetime. I spent many days in the main library in Detroit, as well as in the state archives in Lansing, flipping through microfilm files, searching newspapers for dates that were important in her life, looking for articles about issues important to working-class women and families at the time. I tried to avoid sensational murder cases, although Hearst's papers were known for being sensational. I consulted other newspapers, books and articles. Because *The Detroit Times* is not digitally archived, *The Detroit Free Press* was where I went for articles about specific topics. I also consulted the suburban newspaper, *The South Macomb Daily,* for the 1950s.

> The Times had featured colorfully reported hometown news for the man on the assembly line. It made the greatest circulation gains during the turbulent twenties and thirties by its sensational stories of crimes and scandals. The paper was considered second to none in covering the "blood on the streets" news. Its features and advertising were geared to the lower economic strata and circulation among the growing white-collar class never became widespread. (Louis A Ferman, 10)

When I was an undergraduate at Wayne State University, I interviewed Ferne's sisters for a short biography I was writing for a women's studies class. A few resisted sharing memories.

"You are raising the dead."

"Let her rest in peace."

"She never did anything famous."

So why tell stories and imagine the life of my rather ordinary long-gone mother? Because I am still in love with her, and I want to know her as "Ferne," a woman who lived in a transformative time: born when women first got the vote, a child during Prohibition and the Great Depression, then coming into her young adult life as World War II changed everything. By writing this book, I hoped to have a better understanding of my own life and time in relation to hers and to leave a record of that understanding for the next generations.

NOTE: When newspaper clippings are from articles in *The Detroit Times*, I include only a date. Clippings from *The Detroit Free Press* are noted as "DFP" and *The South Macomb News* as "SMN." With passages from other sources, the author or title is listed and further information is in the bibliography. When I comment in response to passages, the text is italicized.

DRAMATIS PERSONAE

Ferne's father and mother:
Luke Hostetter, Sr.
Hattie Mae Grundy

Hattie's father and stepmother:
Joseph Grundy (Grandad)
Mary O'Brien

Hattie's sister:
Mary Ida Grundy
(six other siblings)

Ferne and her siblings, their spouses and children:
Luke Jr. and first wife: Rose
Catherine (Katie) and husbands: Evan and Art
    Children: Richard (Dickie)
        Barbara and husband: Robert
John and wife: Agnes
Esther and husband: Jack
    Children: John and Carol
Ward and wife: Betty
    Children: Terrance (Terry) and Bruce
Helen (died in childbirth)
Lynn and wife: Helen
    Children: Shirley, Patricia, James
Ferne and husband: Robert (Bob) Henning, Jr.
    Children: Barbara, Robert (Bobby), Virginia (Ginny) and Patricia (Patti)
    Ferne's high school boyfriend: George B
    Ferne's first husband: Robert (Rob)
    Ferne's second husband: George (Abe)
Jeane and husband: Marvel
    Children: Karen, Marvel Lynn, Linda, Denise and Diane

Robert (Bob) Henning, Jr.'s parents and their spouses and his siblings

Robert Henning, Sr. and first wife: Anna

    Children: Harold, Irwin, Fred, Florence, Elna

Robert Henning, Sr. and second wife: Virginia Dubois

    (her other husbands: George and Frederic)

    First child 1: Virginia Rose (Ginny)

        Virginia Rose's husband: Al

    Second child: Robert (Bob), Jr.

        Robert, Jr.'s wife: Ferne

            Children: Barbara, Robert (Bobby), Virginia (Ginny),
                Patricia (Patti)

Robert (Bob) Henning, Jr.'s aunt; Virginia Dubois' sister:

Aline Dubois

Henrietta (Hattie) Mae Grundy
(Ferne's mother's line)

After many generations of farming in France, in 1874, Hattie's family (the Grundys) left for Quebec and Ontario, finally moving to Grosse Isle, a city south of Detroit where her father, Joseph, worked as a farmer and fisherman: he operated a horse-drawn seine to catch whitefish and sturgeon. Every year or so his young wife, Madeline Matilda Renaud, had another child. By the time Hattie was born in 1884, her mother already had five children. Three more children followed. When they moved to Detroit in 1913, Joseph was working as a bricklayer. After that, he was an inspector for the railroad. Hattie's mother Madeline died in 1910 at 58 years old. There are no photos of Madeline. Joseph's life was well documented with many photos and news reports. He lived to be 100, dying in 1954.

Luke Hostetter, Sr.
(Ferne's father's line)

In the 17th century, Ferne's father's family (the Hostetters), moved from Switzerland to Germany to the United States, settling first in Lancaster, Pennsylvania, then Ontario Canada and finally Detroit. Luke's parents were both born in the Detroit area. Their ancestors were also farmers—Amish, Mennonite. His father was a carpenter (also named Luke) who lived for 80 years, dying in 1910. His mother, Sarah Lovenia Dains, after giving birth to eight children, lived to 75, dying in 1917. Both of their lives are documented in early photographs, and there are innumerable documents charting out the Hostetter ancestry back to the time of the Revolutionary War.

The tiny laminated birth certificate lists her name as Fern Hostetter, born at 2:30 a.m. Later Hattie will add the middle name Elizabeth, and at some point Fern and her sister Jean both added an "e" to their names: a flourish, a little decoration. My middle name is Jeane: even on my birth certificate there is an "e." Jeane always called her sister "Fernie" and my mother called Jeane "Jeanie."

CHAPTER 1

FOR THE COUNCIL

Luke Hostetter

299 FLORENCE AVENUE.

(North End)

I favor a progressive, economical business administration, full fire protection and adequate sewer facilities.

Registration day for newcomers:, Saturday, March 11. Polls open for both election and registration from 7 a. m. to 8:30 p. m.

A vote for me will be sincerely appreciated.

Election
Monday, March 13, 1916

HEMLOCK 3973-M

Highland Park swelled in population between 1910 and 1920, increasing tenfold. Families flocked to the community, drawn by well-paying manufacturing jobs at Ford's 120 acre Woodward Avenue complex. New Model T's rolled off the assembly line in mesmerizing numbers one every three minutes. In 1925, just blocks away Chrysler christened its new headquarters close to the railroad lines attracting even more residents to the bungalows and apartment complexes that lined leafy streets." (Stanton, 36)

On the 4th of November in 1921, the Hostetter family awoke to the sound of Hattie Mae moaning. The night before over a foot of snow had fallen, and Hattie was in labor with her eighth child. Her sister Ida had taken the morning train from Grosse Isle and then a streetcar from downtown. The thick snow made the trains and streetcars slower; men were out shoveling around the tracks. In the late afternoon, Ida jumped off the streetcar and ran three blocks, and was almost run over by a crazy car plowing through the snow on Hamilton Avenue.

Out of breath, she immediately sent the girls downstairs to boil water and bring up towels. Luke had gone to work in the morning. He was a city inspector and the family could not afford for him to lose a day of work. All would be well. His daughters, Esther and Katie, were home to help Ida take care of Ward and Lynn. The doctor would check in later in the afternoon. The labor was slow and not so painful during the day, but when Luke came home from work, Hattie was still moaning. At 2:30 in the morning Ferne emerged headfirst from her vagina. She made a tiny cry and then all was quiet. When she looked around the room for the first time, she saw the blurry faces of her sisters, her aunt, her father and her mother. In the morning, she blinked from the sun coming through the lace curtains. She could hear the muted sounds of her brothers and sisters excitedly coming into the room. Ward and little Lynn got into bed with Hattie, and when Lynn looked down at the baby, he said, "She has hazel eyes like mine."

BIRTH CONTROL URGED BY WOMEN

By WINIFRED VAN DUZER
Universal Service Staff Correspondent.

NEW YORK, Nov. 5.— Family limitation through birth control, will be presented for endorsement at one or more of the sessions of the disarmament conference in Washington next week.

This announcement was made today in the offices of Mrs. Margaret Sanger, pioneer limitation propagandist in this country, where a staff of workers is preparing for the first Birth Control conference ever to astonish America. It will open at the Plaza here on Nov. 11.

Nov 5, 1921

ARMY OF WOMEN MAY PICKET ARMS MEET

Thousands to Parade in Favor of Disarmament

By MILDRED MORRIS
International News Service
Staff Correspondent.

NEW YORK, Nov. 1.—Picketing of the president's armament conference by an army of women became a possibility today, with the announcement of the woman's peace society, a national organization, that it would use suffrage tactics to put through its program for complete disarmament.

WOMEN WILL END WARS, SAYS JANE ADDAMS

By Universal Service.

CHICAGO, Nov. 1.—Women will save the world from future wars in the opinion of Jane Addams who spoke before a meeting of congregational ministers.

"Through the organization of the women of every nationality future wars will be averted," she said "The women's International League represents of the flower of womanhood and the highest of civilization of every nation."

She has just returned from Europe where she was elected president of the league She said she believed the women would save the League of Nation

Nov 1, 1921

TROIT EVENING TIMES, FRIDAY, NOVEMBER 4, 1921

-ON
Kari
lache
Ger-
acial

WED AFTER COURTSHIP OF 12 HOURS, BRIDE HAS WORD "OBEY" LEFT OUT

Nov 4, 1921

Bride Gives Up Her City Job to Help Unemployed

MRS. LOUIS F. FESLER

BRIDE GIVES UP JOB TO HELP THE JOBLESS

With Husband Employed Mrs. Fesler Says She Will Manage

The first married woman to heed Mayor Couzen's request to resign city positions developed today in Mrs. Louis Frank Fesler, an employee of the department of safety engineering.

Mrs. Fesler's resignation will take effect Nov. 15. She said that she had heard the mayor's request and thought it only right to let some one who really had to earn a living take her job.

"Some of the other girls in the office who are married did not like my action," said Mrs. Fesler, "because they will feel obliged to follow suit. But I don't care—some of them are better off than my husband and I are, and we will get along all right.

"My husband is very glad to have me resign. He says that he will feel more like a "real man" when he is supporting me by his own labor. And then we both realize that I am making a place for someone who needs the opportunity to earn a living.

Nov 1, 1921

CO-ED WEARS KNICKERS TO CLASS BECAUSE THEY'RE MORE COMFORTABLE

MISS HELEN F. LYNCH

This be-knickered miss is a junior in the University of Michigan. This is her class room garb which she wears, she says, because it's convenient, comfortable and practical.

Nov 3, 1921

4

60 INSANE WOMEN FREE IN CITY, SAYS TOY

Assistant Prosecutor Acts to Have Violent Mad-Woman Confined

BOOK BARRED, MAMIE IS SET FREE

"Witnesses Fixed," Says Judge When Girls Refuse to Testify

Mamie Smith goes free! And she owes her liberty to what Judge Heston from the bench declared to be: "the best set of fixed witnesses that I have ever known."

Everyone of the four girls that the police hoped to use as witnesses against Mamie stood on their "constitutional rights" and refused to answer questions.

"They are not compelled to answer," declared Mamie's flock of lawyers in indignant chorus.

"It's contrary to the constitution

... A city or at least as much of it as could squeeze its way into Judge Heston's court—was there to learn all about Mamie's alleged brothel where the shimmy and toddle were nightly danced by her "good fellow patrons." ... A score of club women were there in the full panoply of moral armor to defeat those who were hitting it up at a livelier pace than existed the last night in Babylon.

Nov 4, 1921

Mayor Praises Married Woman Who Quit Job

By MADELYNNE MILLER

Mayor James Couzens today praised the action taken by Mrs. Louis Frank Fesler, the first married woman employed by the city to resign to make a job for an unemployed male.

"Her action will do more good than any words of mine could do. Example is what we follow after all, not words," declared the city's executive.

"As is too often the case with the utterances of men in the public eye my statements concerning the married women in city jobs have been misconstrued and misunderstood," said the mayor when asked to state his position in regard to the jobs held by married women in the city.

"Letters are being written to the press, the women's clubs are condemning me and I am receiving all kinds of criticism because I have not been clearly understood.

Do Not Need Jobs.

"It is my knowledge that married women throughout the city are holding positions when they do not need to do so. Often they retain the jobs held before they were married.

"I have been trained up in the idea that the woman's place where possible is the home, and if there is a question of whether a man or woman should be dismissed from a place if both cannot be retained, that the woman should go.

"We may be wrong. I do not know.

"I know of several cases of mar-

jobs for a few months and give employment to some of the needy."

I asked the mayor if he had any objection to women in industry. Our distinguished - looking executive pursed his lips doubtfully and strummed his fingers on his desk.

"I disapprove of women in several kinds of industry.

"Any occupation that unfits women for motherhood should be forbidden to women. The woman should be trained for the home.

"A girl may not think at the time she is engaging in dangerous work that she ever wants to marry; she works at this hard labor, and later if she marries she is unfit for motherhood."

"How would you regulate the occupations of women? Either by state supervision or by education. I prefer education, but we may have to have state supervision of anything before we can get the people educated to it. The hours of women in industry, the conditions surrounding their labor are regulated, why not their occupations?"

Women in Politics.

Women in politics was lightly touched upon by the mayor. He is a trifle reactionary in his views on this subject: in other words the women "have to show him" before he believes that they will make a success of it.

Nov 1, 1921

Ferne (1922)

Hattie, Luke Sr., Luke Jr., Katie, John, Esther (1914)

The squares in the quilt were sewn together by Hattie and her older girls. It was warm outside that day, probably early spring. Ferne is about seven or eight months old, so that would be the month of May or June. The baby is mesmerized by the world around her, like a curious puppy who stands before a puddle watching her own reflection. Who will Ferne become in a world where automobiles are becoming popular, where women can now vote and work? She may become a wife like her mother or, the fear of many women of the time, a spinster. How will Ferne live in her body? Will she see it as an object of someone else's desire? Perhaps she will gamble with her body or usher a group of children into a Sunday School. Her mother and father have no doubts; like the others in their extended family, Ferne will marry and have children.

Not quite 100 years later, in 2019, I put "299 Florence" into my GPS and drive toward the address in Highland Park where the Hostetters lived for 12 years. As I approach the address, I am shocked at the devastation. Shells of houses once lived in, now skeletons with collapsing roofs and overgrown fields with garbage everywhere, loose paper, bottles, glass, plastic, some flying in the wind, most of it heavy and sinking into the surface. I'm nervous driving through the neighborhood even with the car windows rolled up. A ghost town in the middle of Detroit. I turn the corner into another lot with two rundown houses that might be inhabited, but no sign of a car or anyone on the street. My mother lived here as a baby, born at home in a house that no longer exists; at this longitude and latitude, she crawled, sat up and listened to other children thundering in and out of the house. "Be quiet," Hattie would command in her own quiet way. Ferne's first experience with the outdoor world happened here, on this spot. None of the trees are old enough to remember, but the wind passes today as it did 97 years ago, although maybe that too is a little fiercer with global warming and the arctic ice melting.

CHAPTER 2

Fernie would curl around Hattie's growing belly as they rocked together. Sometimes she could feel the baby moving under her. When Jeane Lucille was born in 1923, Katie brought Fernie over to see her. "Be gentle," Katie said, guiding her hand softly over the baby's head and hands. "This is your new sister." When Jeane scrunched up her face and started crying, little Fernie backed away. Then she ran over to the window, looked outside at the people walking past their house and back at their dog Jo-Jo who was sticking his nose into her neck. She laughed and ran after him, from one room to another, stopping now and again to study the baby wrapped in a blanket on the couch.

Not long after Jeane was born, Luke got a new job at Burroughs, repairing adding machines. When a coworker told him about a two-story farmhouse for very reasonable rent in Algonac, close to the St. Clair River, he told Hattie about it and she begged him to say yes. She wanted to move where the air was cleaner and there weren't so many cars. "It will be much better for the children. I can garden there, Luke, and can vegetables for the winter months, and we could save more money that way, and later buy another house." Luke agreed even though this meant that he and the older children would have to commute back and forth to Detroit for work, perhaps sleeping over with relatives during the week.

With most of the family gone during the week and the older children in school, Hattie would sit on the porch with the baby and watch Fernie wandering in the yard, looking at leaves and flowers and playing with the dog. The wind from the lake would lift up Ferne's hair and then flicker through the leaves in the oak trees. For Fernie's third birthday, Hattie took some scraps of cloth out of a drawer and fashioned a little doll for her. She sewed the edges and shredded some fabric to make hair, then she embroidered the eyes, nose and mouth. She found an old red ribbon and dipped it in a bowl of warm water, scrubbed it lightly and then rinsed and hung it to dry. She cut the ends, sharpened it with a knife and rolled it into a bow that she put around the doll's neck. When she gave the doll to Ferne, she said, "Call her Maddie." Ferne carried Maddie with her everywhere; she was small enough to fit in her pocket.

Lynn, Ward, Jeane, Ferne

me Esther '1923 Elizabeth Smith

thea. Jeane. me

1.9.2.4

In the 1920s, there were articles in *The Detroit Times* about crimes associated with Prohibition. The religious right, including some suffragettes and members of the KKK, and big factory owners like Edsel Ford had gotten together with political leaders and decided to solve the problems in the family and the workplace by lobbying for laws to outlaw production and sale of alcohol. Michigan made it illegal in 1916, and then in the early 1920s the 18th Amendment made it illegal throughout the country. Soon crime syndicates formed throughout the country. Many locals didn't pay attention to the law, like those on Harsens Island across from Algonac where there were clubs and speakeasies and a burgeoning smuggling industry. Also, it was easy for people to bring alcohol across the St. Clair River from Canada. Detroit's infamous Purple Gang and Al Capone, a Chicago gangster, often hung out in the Algonac area. As people came across the river (walking on the ice or in boats) with their alcohol stash, the gang would sometimes kill them and steal the alcohol. It's no wonder that Hattie insisted Luke Sr. travel back and forth on the Interurban train with Katie, John and Luke Jr. With his presence, they would be less likely to inadvertently interact with gang members.

The electric railroad ran through New Baltimore and followed the water to Port Huron. New Baltimore's broom factory was in its heyday manufacturing some 1,800 brooms a day. Harsens Island and the St. Clair Flats were going through a "Golden Era." With its many palatial hotels and clubhouses, the Flats became known as "America's Venice." Nearby Mt. Clemens became known worldwide with the healing waters of its many bathhouses and hotels. Alan Naldrett (*The Voice News*)

POLITICAL-RUM RING HUNTED BY ST CLAIR WOMAN

Startling evidence is being gathered throughout St. Clair county in preparation for a grand jury investigation of an alleged political-bootlegging alliance. . . .the work of gathering the evidence is being done quietly. . . . The real movement are those of a grey-haired woman, mother of several children—she does not wish her name revealed at this time.. . . [B]ecause of the lack of enforcement, moonshine is being made in an average of almost every third house in Port Huron. June 4, 1923

Lake St. Clair smugglers falling through the ice

While the Hostetters were living on the outskirts of the city, the Ku Klux Klan's membership had been growing in Detroit. On Christmas Eve, 1923, the KKK burned a cross on City Hall grounds. By 1924, there were four and a half million members in the country. In that same year, a member of the KKK ran for mayor of Detroit and almost won. "The Ku Klux Klan is not merely supporting Charles Bowles, 'sticker' candidate for mayor—it is practically running Bowles' campaign" (*The Detroit Times,* Oct 26, 1924). The group wasn't organized enough to get him on the ballot in 1924 so he was a write-in; but he would have won if so many people hadn't misspelled his name as Boles.

Nov 4, 1925

As automobiles like the Ford Model T became less expensive and more people were driving, St. Clair County couldn't afford to keep the train running. In 1927, they sold the Interurban train to a private business. After four years of country living, the Hostetters had no choice but to move back to the noisy city. They took their savings and bought a house with two flats on Alter Road near Mack Avenue in Detroit. It had a three-car garage they could rent, and the streetcar stopped on the corner right in front of their house.

Today

FUTURE progress will be amazingly rapid. Discovery of radio makes it certain that other bodies in space will talk to us, as soon as they think we are worth talking to. There is probably no inter-planetary baby talk. We know that space is not "empty" between us and our neighbors in space. If it were, Newton's law would not work. Something fills the 40-odd million miles between us and Mars, and we shall talk over and through that connecting link, whatever it may be.

MISS LILLIAN KRAUS is only 19 and reporters marvel as she talks calmly of her fourth trip around the world.

Flying machines, permanently stationed six or eight miles up above the thin storm belt of our atmosphere, will sail around our earth in 24 hours. If it seems worth while to go so fast. An ambitious girl of the next century might conceivably sail around the earth 10 or 50 times in a year.

The things we shall do years hence would not be believed now. The things we do now would have seemed impious magic 100 years ago.

Nov 4, 1926

Women Voters' Booth in Downtown Store Like Bargain Counter

Women voters', interest about the Wayne County League of Women Voters' booth on the first floor of Newcomb-Endicott's store yesterday looked like a great bargain sale.

Throngs of women took advantage of the opportunity for instruction in correct ballot marking. League members in charge gave voting instructions and passed out sample ballots.

Mrs. Henry Steffens, assisted by Mrs. William Butler, Mrs. E. E. Bross, Mrs. E. L. Rice, Mrs. Guy Copley and Miss Mae Howe directed the work.

Nov 4, 1924

CHAPTER 3

Ferne (1927)

Luke with his Sunday school class

1926

1929

In 1929, Ferne's oldest sister Katie asked her parents for permission to marry her boyfriend Evan. Ferne and Jeane overheard their mother and father talking about Evan. Hattie told Luke she wasn't too happy about Evan because he seemed a bit sullen at times.

"But Katie says she loves him and, after all, Hattie, she's already 22 and this is her first boyfriend."

"Yes, dear, but I'm worried about her. She doesn't stand up for herself enough, but what can we do? We have to say yes, we have no choice."

The girls were ecstatic, especially about the party. They ran down the stairs to the basement where Katie was working on the washing.

"Katie, they said yes, they said yes!" Ferne hollered.

Katie turned to look at them, smiling. "You two go upstairs and help Ma with dinner."

On the morning of the wedding, Ferne and Jeane knocked on their mother's bedroom door. She was still sleeping. They declared that they wanted to wear their Easter dresses, but Hattie had a surprise. All week she had worked at the sewing machine making lightweight summer dresses for them. After all, it was August and very hot outside.

"You look so bee-you-ti-ful," Lynn said chasing them around the house. "Where'd you get that hat, Ferneee?"

When the guests arrived, the girls met Evan's two brothers and five sisters. The Hostetters and the Spires were big families, and they easily made a party without inviting anyone else.

"Jeanie," Ferne whispered, "did you see what's in the bathtub upstairs? Pa made beer in there! We can't tell anyone at school. That's what Ma said."

"I'm not going to tell anyone," Jeane said shaking her head.

"I don't like that tall man. What's his name?"

"Filbert, I think," Jeane said.

"He keeps grabbing me when I go by."

"He just wants to play with you, Ferne, that's all."

1924

Aug. 30, 1929

20

Ferne in front middle. Aug 30, 1929. Take note of the paperboy
standing to the side watching the family posing in the alley.

In October 1929, the stock market crashed and the children were on half
days. Everyone was worried. Some of the teachers weren't coming to school
because they weren't getting paid. John was laid off from his job in the warehouse at Burroughs, and the family living in the flat upstairs couldn't pay
their rent. Luke Jr. was out of work, too, borrowing from his father.

Luke talked to the manager of the office supply where Katie had worked
and they agreed to give Esther, his second oldest daughter, the job, but with
the crash they cut her hours. Ward was still working 15 hours a week at the
butcher counter of the supermarket, rushing to work after school let out.

He said he'd quit school if they gave him more hours, but more hours were not coming. Luke Sr.'s boss reassured him that he could depend on his job at Burroughs: they needed someone with his skill to keep fixing machines. He didn't have to worry but, then again, he didn't have income from one of the garages and from the flat upstairs. He'd have to swing the whole thing. Maybe John would find work somewhere else.

On Monday morning, Hattie walked the girls and Lynn down Mack Avenue. At Marlboro Street, she stopped and waited until Lynn crossed the avenue on his way to Jackson Intermediate.

"Come right home for lunch, Lynn. No dilly-dallying."

"I have a trumpet lesson."

"Are you sure the teacher will be there?"

"Yes, he told me he'll be there one way or the other. He likes the way I toot."

"Well, come home right after the lesson. Don't dawdle."

Hattie and the girls passed by the bank, the Piggly Wiggly, the cinema and the dime store. When they got to Coplin Street, Hattie looked down through the row of houses, porches and trees. A few years earlier the city had planted rows of elm trees along the streets on the east side and they were already growing tall and thick. Women were gathered in small circles along the street and on the porches talking as their children went ahead to the school. Everyone was trying to figure out what they would do next. Would Hoover be able to resolve this problem? How long would their husbands be out of work?

Hattie stooped down to talk to the girls. "Fernie, you hold Jeanie's hand and walk her to the front door. I'll watch you from here. Say hello and nod to your friends, but then go directly to school. Remember, I'll be waiting on the corner here for you at 12:30. Jeanie, you wait inside the school until Fernie comes for you. Do not leave the school without each other."

"Don't worry, Mama," Ferne said, taking Jeane's hand. She kissed Hattie and Jeane jumped up to kiss her too. Hattie watched their blue coats get smaller and smaller until finally they turned left and disappeared into the front door.

One night, Ferne was doing homework on the dining room table when she heard her mother talking to her father about cousin Madeline.

"I wish we could have gone to the dinner at William's. I really wanted to talk to Madeline. This idea of hers about going into the convent: it's William's idea, I'm sure. After Annie died, he pushed them into the church. My sister wouldn't have heard of it."

"There's probably not much you can do about it, Hattie. She'll do what she wants."

"She's so young. Annie would be disappointed. Luke, I tried writing a letter to her. How does this sound? . . . *Dear Madeline, I am sorry we were not able to come tonight, but I have not been well at all today, maybe the heat. But I must write you before you go. Be sure, Madeline, to act sanely, think things out as anyone should and don't act hastily. This is a large world, and I know it is not necessary for you to enter a convent. I don't think your mother would be so happy about it either. When you told me you could not write to anyone outside, I was sorry for you and for your people. Is that all you have to offer them, Madeline, for what they have done for you and the mother that brought you here? Poor mothers. If they knew the misery they were bringing on earth, just because we are too ignorant to read for ourselves and not let priests and nuns dish it out to us. Aren't you able to find things out for yourself? Don't get angry, dear. Before Wednesday, send me your address before you go. Love to you and the rest of the family. Aunt Hattie.*"

"Well, Hattie, you're trying, and it's convincing to me, but I don't think it will make any difference. She seems set on her journey."

"Fernie, are you doing your homework or are you just drawing?"

"I'm done. Ma, why doesn't Madeline want to think for herself?"

"A lot of people can't think for themselves, dear, but I know you will. Come on, let's go to bed now."

1931

Two Eggs That Beat as One

Mrs. Caroline Egg, and her daughter, Eleanor, are a great team of athletes. Miss Egg is the holder of the women's national running high jump record, while her mother is a sprinter of note. Such stunts as this is a part of their daily training programme. Mrs. Egg is holding her offspring aloft to prove that she can and does support her. Although they can accomplish feats of strength that would baffle a man, the Eggs are by no means "hard boiled."

Nov 4, 1927

---

30 COMING IN 10 DAYS FOR D.S.R.

Authorized for Woodward and Grand River; Fare to Be 10 or 15 Cents

City-owned de-luxe, 16-passenger buses will appear on Detroit's streets within 10 days to take the place of the ousted jitneys, and will afford "to those who wish to pay 10 or 15 cents for transportation all the conveniences of the jitneys and none of the inconveniences," G. Ogden Ellis, president of the Detroit Street Railway Commission, announced Saturday.

Immediately after the jitneys deserted the streets under a Supreme Court ruling shattering

Ban on Jitneys Brings Maze of Motor Traffic

One effect of the jitney ban was the crowding of streets with private autos. Many owners who usually travel downtown in street car, bus or jitney, drove their autos instead. The result was that many thoroughfares were jammed with private cars. To add to the confusion were the antics of many drivers unaccustomed to heavy traffic.

their legal status, the D. S. R. Commission met and authorized purchase of 30 of the de-luxe buses, Ellis revealed.

"The first buses will be used on Grand River and Woodward avenues," he said. "They are to be delivered by the Graham-Paige Company and the Studebaker. They are somewhat like the buses operating from the hotel districts to the Ford Airport, only more luxurious."

Ellis indicated the 30 buses, if

(Continued on Next Page, Col. 3)

Oct 27, 1928

Escapes Prison

MRS. THELMA HOLLAND
Kindness tempered justice when 22-year-old Mrs. Thelma Holland, an expectant mother, was granted three years probation after she had been given a prison sentence for possession of a liquor still. Superior Judge Walton J. Woods of Los Angeles removed the danger of Mrs. Holland's baby being born in prison when he granted her probation so she could go to her mother in Oklahoma. Application for leniency was made by Moses Davis, attorney for Mrs. Holland.

Nov 4, 1929

We're Supporting Bowles!

Mrs. Emma Fox: "I am interested in and working for the election of Charles Bowles, a clean, capable, efficient man."

Mrs. George Calvert: "Judge Bowles exemplifies those ideals for which good citizens stand. He certainly has my support and best wishes."

Mrs. Charles E. Mooney: "Any person who says I am supporting anyone other than Judge Charles Bowles has been misinformed."

Mrs. George R. Grimes: "I cannot conceive how any responsible voter can support anyone but Judge Charles Bowles in Tuesday's mayoralty election."

Mrs. E. J. MacDonough: "I am a staunch supporter of Judge Bowles, whom I admire very much."

Miss Edith M. Reubekam: "I am for Judge Bowles, and will do everything in my power to assist him and his friends to assure his election next Tuesday."

E RAIN OR SHINE...YOU SH
LET'S HAVE A CLEAN CITY

Nov 4, 1929

In 1929, Judge Bowles, the KKK candidate, ran again and this time he won the election and became mayor of Detroit. Seven months later there was a recall election with suspicion of vice and involvement in the murder of a well-known journalist who opposed him. He was removed.

When the *Detroit Free Press* and *Detroit News* became increasingly critical of his administration, Bowles responded by refusing to speak to reporters, an action that only earned him more contempt. . . . rumor that Bowles was favoring gangsters . . . *The Detroit Free Press* said Buckley [Gerald E. Buckley, a popular radio broadcaster and well-known anti-Bowles partisan] was dead because the government of the city of Detroit failed to maintain a decent check on banditry and gunmen, but allowed them to think that the town is wide open and 'easy.'"

(Dirk Langevelde)

In 1976, I visited Jeane at her house in Harper Woods. Her five children were grown, and she already had some grandchildren. She talked about my mother, Ferne, as we looked at photos.

"We were lucky Pa had a job during the Depression, Barbara. Of course, Ma would tell us that we were not as bad off as people who didn't have jobs at all. We used to get tired of putting cardboard in our shoes every day or so, but we still had fun. Ma used to tell us how the old days were better. They had more to eat. On Christmas 1932, I was nine years old and your mom was eleven. We went to Sunday school and then came home to sing hymns while Pa played the piano. Your mom loved to sing hymns. She wanted to be a Sunday school teacher like Pa. Because of the Depression, though, we only got nuts and oranges from Santa Claus. John gave Ferne a storybook, and we got underwear from our sisters. Before the Depression it was different. Once our brother Luke gave your mother a pair of roller skates. She loved them, and she would circle around and around in the backyard. And Esther bought both of us a real china doll. I broke mine the first night, but your mother still had hers when you were born. I remember it sitting on the dresser in her room. Once when we were in bed, I told Ferne how I wished Pa would quit trying to hug me. She said, 'I wish he'd try to hug me.' She and I were very close. I guess he wanted to hug me because I was the youngest one, but he scared me when he was angry."

"Hey, Ferne come on, hurry up. Let's beat the other kids to school."
    "No, slow down, Jeane. Let's go across the street to that field. I'm not going to wear long underwear under my skirt. They'll make fun of us."
    "What are we gonna do?"
    "Look here," said Ferne as she quickly revealed a pair of shears from her coat pocket."
    "Mama's sewing shears! Oh no, Ferne, you're not going to . . ."
    "Yes, I am. I'm going to cut the legs right off."
    "Papa will get us with his strap. He just bought these."
    "Don't worry."
Ferne took out the shears and cut the legs off her long underwear just above the edge of her dress. She slipped them off and threw them into the field. Then she did the same with her sister Jeane's long underwear. Spared a few laughs by fellow schoolmates, they chose to arrive home with red legs from the cold wind, only to be made red again from the lash of Pa's strap as he chased them around the dining room table.

"What did you girls do? We can't afford new underwear. Now you'll be cold this winter."

CO-ED—What makes a typical co-ed typical? Take the case of Elizabeth Woolley, 18, of Pasadena, who has been selected as the "typical co-ed" at the University of California. In her case, the following factors stand out. age 18, height 5 feet 5 inches. Age 18, height 5 feet 5 inches, hair blonde and long.

Nov 4, 1928

In late March 1930, Jeane showed up at the side of her mother's bed. "Mama," she whispered, "Fernie's sick again."

"Oh dear, just a minute, Jeanie. I'll move her out here so you can go to sleep." Hattie put on her robe and slippers and walked through the dining room into the girls' bedroom. Fernie was in bed, moaning.

Hattie put her hand on her forehead. She was burning hot.

"Is she okay, Mama?"

Hattie scooped up Ferne and carried her into the living room, laying her on the couch. In the kitchen she shaved some ice from a block and wrapped it in a cloth. She started wiping down Ferne's body. Then she laid a cold cloth on her forehead.

"My legs hurt, Mama. My legs hurt."

Two weeks earlier she had recovered from a terrible sore throat that kept her out of school for three weeks. The doctor had been to their house twice.

"Open your mouth. I want to check your temperature."

"I can't breathe, Mama."

When Hattie looked at the thermometer, she panicked. 104. She took the rest of the ice from the box and cracked it into pieces. Then she iced her body down while Fernie cried, "I'm cold. I'm so cold, Mama."

"What's going on out here?" Luke came out of the bedroom. "Fernie sick again? We'll call the doctor in the morning. Hattie do you want me to sit up with her so you can get some sleep?"

27

"No, no. You have to work. Go back to sleep, Luke."

By morning the fever had gone down a few points and the doctor was called.

When he examined Ferne, he said he thought she had rheumatic fever and would need careful bed rest for several weeks after the fever subsided. "Let's hope there's no damage to her heart." He left Hattie with some salicylate pills and wintergreen oil to apply to her joints. "It's most important to keep her quiet, lots of water and bring the fever down. She must have bed rest to minimize any heart damage."

The Marry-Go-Round
by Helen Rowland

One reason why women even self-supporting, successful women are so much more anxious to marry than men are is because they are so much WISER than men. Their intuition and their hearts tell them that a life without TIES is only half a life. And half a life is not better than none.
Oct 8, 1930

Mother of Twins Destitute, Spurned by Husband

Deserted by her husband, forbidden to enter her home town, and with nine-months-old twins to support, Mrs. Rhea Eisenhaufer, 20, found sleeping in a department store, is in the Women's Detention Home today.

The twins were born to Mrs. Eisenhaufer in Arcadia, O. A few days later her husband, Paul Eisenhaufer, 22, left her and came to live in Detroit with an aunt, Mrs. Hazel Lennen, 344 Dragoon avenue.

A month ago when her funds were exhausted the young wife put her children in the care of county officials and came to Detroit. Her husband refused to have anything to do with her. Mrs. Lennen gave her enough money to go back to Arcadia.

Her mother, who has remarried, refused to support her, and county officials refused to allow her in the town. They agreed to care for the children for a time. She got enough money to come back to Detroit.

Here, she said, her husband still refused to support her and Mrs. Lennen would not let her in the house. Her husband said he was out of work and couldn't do anything about it.

She has been sleeping in all-night movies for the last two weeks. Yesterday her funds were exhausted. She went to the shoe department of a department store and asked if she could rest awhile. She slept in a chair there for hours and, when awakened at closing time, told the store people her story.

Nov 4, 1930

ma   me

1930

me

1930

me Jean Dicky   Pat

Aug 14, 1931

Dicky   Jean   me

1931

Helene Madison sensational mermaid from Seattle Wash. clipped six seconds off the world record for 500 meters when she covered the distance in 7 minutes 12 seconds at the Detroit Yacht Cub pool Saturday night. (Apr 26 1931)

1931 (not 1932)

When Ferne and her brothers and sisters were young, they rarely saw their Grandad. Joseph Grundy had been angry at Hattie for marrying a Protestant. The family was French Catholic and he thought it should stay that way. After he retired from his job at Michigan Central Railroad, he started working at the Ford Rouge plant as a railroad car inspector. That's when he married his second wife, Mary O'Brien. When the Hostetter family came back to Detroit from Algonac, Mary convinced him that he was being pig-headed. Family is family, she said. He and Mary started coming over on Sundays, and Mary would bring along her sister Rosie. Everyone loved Rosie. She used to sing and dance and make Grandad laugh. In 1931, Mary was hit by a car and killed while crossing Michigan Avenue on her way to the grocery store. After that, Joe took a room in a hotel in Highland Park and, even though he was in his 80s, he kept working for Ford. Every Sunday one of the Hostetters would pick him up and bring him over for dinner.

The girls liked to tease him. "He keeps picking up my skirt and laughing," Jeane said to Ferne.

"Just blow through your lips making a farty sound, laugh at him, then run away. He likes you, Jeane."

⤨

One late afternoon, Ferne and Jeane were sitting at the dining room table playing cards. Hattie was doing laundry in the basement.

"Pick one card, Jeane, and don't look at it," Ferne said. "We don't know who's the old maid that way. We'll see at the end."

"I'm not going to be an old maid," Jeane said, as she picked up her cards and started laying out pairs on the table.

"You never know what's in the cards," Ferne said, putting down a pair of aces.

"I'm gonna get married like Ma, like Katie, like Esther and have a big party, too." Jeane stuck out her bottom lip.

"Maybe you will, maybe you won't," Ferne said with a sassy glint in her eyes.

Ferne laid down her last cards, a pair of jacks. Jeane was left with one card, the queen of spades, no pairing possible, just an old maid in an age when women had the vote, but in popular thought were considered pathetic if they didn't marry.

Ferne smiled, "I want to be a secretary, that is, before I get married."

Hattie pushed open the door to the kitchen carrying a basket of clothes. "You girls can help fold the towels while I make bread for dinner."

Hattie put some flour into a bowl and then added milk, baking powder and water.

"What are we having for dinner, Ma?"

"Everything stew, everything left in the icebox and sauerkraut," she said, laughing.

"I'm tired of sauerkraut. Is there any dessert?"

"A little applesauce."

"When will the root beer be ready?" Jeane asked.

"Ask Pa when he's home."

"Ferne, will you ask him?"

"Jeane, *you* can ask him, silly. While I fold, will you put our cards back in the box under the bed?"

"Fernie, you know I'm afraid of the dark in there. *Please*, you do it."

"Jeane, go to the door, close your eyes and take three steps until you feel the bed, then kneel down, pull out the box and put your cards in. It's fun to close your eyes and do something. Try it."

"No! I'm afraid. Come with me."

"Oh, grow up Jeane."

In two months Ferne would turn 12 years old. She sat at the table with one leg crossed over the other, pretending to be a teenage movie star. Then she sighed, stood up, took her sister's hand and together they went into the dark room.

There was a candle on the dresser and a lamp on the wall, but the Hostetters were frugal with candles and gas. Soon John would get his first paycheck. Burroughs had called him back to work. Things would be a little better.

The next morning when the girls woke up, Hattie was in the basement washing clothes. Both girls went into the bathroom. Ferne was brushing her teeth while Jeane combed her hair.

"My hair is so messy," Jeane said.

"You need a haircut, that's why."

"Ma can't afford it."

"Well, I can do it," Ferne said, taking a pair of scissors out of the drawer. "Can you?"

"It's easy you just clip around. Here, let me try."

When she was finished, they both looked in the mirror, horrified.

"My bangs are short on one side and long here." Tears were running down Jeane's face.

"Don't go out there, *please*," Ferne begged, holding her sister's arm.

"I have to. I wanna eat breakfast." They heard their mother in the kitchen and smelled toast.

"Put on your hat first."

"Why are you wearing that hat, Jeane?" Hattie asked. "Why are you crying?" Hattie pulled off the hat and moaned, "Where is Fernie?"

"In the bedroom," Jeane cried.

"Come here, Ferne, right now. Why did you do this?" Hattie demanded, holding some of Jeane's hair between her fingers.

"I was trying to help. She needed a haircut. We don't have money."

"Trying to help? Now we *have to pay* for a barber to fix her hair. What a mess. You are not a barber! Go to your room. Wait until your father sees this."

Hattie opened a drawer in the dresser in her bedroom, looked around for her emergency box, took some change out and marched Jeane out the door and down the block to the barber. "It's a good thing you girls don't have school today. Let's do this before your father sees you."

Ravishing Marlene Dietrich Gets High-Hat About Her Famous Legs

She Won't Show 'Em Hereafter"
by Lonella O. Parsons

You haven't seen the far-famed Marlene Dietrich's legs in still pictures or on the screen for quite a spell, have you? Marlene just up and rebelled against showing her underpinnings after several writers christened her "Legs" Dietrich. Irony of fate or perversity of human nature, call it what you will, that after Marlene's legs became the subject of song and magazine articles she refused to permit them to be shown. She felt that her career as an actress did not depend upon shapely underpinnings. Maybe she is right. July 3, 1932

IN HIS [HEARST'S] OPINION THE HOOVER administration was not only a disappointment but a miserable failure. Already the nation was approaching the second winter of Depression and conditions were worsening. "the shadow" of fear, of a growing economic downturn, one prominent historian put it, "fell over the city and towns," introducing millions of Americans to a humiliating way of life. With joblessness approaching six million, soup kitchens and bread lines signified a dismal daily existence, while Hoovervilles—makeshift shanties of boxcars and tarpaper shacks at the edge of communities sprang up, the name identifying the cynicism and bitterness of the American people toward their government." (Proctor 163) *Because of the state of the country during the Great Depression and Hoover's inability to help the country, Hearst promoted Roosevelt. Later he came out against Roosevelt, in favor of big business.*

The Hoover administration did not merely turn down the Bonus marchers. It crushed them. Federal troops attacked, using tanks, bayonets, and tear gas, and they set fire to the shacks the veterans were living in with their families. . . . Movie theaters across the country were soon showing newsreel footage of the clashes, which the narrator described as "a day of bloodshed and riot." The villain of the story was the current occupant of the White House (Adam Cohen, p. 31).

WOMEN BUILD BONUS ARMY CITY OF TENTS

by Vera Brown

CAMP BARTLETT, WASHINGTON DC. JULY 2. While women of Detroit's bonus expeditionary forces worked Saturday from dawn in the dark building a little tent city on this bare hillside, men of the peace-time army joined the thousands of veterans who massed before the Capitol today in last minute appeal to President Hoover to grant them their cash bonus.. . . The wives and mothers of Detroit's contingent worked madly trying to make the best of the few things the men had salvaged for their tent homes. Early Saturday morning the men of our Michigan division drove tent stakes in line with the hundreds of other tents from the men of many states.. . . here the women established their poor possessions and tried to make their children comfortable. Springs were salvaged from dump lines. Old automobile seats were laid to end as a foundation for beds. Boxes served as tables. . . July 3, 1932

Methodist Drys Open Onslaught on Tobacco

See Particular Evil in Smoking by Mothers; Attack 'Grape Juice'; Detroiters Comment.

THE announcement of the Methodist Episcopal board of temperance of its opposition to the use of tobacco on social and physical grounds, elicited varied comment Sunday from persons prominent in the medical, clerical and social lives of Detroit. In its weekly clipsheet, the board made a joint attack Sunday upon tobacco companies and manufacturers of grape concentrates for fermentation purposes. The board, decrying the use of tobacco, especially cigarets, made the statement that cigaret smoking, especially among young women is, in effect, not to be countenanced.

Feb 16, 1931 DFP

CO-EDS FIGHT SMOKING BAN

Frances Willard, W. C. T. U. Chief, Used Cigarets When Girl, Records Show

EVANSTON, Ill., Sept. 25—(U. P.)—Frances Willard, founder of the W. C. T. U., was once caught smoking a cigaret when a college girl, co-eds at Northwestern University declared today.

"So why can't we?" was the chorus of protest against the no smoking rules, led by Miss Jean van Evera, woman's editor of the Daily Northwestern.

"Miss Willard was just like any other girl," said Miss Van Evera. "According to the old files, a preceptress came into Miss Willard's room and saw smoke curling up from a dresser drawer. In the drawer, she found a half burned cigaret."

The co-ed editor said 85 per cent of the girls at Northwestern want smoking privileges equal to those enjoyed by men students.

"Last spring we took a straw vote," she said. "Out of 333 sorority girls who voted, 282 were for smoking. Of the 51 against it, 30 were unsophisticated freshmen who didn't know any better."

Sept 16, 1931 DFP

Unemployed, single women protesting the job placement of married women before themselves at the Emergency Relief Administration headquarters in Boston, Massachusetts.
Bettmann Archive/Getty Images

BIRTH CONTROL BILL IS URGED

Senators Hear Attacks on Present Law by Mrs. Sanger, Doctors and Clergy.

Washington, Feb. 13.—(A. P.)—Doctors, clergymen, professors and social workers packed a senate committee room to the doors today to urge passage of the Gillett bill to authorize dissemination of birth control information by physicians, hospitals, clinics, and medical schools. Opponents of the measure will be heard tomorrow.

The present law, passed in 1873, prohibiting circulation of contraceptive information, was variously termed "unfair," "unjust," "unscientific," and "obsolescent" by the eight spokesmen for the group which included Mrs. Margaret Sanger, celebrated birth control crusader. Mrs. Sanger said "the effect of this law on our statute books is to keep alive hypocrisy and evasion and increase our disregard for laws."

Rev. Charles Francis Potter, of New York, told the committee there had been a marked increase of champions of birth control among the clergy until now they "number thousands."

Feb 14, 1931 DFP

In 1936, only 15 percent of respondents to a poll in *Fortune Magazine* asking "Do you believe that women should have a full-time job outside the home?" answered, yes. "Simply fire the women who shouldn't be working anyway, and hire the men" wrote journalist Norman Cousins in 1939. "Presto! No unemployment. No relief rolls. No depression." His facetious words reflected how controversial working women were even after Section 213's repeal. (Erin Blakemore)

A few weeks after her twelfth birthday, Ferne started her period. Hattie came into the bathroom with some bulky old rags and one of Luke's belts. She pinned the rag to the belt. Then she told Ferne not to talk to anyone about it, that it would happen every month. "No need for tears, dear. It means you are a woman and you can have babies."

At night Ferne showed Jeane the rag and how she had to wear Pa's belt, and she told her how embarrassed she was walking around with that rag on. "And it will happen to you, too, every month, Jeane. And Pa knows! I can tell by the way he looked at me. And Grandad, too. He made a face at me when he was here yesterday. Why did Ma tell them? How can I go to school wearing this?"

The next morning, Hattie brought her a clean rag and showed her how to wash the blood out of the old one. "Leave it to soak in this bucket in the basement. Then tonight you'll scrub it and wring it out and hang it up. Your bellyache will only last a few days. Don't worry, Ferne. It's normal."

One day when school let out, Ferne walked west on Mack Avenue three or four blocks until she met up with Jeane who was still in elementary school. Jeane was walking with her friend Shirley. The three girls walked together for one block and then Shirley said goodbye and walked down Lakewood toward her home. Jeane and Ferne continued.

"So what happened? You didn't come down to the playground at lunch time?" Jeane asked.

"Mrs. Snyder took three of us who were her best students to the art museum. It's so beautiful there, Jeane, like a gorgeous church. When we walked down the halls, the sounds of our laughter made an echo. Mrs. Snyder was always shushing us to be quiet."

"Did you get to see those gigantic paintings Pa was talking about?"

"Yes, we stopped in the hallway and watched the man on a ladder painting on the walls. He's from Mexico, Mrs. Snyder said."

"What was he painting?"

"Some men leaning together in a big factory."

"Anything else? Did you see anything else?"

"Yes, when we were leaving, we stopped again to look. He was standing on the ground then. And . . . he was kissing a woman."

"Kissing a woman? Right there?"

"Yes, and the kids started giggling . . . and I saw a painting of a baby curled up in a circle. I wish I could have gotten closer to look at it."

"Pa says he's a communist. And because of communists those people were killed at the Ford factory."

"Well Grampa says the people at Ford's just wanted better pay and more work. People are hungry and some people are starving. And Ford's men killed some of the protestors! They shot right into the crowd. And Jeane, Grampa knows because he works there. I heard Ma telling Pa last night that a family on the next block can't afford coal so they are burning parts of their house in the fireplace just to keep warm. Ma says we are lucky and we should be thankful . . . I want to go back to the museum. I could take the streetcar if I could get ten cents."

"Ma would never let you go, Ferne. She said it's dangerous with so many people out of work."

"Come on, let's run home. Katie's going to be at the house and she said we could take Dickie out for a walk in the stroller."

JAIL 40 FORD RIOTERS

FACE MURDER CHARGES IN 4 DEATHS

Reds Led Hunger Marchers Toy Starts Sweeping Probe; 58 Hurt in Fight

Page of Riot Pictures, Page 11

Casualties in the Ford riot of the Rouge stood at four dead, 19 recovering from gunshot wounds, and about 35 nursing broken heads today, as Prosecutor Harry S. Toy considered placing criminal syndicalism charges before the grand jury.

The battle was fought over a half-mile front, paralleling the main entrances to the Ford River Rouge plant in Dearborn. About 4,000 Communist-led unemployed, armed with stones and brickbats, battled police, who used

March 8, 1932

This article is a perfect example of how Hearst's paper abandoned the working class and began to promote paranoia, calling all union members and protestors communists. The Detroit Free Press reports: "The marchers were heterogeneous. All were not Communists, although faces of familiar agitators were in the ranks. In line were known radicals, habitual demonstrators, former Ford workers, professional paraders, and jobless, hoping somehow to obtain work by parading. . . . about 1,200 were on hand—hundreds of them women . . . They marched singing." *Then the Dearborn police used tear gas and the non-violent crowd started fighting back. Later when the historical eye and ear tell the story, we learn that Ford's security force together with the Dearborn Police opened fire on the crowd. The Detroit police stood by because it was for the most part a non-violent protest that was antagonized* (See Tom Stanton; and Detroit Free Press Mar 8, 1932)

Marry-Go-Round

by Helen Rowland

Big Butter-and-Egg Women. The most amusing and certainly the most consoling aspect of women's economic freedom today is the existence of the "Big Butter-and-Egg-Women"—a brand new type of femininity. . . . It used to be always the GIRL who was regarded as "lucky" when she landed a husband who had made good in the world. . . . But it is only since the advent of women's economic independence that a girl could be a "good catch" on her own money. Nov 4, 1932

Roosevelt Will Make Great President, Garner Splendid Aide, Says W. R. Hearst

G OVERNOR ROOSEVELT, more-
over, in both of his terms has
had the handicap of a very partisan
Republican Legislature, unwilling to
advance his claims to political promo-
tion, but yet unable to oppose the
Roosevelt measures, so plainly popular
and so clearly for the general good.

July 3, 1932

Curls Are in Season Again
Curly Hair No Longer a Gift of Gods

Curls distinguish the fashionable coiffure this season. Wherever smart women assemble, you'll see curls massed high at the back of the head, fluffed over the ears or in the form of wavers and swirls. Even bangs have been revived with slightly curled ends.. . . Not even an expert can distinguish synthetic waves form natures own handiwork these days, permanent waving is done so skillfully. Nov 4, 1932

HINDENBURG YIELDS TO FASCIST

Berlin (INS). Adolf Hitler.. . . who began life as a house painter and street sweeper achieved his life's ambition today when he was appointed chancellor of the Reich . . . the sweep of the Nazi movement as a means of ending the nation's latest political impasse. Jan 30, 1933

500 STRIKERS ATTACK MAN; ARREST 10

Three Girls jailed as 2,000 Picket Plant Guarded by Cordon of 250 Police. Striking workers picketed the Highland Park plant of Briggs Manufacturing today stoned a man who, they said, was seeking employment . . . He was rescued by state police. . . . Earlier in the day, 10 persons, including three young women were taken into custody . . . as the strikers reunited their mass picketing to prevent re-employment of workers to replace those who walked out on January 22.   Jan 30, 1933

20 MILLION IN GOLD ARRIVES; MAY CASH CHECKS IN 48 HOURS

Feb 14, 1933

Nov 4, 1933

People milling about outside of a bank that closed, ca. 1933.
National Archives photo.

Ferne was weak and her throat was sore; she could barely swallow. "Ma, I wanna go to school," she said.

"There's no school today, look at the snow outside. Besides you're too sick to go to school. I'm going to take you to the doctor. Get dressed, dear."

"It's cold in here."

"You're cold mostly because of the fever. The coal has to last us for another month. Put on this extra pair of long underwear. Doctor Matthews is meeting us at his office."

They slushed through the snow for six blocks, sometimes walking in the middle of the street where the trolley had cleared some space.

Dr. Matthews looked into Ferne's mouth and at her throat. "I don't think it is strep this time, Mrs. Hostetter. She has a slight fever though."

"I wanna go to school tomorrow," she whispered to the doctor.

"It's good, Ferne, that you like school, but it's important you get better. Keep her home, Mrs. Hostetter, until she's completely better: bed rest, lots of fluids. Give her the salicylate tablets. Her glands are a little swollen. Make some tea, dandelion if you have it, saltwater gargle. If you have some whiskey and honey, that might help."

"Jeane had it last week, but she's much better."

"Are they still sleeping in the same bed?"

"Yes."

"You must keep them apart now, Mrs. Hostetter. That's very important."

"I'll try, doctor. We have a lot of people in the house and only three bedrooms."

He listened to Ferne's heart. "Yes, there's the murmur . . . and your heart is beating a little fast. We're lucky so far that you haven't had any more incidents. Again, keep her very quiet, Mrs. Hostetter, away from the others, in bed until this passes."

Hattie held out her hand with two dimes. "This is all I have."

The doctor looked at her and shook his head. "Don't worry about it now. After the banks reopen, pay me then."

She put the change into her purse, took the tablets and, on the way home, they stopped at the grocery store to pick up a bottle of milk.

A few weeks earlier, to stop the public from panicking and withdrawing all their money, Governor Comstock had closed all the banks in Michigan. Then Roosevelt closed down banks all over the country. Like everyone else in the country, the Hostetters were waiting for theirs to reopen. "Sit tight" was the advice from the public officials. In the morning some men came to the bank on the corner, took down the sign for People's County Bank and then put up another sign: National Bank of Detroit. Two days before the shutdown, Luke, Lynn and Ward had gone to the bank to take out their savings, but they were only given a fraction. Luke got only $50. And he couldn't cash the checks from Burroughs. Many people, especially those who had migrated to Detroit for work, were now starving, and some were homeless, freezing in the cold. Fortunately, in the cellar the Hostetters had many jars of canned fruit, vegetables, pickles and sauerkraut. In the back of the house, Luke had installed an icehouse where he sold ice to the neighbors. The iceman was able to give him ice on credit, and the nickels and dimes he took in helped the family survive for the month. The banks were closed from February 14 to March 24, 1933.

Prohibition was defeated in 1933, and by 1935 the economy had somewhat improved. Ferne got a babysitting job for a Grosse Pointe lawyer whose wife had died. After school she would walk his two children home and prepare dinner for the family. After a while, she had saved up money to buy fabric to make dresses, coats and jackets. At school the girls were passing patterns back and forth to each other. Ferne was now at the sewing machine more than Hattie.

1933

One afternoon in the end of May, Jeane and Ferne met at their lockers.

"Jeanie, come on, let's get home quick," Ferne said. "I'm glad this is my last year here. Just think, I'm going to high school in September."

"Why are you acting so happy? What about me, Fernie? I'll be here alone. I can't wait to get old enough to get a job, do what I want and get away from Pa."

"He's not that bad, Jeane. You should just avoid him."

45

"Jeez, look how your breasts bounce up and down on your books when you run down the stairs."

"They're an inconvenience," Ferne said, jiggling her shoulders so they bounced a little more.

"I wish I had that inconvenience. Why don't you throw them over your shoulder?"

Full of laughter, the two sisters burst into the spring air, arm in arm.

Ferne's junior high school class.
She's in the top row, third from the left.

SECRETARY PERKINS

REVEALS PLANS TO INCREASE SALARIES

Universal Service Wire

NEW YORK, March 25.—Frances Perkins, secretary of labor and first woman cabinet member, made a pledge of service to the wage earners of America last night. She spoke at a dinner given in her honor at the Commodore Hotel, at which a dozen speakers, including Mrs. Franklin D. Roosevelt, sang her praises as an able leader.

Her deep voice forceful, her words tumbling over each other in her enthusiasm and sincerity, Miss Perkins concluded her extemporaneous speech with a statement which was greeted by a 10-minute ovation by the 1,200 guests:

"We in America are recognizing as we never did before that in the leisure of the workers and in the purchasing power of the workers lies the safety of the merchants, the safety of the manufacturers, and I think in the long run, the safety of the financial institutions of the nation."

OUTLINES PLANS

"Madam Secretary" got down to brass tacks at the end of her speech, and outlined her plans for expansion of the department of labor. She said:

Mar 25, 1933

CHAPEAUX TAKE MANY CHIC TURNS

By Minnie Cage

THE SPICE that, according to the saying, is to be found in variety has been added to women's lives this season by the many different styles and shapes of hats from which to choose. Glancing back to a few seasons ago when every woman wore a cloche we cannot understand how we all managed to endure the monotony.

We were musing on this Friday morning at the Cass Town Hall lecture as we watched the many smartly dressed women promenading through the foyer of the theater.

Along came Mrs. John H. French wearing a modish little pill box hat of black hatter's plush trimmed with a tiny red feather on the left side. She was enveloped in black broadtail and silver fox. Her broadtail coat reached to the bottom of her dress and had a wide collar of the silver fox.

Nov 4, 1934

In her ninth grade school photo at Andrew Jackson Intermediate School, Ferne looks like an innocent young girl. Then in another photo taken later in the school year (1935, not 1933), her felt hat is tipped to the side, her lips lined with lipstick, eyes sharpened with mascara: vampy or modest, both possible.

So quickly a child grows into a woman. Snazzy haircut with tight curls, wearing a long checkered cotton dress with big lapels, a bracelet on each wrist, slinky, a little curve to her hips. She looked down at Katie's baby, Barbara, who had just started walking and was pushing her wagon. Hattie stood between her daughter-in-law Rose and Ferne. Long lines that run through the images remind us that this is not reality. It's the imprint of a moment, a moment one month before Ferne started high school.

Luke's wife Rose, Hattie, Ferne and
Katie's daughter Barbara

CHAPTER 4

MR. ROOSEVELT CALLS YOUTH TO AID NEW ORDER

Roosevelt said he and his associates were denounced as 'reformers socialists and wildmen" when they advocated factory regulation laws in the New York Legislature 24 years ago. . . . In the olden days a great financial fortune was too often the goal.. . .The newer generation of America has a different dream. You place emphasis on sufficiency of life, rather than on a plethora of riches." Aug 25, 1935

Joe Louis Knows Rights as Citizen

Joe Louis knows his constitutional rights. When he registered to vote Saturday he was asked if he was a Republican or Democrat.

"I ain't talking about things like that when my lawyer ain't around," Joe replied.

The Brown Bomber was 21 on May 13.

Aug 25 1935

"Joe Louis was one of the greatest fighters of all time. But more than that, he was an icon of his time. After his father died, Louis's mother remarried and the family moved to Detroit, settling in Black Bottom. Louis attended vocational schools and took boxing lessons at Brewster recreational center. Heavyweight boxing champion, Louis was Black Bottom's favorite son." (Williams 102).

Cardinal Replies on Birth Control

Hayes Declares That 'Case Is Closed'

NEW YORK, Dec. 8—(A. P.)— In a blistering attack on birth control advocates, Patrick Cardinal Hayes today described them as "prophets of decadence" and declared that so far as Catholics are concerned "the case is closed."

Cardinal Hayes, in a sermon at St. Patrick's Cathedral, answered the recent demand of the American Birth Control League that contraceptive information be provided for mothers of families on relief. Rabbi Sidney E. Goldstein challenged the Catholic Church to withdraw its opposition.

"For the preservation of the race God has given man the natural faculty of reproducing his kind, the Cardinal said. "The exercise of this faculty for pleasure alone, with the natural result prevented by artificial means, is a perversion of this faculty, and he who does so is as the liar, the glutton and the drunkard.

"He misuses a gift of God, he offends against nature, and so performs an act which is condemned by God and his church, and which nothing can make right."

Holding that at the League's Carnegie Hall meeting last Monday the Catholic Church's position on birth control was misrepresented, Cardinal Hayes said:

"Who are these people that sit in soft garments and offer affront to the poor? Are they taking over from the poor the responsibilities of motherhood? You know that they are not."

The solution of the problem, the Cardinal added, was self discipline.

"Prenuptial virtue," he said, "is the key to marital chastity."

Dec 9, 1935 DFP

BLACK CULT SUSPECTED IN SCORES OF KILLINGS. State and city police joined today by a state-wide investigation of scores of mysterious deaths, including supposed hit-run accidents which they believe may have been killings done by the Black Legion, night-riding band accused of the murder of Charles Poole. Capt. Ira Marmon acting commander of the state police, said two members of the Black Legion told him at least 50 persons in the state were marked for death by the organization's killers. "Every case of mysterious death in the state will be investigated," Marmon said. "We believe a number of hit-run auto deaths and supposed suicides may turn out to be Black Legion murders. May 24, 1936

Cult Passwords Told By Jailed Members

Two passwords were used by members of the Black Legion, members revealed Saturday in detailing the crusades of the band in bringing erring husbands to "justice" that finally resulted in the murder of Charles A. Poole, a WPA worker.

The passwords, "Deeetroit" and "Secrecy Always," were given by Herschl Gill, 31, of 1467 Lansing avenue, and Urban Lipps, 22, of 4800 Commonwealth avenue.

Gill, a childhood friend of Rebecca Booker Poole, widow of the slain man, is one of nine held by police for investigation. Lipps is one of seven for whom murder warrants are expected to be asked. He accompanied Poole on the fatal ride to Gulley road in Dearborn.

BOASTS OF "CRUSADE"

Gill blandly waved aside the atrocious murder, boasting of the Black Legion's fight for "clean politics."

"We were banded together to help each other and to do good generally," he said.

"We don't always use the password at meetings and I have never seen any of the fellows wear robes at meetings," he said.

Gill said Harvey Davis (Colonel of the Black Legion) asked him to join after he met Davis through a cousin when he was driving a truck.

"I signed a pledge that I was born a Protestant and would fight for good government. As I understood it, we had to be good, right-living citizens to belong. I never knew of the club as the Black Legion although I had heard about that band."

Gill said the first time he ever saw the black robes was for "a death procession of the "Black Legion" interrupted last August in a plot in which police said Albert Bates, Ford Motor Company employe, was to be the victim.

Lipps, who said the password was "Secrecy always" and the pass sign was "To wave anything three times," said he "had to kneel, while a man held a gun at my heart and made me answer something after him."

Lipps admitted he was the man who walked into a beer garden at West Fort street and McKinstry avenue to get Poole to go to a "baseball party" the night of the fatal ride. Poole, he said, road in the car alongside of him, asked about the "party" but "that was all."

May 24, 1936

When Ferne heard Mr. Mugridge opening the door, she stood up from the dining room table and put on her coat. Then the phone rang.

"Ferne, stay with the children for a minute while I take this call."

She shushed the children while listening.

"Yes, I am attorney Mugridge. What can I do for you, Mrs. Poole?. . . You're the wife of the man in the news? I'm so sorry. . . . There are three of you and all of you are widowed? Hazen Branch's wife, too? . . . Some people have donated money to help you? And now you want to sue Mayor Markland of Highland Park and the police force? Is there a criminal case against them?... Yes, I agree they are clearly guilty of being involved, but what evidence do you have? . . . Yes, all of you are in need of support. It was very brutal what happened to your husbands . . . . I'm very sorry again Mrs. Poole and I'm glad Marjorie sent you to me, but Mrs. Poole, this is not the law I practice. I mostly work with divorces and mortgages. Give me your number and I'll do some research to see if I can find someone who might be able to help you . . . . I understand you are frightened. Please be careful. Perhaps you should go with your daughters and move back to Tennessee permanently. I'm concerned that your case will never be heard here, given the situation in the city. Maybe that money would be better used to help you feed your children.... Good day, m'am. Yes, I'll get back to you. Goodbye."

Henry Mugridge took off his hat and his coat and hung it in the hallway closet.

"Thank you Ferne," he said, handing her a dollar. "The children have a half day tomorrow. Is it possible you can pick them up, or should I have my sister come by?"

"I'm in school until 2 p.m., but on my way home I could pick them up at your sister's."

When Ferne arrived home, Jeane, Ma and Pa were sitting at the table eating dinner. She went into the kitchen, took the lid off a pot of stew and served herself.

"Why were you late?" Luke asked.

"Mr. Mugridge was late. Then he got a phone call. One of the women whose husband was killed by that Black Legion group wanted his help, but he can't help them. He talked on the phone with her for a while. And I heard him tell her to leave town to protect herself."

Luke shook his head as he pushed his plate into the center of the table. "Shocking, even the police commissioner and the mayor of Highland Park seem to be involved. And some of Ford's security, too. They have cells around the Ford Rouge plant and also in Highland Park. I heard that thousands of people are members. Many of them joined because they were afraid not to. Now that Prohibition is over, we thought the violence would stop, but no, these hate-mongering men think they have the right to organize and kill people. I read that fifty-some people have been killed. You girls stay clear of anyone who talks like this."

"I hope Grampa's okay," Jeane said.

"Don't worry, Jeanie," Hattie said. "Grampa's old, so they'll leave him alone."

"Hattie," Luke said, "did you read how they tried to force one man to leave his wife because she was born into a Catholic family. We had enough trouble with that when I was running for council in Highland Park. You girls never knew this, but that's part of the reason we left Highland Park."

Hattie stood up and started clearing the table. "Jeane, help me with the dishes and be sure you leave Lynn a bowl of stew. Then finish your homework." She stood there by the table for a minute and looked at everyone. "Remember, girls, Jesus taught us to take care of the poor. Everyone is his child."

"Those men have been mostly killing their own kind," Luke said, shaking his head. Then he poured himself a glass of beer and sat down at the piano and started singing *Amazing Grace*. Ferne joined him. That was one of her favorite hymns and she loved to sing.

Ferne's father let her keep 25 percent of her babysitting money. She saved most of it to buy material to make clothes for herself and for Jeane, too. Once she took apart an old dress of her mother's and used it as a pattern to make new dresses for her. She loved looking through fashion pages in the newspaper.

In the three years they were married, Charles A. Poole, murdered WPA worker, never laid a hand on her, Mrs. Rebecca Poole, his widow, said Saturday. "Everything is going crazy," Mrs Poole cried. "It's a lie! Charles never harmed me." . . .

"First they [the Black Legion] murder Charles and after he's dead they say he beat me and that's why they did it," Mrs. Poole cried. "It's not true. He was a wonderful husband." "Justice for those men will come from the hand of God. . . .

"We had occasional arguments, of course, but never anything serious. He helped with the housework and we planned for the baby that was coming. We had heard of some secret organization but never paid any attention. Charles never was interested in any club or organization."

. . . Harvey Burte of 6660 Appoline Avenue, Poole's uncle, said he believed Poole was killed because he would not take the "Black Legion" oath of office. "Charles never beat Rebecca, of course," he said. "They never had any trouble. He just wouldn't join that bunch and they killed him." May 24, 1936

School was out, and on the first warm day, Gerry and Ferne put on the bathing suits they had recently made from scraps of material. They looked at each other in the mirror.

Ferne said, "I'm going to take Lynn's Kodak with us to Belle Isle. There's some film in it, too. He won't mind if we take a few snaps on the roll."

At fifteen years old, their bodies were already womanly. And when they walked, they walked the way movie stars walked in the films they had seen at the Uptown and Cinderella Theaters, strutting and swinging their hips. As they slid into their seats, on the Jefferson streetcar, a couple of young men scanned their bodies up and down, gawking and cat calling. They both smoothed their skirts over their knees and looked at each other.

"Aren't they disgusting," Ferne said. "Isn't that the guy in our history class? You know, he sits in the back row and comes in late all the time."

"Yes, that's Dave Dawson. I'm going to tell his sister how he behaves."

The boys were looking right at Ferne's chest so she turned her back on them.

"I love your sandals, Fernie. Where did you get them?"

"Katie wore them last year and she left them in the closet. One had a broken strap. I sewed it together, polished them. Vavoom." She crossed one leg over the other.

Then the driver yelled out, "Belle Isle," and they went out the back door, and began their walk across the bridge, past the casino and over to the other side of the park. After swimming and photographing each other, they lay together on a blanket, their hair frayed and their bodies drying in the sun.

July 15, 1936

BROAD STOCKS BOOM TRAILS LANDSLIDE

By George R. Holmes
Int'l News Service Staff Correspondent

NEW YORK, Nov. 4. — The Roosevelt landslide continued to expand today as belated returns put all but two states—Maine and Vermont—in the Democratic column, giving the New Deal a fresh vote of confidence from the electorate such as no government in American history ever enjoyed. With him 29 Democratic governors were swept into office and the next congress will have one of the greatest Democratic majorities in history.

. . . Then like a house of cards, the whole Republican structure erected by dint of so much effort and expenditure of so much money, fell apart. State after state fell into the Democratic column. . . . President Roosevelt carried every principal large city in the country and yet it was no city victory over the rural regions for they, too, went overwhelmingly Democratic. . . Just where this political holocaust leaves the Republican Party of the future is something that will be debated at great length in months to come.

Nov 4, 1936

Sandals Come In White or Colors

By Joan Dean

IT'S all very well to have hot feet in the Winter, when you're dancing to the strains of a swing orchestra. But in Summer, nothing raises your temperature and your temper like hot shoes. If you need another pair of air-cooled sandals—and nothing keeps you cool like changing your shoes frequently —look at the pair shown today.

* * *

MADE of an excellent quality of white kid, these sandals provide their own air-cooling system. Smartly cut-out, their open shanks also serve to make your foot look INCHES shorter. And of course the low heels are fashionable—and correct with all informal Summer clothes.

* * *

Pa Pat ma

Sept 12, 1936

Ferne woke up tired. Everyone had been up late the night before listening to the radio for returns on the election. School was closed, and Ferne had to get dressed quickly and make it over to the Mugridge house. He had an appointment this morning that he couldn't cancel.

On her way out the back door and down the steps, she stopped on the bottom step, as their dog Pat came tearing through the yard with a yellow cat perched on his back, her nails digging into his skin. He crawled under the steps, scraping the cat off his back. Pat was whimpering under the porch. Ferne knelt down to see if he was okay, and a paper boy who had just arrived to pick up his papers, knelt down beside her.

"That cat was teasing your dog," he said. "He'll be okay. The same thing happened yesterday morning. I think it's a game they're playing."

When Ferne stood up, she brushed off her jacket and said, "How are you, Bob? I haven't seen you or your sister in a while. Does she have a job or something?"

"Ginny's fine. She's got a job as a receptionist in a doctor's office on Kercheval. Your dad's selling more than ice, eh? "

"Yeah, they're selling bottles of beer, too. They keep it in the icehouse. Did I tell you that I have a job nearby your house, babysitting for a lawyer."

"That's good. I have two paper routes now. I'm hardly ever home. I just bought this one for five dollars, bike included. It's pretty rickety though. Gotta go... See you later."

Bob headed down Alter and over toward Wayburn yelling, "Paper. Get the morning *Times*! Roosevelt sweeps in! Dems win! Get your *Times*!" As he pedaled, the lights came on in some of the houses on the block. He hopped off his bike and dropped it to deliver the paper to their front doors.

Later in the afternoon Ferne and Jeane put on their fall coats and hats and waited for the streetcar to back up onto Alter Rd, in front of their house, the first stop or the last stop depending on which direction you were traveling. They got on the train. It turned left on Mack Avenue and took them downtown to Crowley's where they shopped for fabric and looked at stylish hats they couldn't afford. As the train passed, they saw Bob Henning walking his bike out of their yard. All his papers were gone and he had a block of ice on the back of his bike.

Ferne put two fingers in her mouth and whistled. He looked up, smiled and waved back.

Nov 4, 1936

Lynn's band

John's wife Aggy, Lynn and Ferne

Ferne with Esther's son, Johnny

On a late afternoon in May when the leaves from the elm trees were light green, Ferne was sitting on the porch with her sisters and brothers. John and Aggy had just gotten married and they were now living in the flat upstairs. The group was talking about the new jazz quartet Lynn had joined and the gig he had later that night at Café Madrid, downtown in the Lafayette Building.

"Fernie, do you want to come with us?" Lynn asked. "You've never been to anything like this. You're old enough now. You'd like it."

"I want to go, *too!*" Jeane yelled and stamped her foot on the step where she was sitting.

"I want to," Ferne said, "but Ma will *never* let me go. I'm only sixteen."

"You're almost sixteen," Jeane corrected her.

"It's a dinner club. You look old enough," Aggy said. "I don't think the club people would check her, do you, John?"

"No, they rarely check anyone there. And Fernie, you look much more mature than your friends."

Suddenly the door swung open and Hattie walked out onto the porch with her arms crossed in front of her. She had overheard them talking. "What are you trying to do, Lynn? Ferne is too young for this."

"Ma, look at her. She can pass. Ferne's got a head on her shoulders, too. She's not gonna do anything out of order, especially with all of us there," John argued. "Don't you think?"

"I want to go too," Jeane said again.

Hattie sighed. "Absolutely not, Jeane. I said okay for you to work in the sweet shop after school, but that's all for now."

"I want to hear Lynn's band, Ma! It's not fair."

Lynn stood up.

"Sorry Jeane, there is no way you can go this time," Hattie said. "You look too young. They'll never let you in. Ferne can go but, Lynn and John, you better look after her. No drinking. And bring her home directly afterward."

Ferne had stayed quiet, waiting and hoping.

"That's settled," John said, standing up with his camera. "Before you go into the house and before the sun goes down, let me take a photo. Ferne, you stand over there and Lynn, you get between Ferne and Aggy." Ferne crossed her arms with her breasts resting on her forearms, her dress folding around her legs. Then Ferne took the next photo. She looked through the viewfinder to catch Jeane in her checkered dress leaning against John.

A few hours later, Lynn was driving and talking to John in the passenger seat. "I heard there's gonna be a knockout singer at Cosy Corner tonight, a gal from the east side. After our last set, we can shoot over there and maybe we'll catch the last few numbers."

"I think we should go right back. Ma will have a fit," Ferne said.

"She won't care. We won't be that late. You don't have school tomorrow, kiddo."

Aggy put her arm around Ferne. "I'm so proud of you, Fernie. You made the honor roll. Maybe you'll go to college."

"It was easy this year—shorthand, typing, business English. I wanted to go to college to be a teacher, but no chance of that. They put me on the secretarial track. Something Dad said to Mrs. Murphy about skills for working."

"I'm sorry, but a secretary is fine. You're going to be the first in your family to graduate from high school. That's something."

"It's okay," Ferne said. "We don't have enough money for college anyhow and teachers' pay is getting cut all the time."

On the way home, Ferne was curled up in the back seat, tired from dancing with her brothers. She had her feet in Aggy's lap.

"Aggy. I'm worried about Katie. Did you see the bruise on her arm last week? I don't think Evan is treating her right."

"I saw it, too. I'm worried. They don't seem happy together."

"I hope you had a good time, Fernie," Lynn said. "You sure did dance it up at the Sixes. The cats were dizzy watching you."

She laughed. "I like how negroes and whites are together in that place."

"Yeah, and a white drummer sat in for the last number. That was a surprise. That group was dynamite."

In the thirties, jazz music clubs in Black Bottom were very popular and in some of the clubs (called Black and Tans), blacks and whites mingled and danced together. But most of Detroit was segregated. The Hostetters lived just two blocks from the east side border of Detroit and Grosse Pointe Park in a white working-class neighborhood; the schools the children attended were all white. When Ferne's father and mother were growing up, very few African Americans lived in Detroit, less than two percent. When Ford started producing the Model T on an assembly line in 1914, he sent an announcement all over the country saying he would pay workers $5.00 a day. He couldn't produce the cars fast enough. People flooded into the city. For many, especially the poor and unemployed, Black and white, foreign and native, this was a decent wage, decent enough to migrate to Detroit. Unfortunately, more people arrived than the auto industry could hire and there wasn't enough housing; and blacks suffered additionally because they were segregated into a few crowded areas. When the Depression hit, there were many layoffs; and the poverty was much worse for blacks who had already been given the lowest paying jobs and charged the highest rents, mostly for crowded ramshackle housing.

As Ferne and Jeane traveled on the streetcars, they would see blacks coming and going. And as they headed downtown on the Mack Avenue streetcar when they passed through Black Bottom, the girls would look into the neighborhood wondering how different their family life might be from the lives of these darker-skinned people. Sometimes one of their friends would say something disparaging about blacks, but never in the Hostetter household. Hattie wouldn't hear of it. She and Luke had raised their children to recognize everyone as children of Jesus.

Harold Dumas + Gerry

May 19, 1937

Lynn + Agnes
July 10, 1937
St. Joe, Mich.

Lynn and John's wife, Aggy

Sept 12, 1937

Katie, Evan, Barbara and Dickie

Woe to Girls Who Scorn The Advice of Parents

by Irene M. Hawkins
Women's Editor, The Detroit Times

Dear Hostess of the Open Door: I have been married a year and am very unhappy. I married against the wishes of my parents. They warned me many times that we would not get along. Because I had known him for three years and I thought I knew all there was to know about him. So they relented and gave me a nice wedding. My husband comes from a nice family and so do I and I am well liked by everybody. The trouble is he is so jealous that he accuses me of going out with other men, call me names and insults me every chance he gets in front of our friends. The truth is I never go any place without him. I make all my own clothes, canned 150 quarts of fruit this year, make my own bread and am considered a good cook, saving every cent I can out of his salary. He makes good wages, but when I ask for new clothes he tells me to go to work and earn them. Before I married I had a good job at $30 a week and kept it until last April, when I was dismissed because they do not employ married women where I worked. Since then he has been disagreeable. We have a nice home, a car all paid for and nice furniture, but I feel that I am not wanted. I left last July but came back again. I don't know what to do. I could have my old job back again—if I left him—so what would you advise? MISTAKEN SUE.

WHAT TO DO? So—it looks as though mothers DO know what they are talking about when they disapprove of daughter's choice of a husband. It's pretty obvious to a mother from a young man's behavior how he will stand up under the problems of marriage—whether he is kind and responsible.—two important factors in lifelong companionship.. . . Everything's all right except his disposition.. . . Is it possible for your mother and his mother to take him to task and tell him that he just can't go around calling his wife names, accusing her of things she hasn't a thought of doing and that he has a pretty sensible wife, to be baking bread, canning fruit and making her own clothes." Perhaps he is just a little contrary and could be coaxed into good humor. Why not have a talk with him and inform him that since YOU are playing fair and doing your part, you are not going to be abused. And it is abuse to be called names, told to go to work and be embarrassed before friends. If you cannot make him understand or come to an agreement, then ask your mother's advice before really giving up the ship. You have such a nice start, it is too bad you cannot get along. Nov 4, 1937

John and Aggy

July 26, 1937 DFP

Ferne and friend, Bette Wilke

GM to Keep Plant Closed
Till UAW Stops Picketing

KNUDSEN HITS 'COERCION' OF WORKERS. The Fisher Body plant
NO 1 in Flint, which employs 3,700 will remain closed, William S Knudsen
General Motors President, announced today until the UAW stops what
he termed "coercion or intimidation" of workers. The plant closed for
the second consecutive day today when the management charged that 400
employees were kept out by the UAW pickets. The Buick final assembly
line, employing 1,200 was also shut down. . . Men can work in our plants
whether they belong to the union or not. Apr 19, 1938

June 1, 1938

June 1, 1938

Gerry and Earl Spies

One summer Sunday after returning from an early church service, Hattie, Jeane and Aggy were in the kitchen cooking. Ferne stood in front of the house looking down the road for Esther and Jack's car. She couldn't wait to see little Johnnie. He'd just started walking. As she stood there, the wind whipped her hair back and pressed her long dress between her legs. As the streetcar passed, some guy standing at the door whistled.

When Jack parked their car, Ferne opened the door and scooped Johnnie up.

"Auntie Fernie," he screamed. Then Fernie took his hand and walked him into the corner of the yard where there was a bit of soil and a lilac bush in bloom.

She picked a flower for him and said, "Let's go give it to Gramma." He held the flower proudly in his hand as she walked him up the stairs and into the kitchen.

Within half an hour, the house was full of people and the dining room table was covered with food.

John said, "Fernie, let's take the children behind the garage."

Ferne sat Dickie, Barbara and Johnnie in a row on some bricks, and then John made a shadow show with his fingers. Dickie started laughing when the doggie shadow chased the daddy and mommy into the dark room, the black square shadow created from the sun hitting the icehouse. Then John picked up Dickie and flew him like an airplane back into the house.

At the table, Hattie passed around a bowl of potatoes. "Thanks, Ward, for bringing milk. How did you get it with the strike?"

"The Piggly Wiggly is still getting some deliveries," Ward said. "And our friend Denise works there. I gave her a good deal on meat in the butcher shop."

Evan took Dickie into the bathroom. Everyone could hear him hollering, "Did I tell you to wash your hands, young man? Do what I tell you." Dickie started crying.

Everyone at the table was quiet.

When they came back into the room, Katie called Dickie to sit on her lap and Evan went outside for a smoke. "Daddy's had a hard week, honey," she said. "Don't pay attention."

Oct 27, 1936 / WPA

Scarlet Fever Cases Mount

Warning that the annual late Fall increase in scarlet fever cases is above average this year, the department of health today asked parents to inspect their children every morning for signs of the disease.

Children having sore throats, accompanied by vomiting, headaches and fever should be sent to bed immediately and a physician called. Franklin H. Top, director of the communicable disease division of the department said.

He warned that it was particularly important that infants and young children be kept from contact with their older brothers and sisters who complain of symptoms.

The department reported 83 cases of scarlet fever in the city in the week ending October 29, as compared with a norm of 48 cases. There were 63 deaths from all communicable diseases during the week.

Nov 4, 1938

June 22, 1938

from Sept 23, 1939 DFP

August 25, 1938

May 24, 1938 DFP

68

Jeane was combing her hair and pinning it up for the night while Ferne was sitting on her bed looking through some photos from last summer. In one of the photos, Ferne was sitting on the bumper of a car, wearing a halter top and baggy calf-length pants. Her hair was windblown and touched around the edge with sunlight. She had a bracelet and something in her left hand. Jeane looked closely, "You're smoking in this photo! You better not show that to Ma. She'll throw a fit."

"I'm fine," Ferne said, laughing. Then she turned out the lights. They could hear the radio playing in the living room and the muffled sounds of their mother and father talking.

Jeane turned over on her side and began tracing with her finger the edge of a rose in the wallpaper. "I think Lynn's going to marry Helen. I hope you don't go off and marry George and leave me here all alone with Pa picking on me all the time."

"Don't worry, George is my one and only. We want to get married, Jeane but not until after I graduate. That's months away. We haven't told anyone, so don't say a word. Did I tell you his father is the lawyer who's taking care of Katie's divorce?"

Both girls were silent for a minute or two, listening to the rain hitting the window.

"You don't know what I go through here, Fernie. I don't start work until noon and all morning Pa is telling me: *do this Jeane, do that Jeane.* As soon as I have money saved, I'm looking for my own place."

"I'm glad you don't have enough money. What would I do without you?... Do you want to go to Belle Isle with Gerry and me on Sunday, and maybe her husband, too—if he isn't still picketing in Flint? He's trying to find a job in Detroit or soon they'll be moving to Flint. We might ride bikes around the island. It's supposed to be a warm day. And the leaves will be gorgeous red and yellow."

"Maybe, I have to see what else is going on. Is Henry still heartsick over losing Gerry?"

Ferne laughed. "I haven't seen him lately, but I heard he's taken up with Marjorie."

Hattie opened their door a crack. "Everything okay in here, girls?"

"Yeah," Ferne said.

"I thought I smelled smoke in the bathroom."

The girls looked across the room at each other. "Not me," they both said.

"Maybe I'm wrong. Maybe it's coming from outside," Hattie said as she shut the door.

"See," Jeane said. "With everyone gone, we can't get away with anything anymore."

Roosevelt Plea To Voters Set For Tonight

By George Durno
Int'l News Service Staff Correspondent

HYDE PARK, N. Y., Nov. 4.— President Roosevelt will place the New Deal's record of the past five years before the nation tonight in his political broadcast, he disclosed at today's press conference.

Social legislation, such as the Wagner Labor Act, social security, aid and care for crippled and destitute children, will be reviewed in connection with the President's appeal to the voters to elect those next Tuesday who are in sympathy with the program.

Nov 4, 1938

Ferne's visit to Michigan State University with her two friends

The day after Ferne graduated from high school, she and George took the streetcar to Belle Isle. They walked over the bridge and cut through the middle of the island, stopping to sit on the grass at the edge of a small forested area. They looked out across a meadow and across the river at the buildings in Windsor, Ontario.

"Did you like Lansing?" he asked.

"The school's beautiful, and Marjorie is lucky to be able to go."

"Her parents are quite wealthy, and they want her to go to school."

"Both Maria and I were envious. We saw the dorm rooms and students studying in the library. But we all have different paths... George, why is your father so against us getting married? I don't understand." Ferne pulled out some grass, holding it in her hand and staring at it. "Doesn't he understand that we are in love?"

"Fernie, my father has his own ideas, I have mine. We don't get along. I don't like the way he treats my mother. That's why I left last year and rented a room on Nottingham. My father thinks if we get married, I will never go to college. I told him I don't want to go to college anyhow. I just want to work and marry you." She started crying and George put his arm around her. "I'm going to wait a few weeks and try talking to him again. We could run away, but then I wouldn't have a job."

Fernie looked down at the ground and started searching through a patch of clover. "Maybe I can find one with four leaves," she said, but each one she pulled had only three.

They stood up and started walking toward the river. When they sat down on a park bench, George took out his pipe. What Ferne liked about George wasn't just his love of dancing, it was also his way of talking and how he knew so much about history and politics. He explained to her what was going on with the auto industry and the Depression and why so many people were homeless and poor. He was polite too, not like her brothers who were always kind of rowdy and drinking. Loving yes, but rowdy. George had grown up in a house where he was the only boy and his father had gone to college.

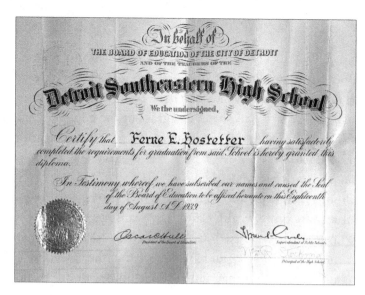

1939

MARJORIE HILTON
4616 Chalmers Ave.
Jackson.

PHYLLIS VYVYAN HILTON
525 Ashland Ave.
Jackson.
Alchemist Club, President;
Michigan State.

ELAYNE E. HINES
2535 Lycaste Ave.
Foch.
The Business Institute.

EUGENE HIRSCH
3954 Coplin Ave.
Jackson.
"S" Club; Track Club,
Treasurer; International
Relations Club; Varsity
Track, Football.
University of Michigan.

WILLIAM HOCK
5115 Lillibridge Ave.
Foch.
Hi-Y, Jungaleer Chapter;
"S" Club; Track Club;
Varsity Football; House
Football, Golf, Bowling;
Senior Social Committee.
University of Michigan.

RAY HOEFLER
4660 Beniteau Ave.
Foch.
House Foul Shooting.

MILTON C. HOFFMAN
5950 Newport Ave.
Jackson.
"S" Club; Hi-Y, Jungaleer
Chapter; Varsity Tennis,
Captain; House 202,
Councillor.
University of Texas.

JUNE HOGELAN
2147 Alter Rd.
Jackson.
Girl Reserves; Glee Club.
The Business Institute.

RONALD HOLMES
10441 E. Warren Ave.
Barbour.
House Wrestling, Track;
Varsity Football.

MARGARET HOLOHAN
2551 St. Jean Ave.
Foch.
Detroit Business University.

REESE MARTIN HONN
825 Emerson Ave.
Foch.
International Relations
Club.
Wayne.

PAUL HOPFNER
5960 Newport Ave.
Jackson.
P.A.I.S.

MARION HORNING
2546 Manistique Ave.
Jackson.
Traffic Club.
Vocational School.

FERNE HOSTETTER
5187 Alder Road.
Jackson.
Dorcas, Bowling Clubs.
Burroughs School.

CHARLOTTE M. HOUSTON
5126 Cooper Ave.
Barbour.
Wayne.

C. RICHARD HOWARD
1055 Lenox Ave.
Foch.
Hi-Y, White Chapter.
University of Michigan.

FREDERICK HOYER
2971 Harding Ave.
Foch.
House Golf.

ROBERT HUBBARD
606 St. Clair Ave.
Foch.
Reserve Basketball.
Wayne.

JOHN HYLAND
609 Emerson Ave.
Jackson.
House Football, Baseball.
Michigan State.

RUTH BARBARA INMAN
567 Lenox Ave.
Barbour.
The Business Institute.

MINNIE ISLES
644 Lenox Ave.
Foch.
The Business Institute.

RAYMOND IVORY
4100 Haverhill Road.
Ottawa Hills High, Grand
Rapids.
House Golf; Varsity
Basketball; Senior Band;
Orchestra.

BARBARA LEE JACKSON
6129 Yorkshire Road.
Foch.
Spanish Club; Printing and
Publicity Committee.
Michigan State.

CLEDA MAE JACKSON
3515 Lycaste Ave.
Foch.

JACK JACOBS
1406 Lakewood Blvd.
Jackson.
House Basketball; Varsity
Golf, Tennis.
Northwestern University.

RICHARD JANKOSKA
3575 Nottingham Road.
Jackson.
House Football; Senior
Band.
Michigan State.

PHYLLIS JENKS
713 Drexel Ave.
Foch.
Story Tellers Club, Treasurer.
The Business Institute.

[42]

JUNE

72

May 21, 1939

George Bixler and Ferne, Aug 1, 1939

Link Spinster's Death
To Vanished Wealth

BODY IN RIVER LINKED TO LOST CASH. The body of Miss Annette Hawkins, 51, a once well-to-do Royal Oak spinster who disappeared under strange circumstances last January . . . Police found the body Wednesday in the Detroit River at Third Street. She had dropped into a nearby beer garden and drank a cup of coffee and told a friend she was on her way to a 'bookie.' She never returned. . . She was an enthusiastic devotee of horse race betting . . . She was engaged in the business of raising squabs in Royal Oak and had a flock of several thousand birds. . . Friends described her as a likeable and energetic person of many interests.. . . "Ann and I used to have a few drinks together at a beer garden in Royal Oak. Last Summer we met a man in this place whom we used to call Tex. . . [He] made quite a play for Ann. . . . He finally invited her to Mt. Clemens. When Ann returned she told me that Tex and another man in Mt. Clemens wanted her to go into a deal in which she would make a lot of money. She was supposed to put up $2,500 before Saturday." May 12, 1939

May 6, 1939

Hitler Pays 6th Visit
To 'The Merry Widow'

LONDON, May 12—(INS)— For the sixth time, Chancellor Hitler attended a performance last night of his favorite operetta, "The Merry Widow," at Munich, the London Daily Express reported today. The paper said that Miriam Verne, American dancer favored by the chancellor, starred in the production.

May 12, 1939

200 Persons Divorced Weekly in County; Half Shun Court to Read Results in Papers

Dec 3, 1939 DFP

Hattie sent Jeane and Ferne to the grocery store. They took Katie's little girl Barbara along with them.

"If you get married, I'm not staying here," Jeane said.

"Jeane, what's so terrible? You love Ma and she needs you. Pa isn't feeling well. He's not going to be able to work for long. You should stay home until you get married. It won't look right."

"I have enough money to rent an apartment."

"But you're only 16."

"You're lucky, Fernie, that you landed that office job at the insurance company. I wish I could get a job like that. I'm still working part-time as a candy sales girl."

Suddenly Barbara tripped, fell down and started crying. Ferne knelt beside her and consoled her. "I want Mama," she wept, laying her head on Ferne's knee.

"Oh sweetie, your mama will be here in a few hours."

They walked along, each holding one of Barbara's hands. "I don't think you'll be alone, Jeane. Maybe Katie and her children will be back living with us. They're already here all the time."

When they turned the corner to the alley, Ferne stood still, standing behind a brown bush.

"Wait! Jeane, that's George's father's car!" she whispered loudly. "What's he doing here? I can't go in the house. I can't go in the house," she said nervously. "Let's walk around the block."

When they returned, the car was gone. Jeane took Barbara upstairs to see John and Aggy, and Ferne went into the living room where her parents were sitting.

"Ferne," her father said, putting his newspaper down. "We need to talk."

She sat on the couch and tucked her skirt under her.

"Mr. Bixler stopped by."

"I know. I saw his car."

"He does not want you and George to get married. He's very firm about this. He wants George to wait until he is older and has finished college. He asked us to intervene. I'm sorry, Fernie, I know how much you like him."

"He doesn't want to go to college."

"Ferne, that's their family affair. He asked me to break off the relationship. Otherwise Mr. Bixler won't offer any support and he will cut George off. I agreed to talk with you."

"What kind of father is he?" She started crying. "We're in love."

Hattie got up and sat next to her, consoling her and hugging her. "There will be someone else for you, Ferne. Don't worry. There's no rush. You are very young."

Ferne ran into her room, shut the door and threw herself on the bed.

At dinner, Ferne did not leave her room. When Jeane tried to talk to her, she said, "Leave me alone, Jeane. Leave me alone."

George told Ferne he would try to get a transfer so they could move to Florida together. Who cares about his father, he said. Ferne thought about it, but she couldn't leave her family, and she didn't want to go against her father. So she said it wouldn't work.

august 20, 1939

76

I zoom in on the photo of Ferne. She is about 4 inches taller than Jeane. Their noses and mouths look identical, but their cheekbones and foreheads are different. Jeane has a widow's peak. Ferne is wearing a cotton print dress she made from a McCall's pattern—it has puffy sleeves, a white belt and a bow tie at the collar. Her hair is parted in the middle, rolled and braided. Her teeth are straight with an eyetooth overlapping. They didn't last long. In their 30s both Ferne and my father had their teeth pulled. False teeth. Strange to imagine now, but quite common then.

CHAPTER 5

Jeane and Ferne were walking east on Jefferson Avenue. They had just left the Cinderella Theater.

"It's really chilly tonight," Ferne said, pulling her coat around her. "Seems like winter's coming early this year."

Jeane put her arm into Ferne's. "It was really scary when Ida Lupino was caught in the brambles with all that fog and that guy stalking her, wasn't it?"

"She's beautiful with her tiny waist and her shoulder pads. They make her waist seem even smaller. I could make a jacket with shoulder pads like those."

When they walked past the sweet shop where Jeane worked, she pointed to a sign in the window. "They're looking for someone else to work in the evenings. I'm trying to get Margaret to apply, but her father won't let her work evenings."

When they turned onto Marlborough Street, a damp wind from the river blew a clutter of leaves off the trees, adding to the piles already crunching underfoot.

Ferne put her arm around Jeane. "The newsreel was horrifying, the German soldiers just marching into Poland and taking over, bombing buildings, blowing up their bridges. I'm worried. Maybe they'll come here. Ma is scared the U.S. will get involved. Lynn and Ward were talking in the kitchen. They're worried they'll be drafted."

"How's Ma?"

"She started crying when I told her I was going to stay with you, that I didn't want you to be alone. You're too young. She told me she was going to call the police to bring us home."

They turned in front of a two-story bungalow and walked along the side to the back door. They climbed up the steps to a small apartment with torn wallpaper and peeling paint on the ceiling.

Ferne looked around at the old furniture. "This place is a mess."

"It's the only place anyone would rent to me."

"Jeane, Dad's having trouble breathing. He's walking very slowly. They want us to come home."

"I thought I'd like it here, but all week I've been crying. Even though Margaret comes over, it's just too quiet and lonely. I'm used to being around people."

"Let's go back home tomorrow morning. Everyone will be happy to see you. Pa wants you home, too. We go home tomorrow, right? I'll take the day off work. Come on."

"Okay."

Ferne sat down on the couch next to Jeane. "There's something I didn't tell you."

Jeane looked at her, "What now?"

"I got another letter from George. He left home and moved to Florida where his aunt lives, and he said he's not going to college. His father is furious. I would've gone with him—he wanted me to—but I don't want to disobey Pa. So now George is going to marry some girl from there."

"What? Why is he in such a hurry? I'd like to tell him a thing or two."

"The draft. They're worried about the draft. If you're married, you might not have to go."

"What are we gonna do?"

Ferne stood up. "I know what I'm gonna do. I'm gonna go to the Vanity Ballroom night after night until I meet the right boy. That's what I'm gonna do."

Then she turned on the radio. The Ink Spots were singing,

If I didn't care, would it be the same?

And then they stopped singing, and one of the men said in a very deep voice,

If I didn't care, honey child, more than words can say,

If I didn't care, would I feel this way?

Would my every prayer begin and end with just your name?

"Are you okay, Fernie?" Jeane knocked on the bathroom door.

Ferne was putting her hair into pin curls. She looked into the mirror and Jeane looked over her shoulder. "I was in love with George, Jeanie, but I'm certainly not going to wallow in it."

Senate Passes a Bill to Ease Divorce Law

LANSING, April 11—The Senate acted to liberalize Michigan divorce laws Tuesday by approving Rep. Robert M. Sawyer's bill to require only one year of residence, instead of two, to obtain a divorce on grounds of desertion.

The Senate also passed a bill to make refusal to support children under 17 a felony, and to permit delinquent taxpayers to pay up taxes for 1935 and before without penalty. The tax offer expires Sept. 30.

Apr 12, 1939 DFP

Mr. Roosevelt To Lift Arms Ban Today

By EDWARD B. LOCKETT
Int'l News Service Staff Correspondent

WASHINGTON, Nov. 4. — President Roosevelt at noon today was scheduled to sign this nation's newest instrument of foreign policy—a neutrality bill substituting cash and carry sale of munitions as well as nonmilitary commodities to warring countries, for the arms embargo of existing law.

This action will make law of legislation which Mr. Roosevelt plainly made known he wanted early last Spring, and which the regular session of Congress failed to enact.

After war broke out in Europe, he called Congress into special session to write the new measure, and after 28 days of debate his bidding was done.

Operation of the new law is expected to mark the start of a billion dollar war business boom, channeling foreign funds into almost every one of the heavy industries of the United States.

Nail Biting Denotes Lack of Poise

By DONNA GRACE

The Answer

Perfect nails may be the answer. When the nails are long and beautifully formed, we are not going to injure them and we believe the best way to go about this reform is to visit the manicurist every day. This is the training that will cure one's urge to chew when a bit flustered.

There are ways of building the nails to beauty. They begin with good health, then a well-balanced diet. Milk, eggs and leafy salads will grow nice nails. One must keep the cuticle smooth. The least bit of horny surface will be an invitation to bite. Nail brushes should be firm but not too stiff, and whenever soap is used it must be rinsed off thoroughly.

Nov 4, 1939

Woman's Work Is Never Done---
---At Least,

Girls in boots and khaki going cheerfully about the big task of caching Great Britain's home-grown food supply (only half of the nation's needs) for a long grim Winter. These are some of thousands who enlisted in the Land Army (just one of many formal women's organizations with a total enrollment of more than 1,00,00), took a month's course in farming, took men's places in the fields to do all farm chores. Farming is so important that England has already put under cultivation parks, hunting preserves, estates of wealthy and nobility. Nov 4, 1939

Jeane was shy, ladylike and a little silly when she was around young men, but at home she was stubborn and this drove her father crazy. She was the youngest, and he had often watched Hattie and her older brothers and sisters let Jeane have her way. Perhaps he too had been guilty of the same thing. But when she quit school, Luke was worried what would happen to her if she didn't have a skill, if she didn't find a husband. She didn't stay in school long enough to learn shorthand and typing. She told him she wanted to be a beautician.

"Are you sure?" he asked. "I'll pay the tuition to send you to beauty school, but you have to promise to finish."

"I definitely will, Pa, definitely."

"And Jeane, if you finish, maybe I can help you get started."

Jeane enrolled and went to school for a little over a month. But she didn't like washing other people's hair, the endless rolling and pinning. She didn't have the personality of someone who could endlessly attend to others. And they said she had to wear a white suit and wear her hair the same as the others. That really bothered her. Who wants to look like everyone else? So she quit going. Pa was more angry at her than he had ever been. She was throwing away his hard-earned money. When he hollered at her, she packed a suitcase and stomped out. Then yesterday Ferne left too, so she could look after her. He was bereft. Suddenly his last two children were gone and the flat was empty.

When he looked out the window and saw the two girls walking up the steps of the house with their suitcases: what a relief. "Hattie, they're here," he said, raising his voice a little and pretending he wasn't ecstatic.

"I'm sorry Pa," Jeane said, looking to the side. "I'm not that good as a stylist. You should have seen how they laughed at me."

He sighed.

"Put your things away, girls," Hattie said, "and have lunch with us. Grandad's moving in this afternoon. I need some help setting up the sunroom for him. I also have laundry to do for Mr. Munjall. Ferne, can you help me in the basement? My shoulder is sore. You can feed the clothes into the wringer and help hang them."

"Sure thing, Ma. I thought Munjall was going home to India. Didn't he lose his dishwashing job?" Ferne asked.

"Apparently he begged Louie. For the time being he'll have his job. Thank the Lord. He says he'll be here until fall and then he'll go home. Then Grandad will have that room."

Curly, Marion, Johnnie, Agnes, May 1940

On Mother's Day, the whole family, wives, husbands and children, came home to eat dinner and to celebrate their love for their mother, now a grandmother, and the young mothers, Katie, Esther and Ward's wife Betty. They gathered around the dining room table and in the chairs in the living room. There wasn't enough room now for everyone at the table.

Katie came in the back door with her children. "Happy Mother's Day, Gramma Hattie," Dickie yelled jumping up to hug her, handing her a bunch of daisies.

When the family was sitting at the table, waiting for Luke to say grace, John looked straight at Katie, staring. "How'd you get that bruise on your face, Kate?"

"I slipped and fell down the stairs," she said, her eyes welling with tears. "Such a stupid thing wearing those slippers."

John stood up and turned around. "You're bruised all over. Where's Evan? Where's that shithead? What the hell's wrong with him?"

"He couldn't come. He's busy with some work he brought home and then visiting his mother. I told you, John, I fell down the stairs. He didn't have anything to do with it."

Everyone was quiet.

Luke Sr. stood up from the table. His voice was weaker than usual. "Listen, let's not talk about this now. The children are here. We are celebrating our mothers today. Fernie move over. I want Katie to sit beside me." He put his arm around her.

He cleared his throat. "Before we eat, I want to thank everyone for coming to honor Ma today. We're sorry to have lost Pat. He was a good dog, but that fight last week with the Airedale was his end. We made a little grave for him behind the garage. Let's say thanks now to God for granting us our health, love for each other and the food on this table. Please God protect us and protect our country in this difficult time. Amen." A chorus of amens and then everyone started eating dinner and chatting.

After dinner, Ferne hollered through the back screen, "Ma come outside, and take that apron off. Jeane's gonna to take your photo with me, and I'll take hers with you."

Jeane directed them to stand in the back of the bank. Ferne put her arms around her mother and Hattie reached up to hold her too. Cheek to cheek. Hattie was dressed for Sunday, wearing dark clothes, black shoes and her wire rim glasses. She took one step forward, as Ferne's hips flew out and about, her skirt catching the wind, her ankles crossed. It was high heel Sunday. Click and click again. Ferne and Jeane were in love with their mother. Behind them the bars on the windows of the bank.

Later in the afternoon, there was a lot of racket going on in the back bedroom.

"John," Hattie said, "would you take the children outside for a while. I want to talk to Katie."

When John opened the door to the bedroom, he found Dickie watching while Barbara, Johnnie and little Carol Lee were jumping on the bed. "Hey! That was my bed when I was a kid! If Gramma catches you children doing this, you'll be in a lot of trouble. Come on outside all of you. I'm going to teach you how to make a city of people from those hollyhocks." They trailed out behind him as if following Johnny Appleseed.

Ferne smiled as she watched them marching toward the cinderblock seats behind the garage. She remembered John putting on hand shadow shows for her and Jeane when they were small and he was a teenager. She sat down at the kitchen table and poured a cup of coffee. She could hear Katie and Ma talking.

"We are working it out," she heard Katie say. "It was my fault, really Ma. You know how moody he is. I was frustrated after being with the children alone for too long and I nagged at him. I saw the lawyer, but we don't need another divorce in the family right now. And I have the children. I don't want to leave Evan. What would happen to the children?"

"Dear, you cannot let him push you or hit you. That's unacceptable. Perhaps he only meant a little push, but the fact is you fell down the stairs. And you could have been seriously injured. Maybe you should stay here for a few days and let him think about it."

"I need to go home, but if you and the girls wouldn't mind, I'd like to leave the children here for a few days."

Katie sat down beside Ferne on the front porch. "You don't mind, do you Fernie, helping Ma with the children."

"No, Katie. I wish you would stay with us too."

"I've got to straighten this out. Everything will be all right. I just have to talk to him. You know, Fernie, it's different once you're married to someone."

When she left, Ferne watched her walking down Alter Road toward Harper. Her striped dress got smaller and smaller until she turned the corner, heading west.

May 1940

Grandad   me   Dad

June 16, 1940

Ward and his wife Betty and son Terry—Mother's Day / Father's Day—Lynn and Helen

May 26, 1940

London Lists German Toll At 52 Planes

By FRAZIER HUNT
Int'l News Service Staff Correspondent

London, May 25.— Britain's tireless sky fleets, lashing back at the first real German air attack on England proper, dealt a crippling blow today to the vital communication - arteries feeding and supporting the Nazi surge to the English Channel, the air ministry announced tonight.

May 26, 1940

The War in Brief

FRANCE. The battle of Flanders is just beginning. . . Heavy losses have been suffered by all German troops . . . American bombing planes, many of which have arrived in France within the past few days went into action against Nazi troop concentrations.

•

GERMANY. Strangulation of allied forces in Flanders is "rapidly progressing". . . German legions . . . pouring through the gap . . . A new secret weapon . . . The pound sterling has been thrown out of the European continent and the German mark is circulating everywhere.

•

AMERICA The prospect of turning industrial "ghost towns" into production centers to manufacture munitions and possibly aircraft is being studied. . . New Castle, Pa, Mingo Junction and Martin's Ferry where unemployment figure are high . . The army has developed a new and highly secret aircraft warning device considered superior to any other detector in the world.

May 26, 1940

After going out dancing two or three times a week for a few months, Ferne told her mother she was going to volunteer for the army. Hattie begged her to reconsider. Ferne went down to the recruiting office in Grosse Pointe, but after the doctor examined her, he declared that she could not join the WACs because she had an irregular heartbeat.

She was very upset. "I'm completely healthy," she said. "What can I do?"

"Do you type? File?"

"Yes."

"We need someone here. If things continue as they are in Europe, we'll soon be flooded with work."

She took the job and on Monday she started working as a receptionist. The pay was low but she liked Loretta, the young woman she was working with. They would chat all day long, and sometimes they went out together at night to dance at the Vanity or at Eastwood Gardens. Loretta lived with her mother and her brother. Their father had died ten years earlier in a car accident. Like many other families during the Depression, the children had to leave school after sixth grade and find work to help their mother.

Sometimes her brother Rob would come along when they went out dancing. He was almost six and a half feet tall, a hefty young man, two years older than Ferne. She taught him how to jitterbug and, even though he was a bit awkward, he could pick her up and swing her around the dance floor. After that, most nights they were together sitting on the porch at the Hostetter house planning for their future. After dark, they would walk around the block and then cut through the alley to sit behind the garage where no one could see them. Rob kept saying he wanted to marry her, but Ferne wasn't sure. She liked him, but not as much as she had liked George.

"If we were married, we wouldn't have to hide like this, Ferne," he said as he stroked her hair. "I could bring you home with me."

"Oh, your mother would really like that."

"She would love it if I were married. She keeps telling me to get married. Loretta's getting married and moving out soon. There'll be more room in the flat for us."

"Maybe, but maybe not. I want to have our own place. Couldn't we rent our own apartment? We both have jobs," she said standing up and straightening her skirt. He slipped his hand under her skirt and stroked her inner leg.

"Stop it," she said, laughing.

"After a while, of course, we can save money."

As the weeks passed, they started talking about having children.

When her father got an inkling of their intent, he was concerned. Not only was it too soon after George, but he and Hattie both thought this young man was too big for Ferne. When Luke spoke to Ferne, she cried and begged him to say yes. He hated it when she cried like that. Against his better judgment, he gave in, but he made them promise to wait at least six months before they married. He posted an announcement in the *Detroit Free Press* about their engagement and also Lynn's engagement to his girlfriend, Helen.

FERNE HOSTETTER'S
parents, Mr and Mrs. Luke Hostetter, of Alter road, announce her engagement to Robert L. Trump of St. Jean avenue. Helen Kula's father, Alex Kula, of Crane avenue, announces her engagement to Lynn A. Hostetter.

October 29, 1939

April 1940

April 1940

On the morning of September 14th, 1940, Ferne and Rob were married at Knox Presbyterian Church. That evening, Ferne moved in with Rob and his mother in their flat on St. Jean Avenue. Loretta was still there, but only for a few weeks. After a week and a half, Ferne started coming home to her mother and father's house after work, hanging around with Jeane and her mother.

"What's going on, Ferne?" Hattie asked.

"Oh nothing, Ma. I just miss home."

"You're married now. You must live with your husband." Hattie put her arm around her and kissed her. "You must go home and help with dinner."

Ferne picked up her purse and her coat and slowly walked up to the corner for the Mack Avenue bus.

Three months after the wedding, Ferne showed up at her parent's house in the morning with a suitcase. She didn't like Rob's mother, she said, and she was depressed living there. Gerty was nothing like Ma. She nagged continually, wanting Ferne to do all the housework after she came home from working all day. And she and Rob couldn't get enough money together to have their own place, even with his salary at Chrysler and hers. And he never wanted to go out dancing or have fun. Ferne was adamant—if they couldn't get their own place, they needed to live with her parents. But he wouldn't leave his mother.

90

"You've only been with him a few months, Fernie. Married love isn't supposed to be that easy," Jeane said.

"Who said this marriage was about love?" Ferne turned on her side, sobbing. "It was torture living there. He didn't love me, not the way I love. It was more about his mother. She didn't want him to lose his job and go into the army. Pa was right, it was too soon. I wanted George. I feel smothered by Rob and unappreciated by his mother. And, Jeane, sex is not all it's been built up to be. That's all I'll say about that."

The next morning Ferne was throwing up in the bathroom with terrible cramps and a few drops of blood. Hattie asked, "Did you skip a period?"

"Yes, I'm two weeks late," she said, weeping and moaning.

John drove them to the emergency room. Finally, a doctor told Hattie and Jeane that they were taking her into surgery. He thought it was a tubal pregnancy.

When Hattie was young, many women had died from tubal pregnancies, including one of her friends. A few hours later, the nurse told Jeane and Hattie that Ferne was fine. They had to remove one of her fallopian tubes and a blood clot, but the operation was successful. "She should wake up in an hour or so."

When Ferne woke up, Jeane was sitting beside her holding her hand.

"Oh Jeane, why does everything go wrong for me?"

"Fernie, the doctor said the operation was successful."

"I probably won't ever have children," she said weeping.

"That's only a *chance*, Fernie. Remember that. It could happen to any of us. Try not to focus on the negative."

"Where's Ma?"

"She had to go home to take care of Pa. She'll be back in the morning. Katie's coming soon, and then I'm going home for a while."

When Ferne came home, Rob stopped by to see how she was and to try to talk her into returning.

"We'll have a big family and I'll look after you."

Again, she explained to him that she had made a mistake. When she refused to go back with him, he turned around and never returned.

Luke thought she could get an annulment, but he insisted that she wait three months just to be sure she had made the right decision. When she explained to the judge that they had lived together for only a few months, he wondered why she hadn't come directly to the court.

"My father made me wait," she said. When she explained that Rob had promised they would get their own apartment, the judge would not entertain this argument. This was not a good reason, he said, to undo marriage vows. She could have lied and said that he was cruel to her or abusive, but she couldn't do it, so Ferne would now have to work and save money to pay for a lawyer.

She took her wedding portrait out of the envelope and stared at it. She was wearing a dark dress with a white lace lapel and little white buttons down to the waist. Her hands were crossed one over the other, a wedding band on her left hand. She wore a large dark hat with some feathers and her hair was rolled in the fashion of the time. When the lights flashed, Rob was standing beside her. She took her scissors and clipped around the edges, leaving only a foot, a lower leg and one shoulder. The three Hostetter sisters and sisters-in-law also did exactly as Ferne had requested and clipped him out of all the photos. "Out of your life, out of the picture," Jeane said as she clipped him out of hers.

In November, Ferne was in the post office waiting in line when she saw Rob up ahead. He was wearing a U.S. Air Force uniform. He must have enlisted, she thought. She tried to say hello to him, but he looked in the other direction. As he was walking past her, she said "I'm sorry, Rob," but he walked straight out the door.

When she filed on April 26, 1941, the only way she could obtain the divorce was to claim cruelty and non-support. Rob did not contest.

CHAPTER 6

Home

May 1942

At 87, Hattie's father Joe was still an active employee at Rouge, but lately he had been having some difficulty getting to the plant from the rooming house where he lived in Highland Park. The streetcar on Mack and Alter was a more direct route, and Hattie was concerned that he wasn't eating correctly, maybe drinking more than eating. That's why she and Luke had decided to build the addition on the house. They knew that sooner or later, he would need to live with them. On Sunday John and Aggy brought him to the house with his suitcases, his books and all his things. He was a big man, so they put a large armchair in his room for him with a stool for his feet. He sat in the chair like the king of the house while the girls waited on him.

"Do you want coffee, Grandad?" Ferne asked.

"With milk and toast," he said.

When the older children came home with their children, each child was instructed to go into the sunroom, stand in front of him and say, "Hello Grampa Grundy." Then he would reach out his long finger and poke the child, asking, "And *who* are you?"

"I'm Terrance," the three-year-old said, standing by his father.

"Terrance who?"

The child looked up at his father who whispered in his ear.

"I'm Ward's son," he said proudly and then Grandad laughed and patted him on the head.

In the afternoon, Joe would go around the corner to the tavern on Mack Avenue and Wayburn to play cards with his friends. Jeane and Ferne collected him there at around nine p.m. Sometimes the bartender would call the Hostetters to send someone for him. He'd hold on to their shoulders as they guided him home. "Your mother is a saint," he said. "The only time she ever disobeyed me was when she married your father." Then he laughed deep and hard. When he was in bed, the sound of his snoring filled the house.

One night in March when Jeane and Ferne were at the Vanity Ballroom, a tall thin young man with a big smile approached Ferne. She was sipping a coke and sitting at the side with her legs crossed, wearing a new pair of high heels with a strap around her ankle.

"Whew, look at those legs," he said, whistling. He moved and talked as if he thought he was starring in a movie. "You sure are a good looker, honey. You wanna dance?"

She raised her eyebrows, tilted her head, looked at his wide brim fedora tipped to the side, and she said, laughing, "You talk just like my grandfather. Of course, I'll dance."

Then he swung her to the side and she dipped under his arm. Again he swung her out to the side, wiggling his hips. "Wiggle it, girl," he said, laughing, and dancing fast and wild. "Just do what I do." Later he introduced himself as Abe, short for George Abriel.

When Ferne looked around for Jeane, she couldn't find her.

"Are you looking for your sister?" Abe asked.

"How'd you know she was my sister?"

"She looks a lot like you, especially her legs. She's over there, dancing with my friend, Frank."

Ferne looked around again and there Jeane was dancing with an agile young man with black hair and a big grin.

At ten o'clock, the girls explained they had to head home; they were already late. Abe and Frank walked along with them, Jeane and Frank following Ferne and Abe. When Abe reached around Ferne's waist to kiss her, she pushed him away. "That's a little fast, buster."

He laughed and took her phone number. On the corner of Kercheval and Alter, the men stopped, said goodbye and watched the young women walk their last block home.

"I like him," Ferne said. "He likes to dance and have fun. He makes me laugh."

"Frank's nice, too," Jeane said, "much nicer than that creep I met last week. That boy offered to give me a ride home and then unzipped his pants. Can you imagine? I was out of that car like lightning. I ran all the way home."

"What? Jeanie, don't go home alone with a stranger in a car! It's dangerous. Whew, sometimes I worry about you. So now you like Frank? What about Eddy?"

"Well, maybe I'll see Frank one time and then decide who I like best."

Despite the Depression, the Vanity was one of the most popular dance venues in town and a place generations of Detroiters went to hear live performances by Duke Ellington, Benny Goodman, Louis Prima, Jimmy and Tommy Dorsey and Cab Calloway. . . . Such spectacular venues were popular places for Detroiters to go dance the night away and socialize. In its heyday, the Vanity hosted huge crowds – up to a 1,000 couples. Five nights a week, they danced to the big bands on the 5,600-square-foot maple dance floor, where couples "floated" on springs that gave the floor bounce. Patrons - who paid 35 cents to get in - would enter from the first floor and ascend a grand main staircase before entering a ballroom that took them to a different time and place – an ancient Aztec temple.. . . "It was just dancing, no liquor or any of that," said [Theresa] Binno, now 80 and living in Waterford, Mich. "We'd go in the early evening and spend three or four hours dancing, drinking Cokes. … Someone would always ask us to dance. We were always dancing. . . . I said I'd never get married unless the guy knew how to dance. … It was a great time to be young." (Dan Austin)

After Ferne and Abe started dating, Ferne would come home from her job at the draft office and he would be waiting on the front porch. Everyone liked him.

The first time Frank rang the doorbell to pick up Jeane, Grandad answered with a surly voice, "Who are you? What do you want here?"

"I'm here for Jeane."

"My Jeanie? No way, young man, not with the likes of you. Get out of here. Get away!"

Jeane came out of her room. "I heard the doorbell. Where's my friend, Grandad?"

"You're not going out with a colored man. I sent him on his way."

"What? You did what?" She looked out the window and saw him standing across the street. She grabbed her purse and ran out the door.

Grandad grumbled and walked into the kitchen. "Hattie, Jeane is very disrespectful. That boy was colored. I sent him away and she almost knocked me over chasing after him. She should find a nice white boy."

"Pa, he's Italian, and Jeane's free to go out with whoever she wants. Let her be. By the way, he's also Catholic. Do you want some lunch?"

"No, I'm going to the tavern," he said, heading toward the door with his cane. "I knew he was Italian," he said. "That's what I meant."

Blond or Brunet?

Would-Be Army Hostesses Apply by the Thousands; Must Be Mature, Department Rules

By KENNETH M. SCHEIBEL
Int'l News Service Staff Correspondent

WASHINGTON—The next few weeks will tell whether generals prefer blondes or brunets as hostesses to help boost the morale of America's new civilian-soldier army. It's up to the commanding officer in each corps area to choose the girls who will make life brighter around the army camps. . . . Officials in the "activated morale division" however dropped a hint to the boss who will soon be singing "The Gal I Left behind" as to just what sort of a person their camp hostess will probably be.

First of all, the 1940 hostess will "not be just a gay entertainer" She must possess "maturity and energy" because "she'll have to work as hard as the soldiers themselves." Senior and junior hostesses will be paid $2,100 and $1,620 a year respectively. Further affecting the picture the potential draftees might have had about finding glamour in camp, an official further emphasized: "We're not picking these girls for looks alone, although it's safe to bet they won't be too hard on the boys' eyes." But in order to rate the job, she must be also a high school graduate or equivalent have experience as a hostess as well as "administrative ability, intelligence, tact, high type character and physical stamina

. . . Reports have reached the war department that army recruiting stations have been besieged by hundreds of would-be hostesses. "We're not enlisting hostesses. We're only hiring them!" the official emphasized." Nov 4, 1940

IN 1941, YOUNG FILM DIRECTOR ORSON WELLES produced Citizen Kane, a thinly veiled biography of the rise and fall of William Randolph Hearst. Nominated for nine Academy Awards, the film was praised for its innovative cinematography, music and narrative structure, and has subsequently been voted one of the world's greatest films. Hearst was not pleased. He mustered his resources to prevent release of the film and even offered to pay for the destruction of all the prints. Welles refused, and the film survived and thrived. biography.com May 14, 2017

Hattie and Ward's son, Terry 1941

Jan 24, 1941

Nov 4, 1940

Sept 19, 1940

DFP The Detroit newspaper mentioned in this article is *The Detroit Times.*

The next day when Luke came home from the doctor's office, he went into the bedroom and straight into bed. He was exhausted. Hattie called Ferne, Jeane, John and Aggy to come outside.

"The doctor says that Pa's heart is very weak, and he doesn't expect him to live much longer. Maybe a month at most." As Hattie talked, tears began to stream across her cheeks. She cleared her throat and tried to steady her voice. Just seeing their mother cry gave Ferne permission to cry too.

"We must restrain our grief," Hattie said, "and stay steadfast with our love and support."

"Ma, we'll help you with everything," John said, putting his arm around his mother. "Don't worry about money, don't worry about anything."

"That's right, Ma, we'll all help you," Ferne said.

"Please children, don't tell Grandad until he can't help but notice. Otherwise he'll say something."

"Grandad will outtalk and outlive us all," Jeane said.

"God bless him. Now let's go inside."

While kneading dough for bread, Ferne told her mother that she and Abe were going to get married as soon as her divorce was final. She wanted to get married before Pa died, but now that might not be possible.

"I think for next Sunday's dinner, we could celebrate your engagement," Hattie suggested. "What do you think? That way Pa can celebrate with you... Fernie, will you call Ward, Luke and Lynn and tell them about the dinner. I'll call Katie and Esther."

George and his friend, Jay

100

Abe MA Say

June 29, 1941

Some days Luke had enough energy to get dressed and go outside. Other days he was so weak that he'd stay in the house in his robe. Every day one or more of his children would stop by and sit with him. At night Ferne would often read him passages from the New Testament. She hoped that she and Abe might have the same luck as her parents, long lives with many children. After all they shared an attitude toward life that was similar: they both were hard workers, they loved having fun and socializing with their friends and they both wanted to have children.

Whenever they weren't working or helping Hattie, they would go out dancing or picnicking in the parks with their friends. Their favorite dance spots were still the Vanity Ballroom, Lake St. Clair Ballroom, Bob-Lo Pavilion and out at 8 Mile and Gratiot at Eastwood Gardens. Abe spent many nights at the Hostetter house sleeping on the couch. His family house was out in Trenton, but he worked nearby at Bud Wheel on Connor and Mack. Very quickly, he became part of the family.

One Saturday, Ferne and Abe went to Eastwood Gardens with Jay and his girlfriend Delores. Jeane came along with her boyfriend Eddy. Everyone was dancing except Ferne and Abe. She took out her camera and snapped his photo, with his elbow on the table, his cheek against his fist. He smiled at her in a flirty way. Then she passed the camera to him.

"Here comes Jeane. Why don't you dance with her," she said, standing up, "while I go to the ladies room."

As she was walking along, she heard a commotion outside the gate. A group of African American teenagers were waiting in line.

"No N——s allowed in this park," the man said, and the teens started yelling and throwing pebbles at them. "We want to dance too. We have the money to pay. We have a right."

"No, you don't. The law says I can let in whoever I want to let in. Go your own way," the man said loudly, slamming shut the gate. "Gate closed for the time being," he yelled to the other whites outside the gate. Then a scuffle started between some of the people in line.

"Why don't you boys go to your own places and let us get into ours," one woman yelled.

"Who are you calling a boy?" the teen hollered.

"Are you yelling at my wife?"

There was a lot of pushing and shoving until the police arrived and broke up the fight, putting two of the young black men in the back of the car.

On the way home, Ferne said to Abe, "When I came here to dance a couple of years ago, Billie Holiday was playing. Then last year Duke Ellington was here with his orchestra. Ever since then all the performers have been white. Why is this happening?" Then she told Abe about going to the black and tan clubs with Lynn a few years back.

"That was probably a dangerous thing to do. I'm surprised your brother would take you."

"It was great. We had a lot of fun."

"With all the people coming here, clamoring for work, even at Bud Wheel," Abe said, "there's tension between the workers. Everyone's worried about their jobs."

"The black sections of town are very overcrowded and rundown. Everybody wants a better life."

"Lately, it feels like a keg of dynamite, doesn't it, like the Old South is alive and well in Detroit."

Eastwood Gardens

July 20, 1941

Eastwood Gardens

July 20, 1941

Me

July 27, 1941

me

August 3, 1941

Me Betty Jay Shirley Tommy Susy Bobby

August 3, 1941

Jean

August 10, 1941

103

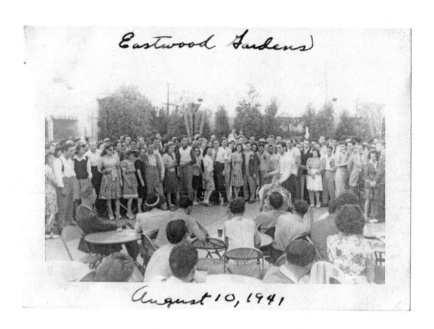

Eastwood Gardens

August 10, 1941

Eastwood Gardens

August 10, 1941

Jeane   Eddy

August 10, 1941

Me

Eastwood Gardens

August 10, 1941

Abe

Eastwood Gardens

August 10, 1941

10 Nazi Divisions Smashed Near Kiev, Russians Say

U. S. SHIPS RUSH TANKS, PLANES TO SAVE RUSSIA

Nazis in Paris Slay 12 More Hostages

Sept 20, 1941

Flu Germ Isolated

Cape Town Scientists Discover Source of Scourge; Promise to Produce Vaccine Soon

International News Service Cable

CAPE TOWN, South Africa, Sept. 20.—The institute of medical research in Cape Town announced today that the influenza germ has been isolated for the first time in history.

The statement said the germ was tracked down as a result of experiments undertaken at request

of the South African defense department to prevent "repetition of the scourge which swept the world in 1918."

Dr. E. H. Cluver, director of the institute, declared:

"We are absolutely certain we have isolated the germ.

"A vaccine soon will be prepared and we hope it will be wholly successful."

Sept 20, 1941

Planned Parenthood Gaining Favor

BY ELIZABETH MAURY

THE WORLD do move! Twenty years ago the only time the subject of birth control was mentioned in the papers was when Margaret Sanger got herself jailed for proposing that literature about it should be allowed in the mails.

Today, the theory of planned parenthood is considered a vital element in the national defense program and a third state, Alabama, has just included the maintenance of maternal health clinics under the state public health service. Both North and South Carolina had previously authorized tax supported clinics where married women could obtain information on spacing their families.

Progress in the field was highlighted at the annual meeting of the Maternal Health League of Michigan at the Women's City Club Tuesday afternoon. Among other things the Detroit Chapter reported the opening of a fifth clinic in Detroit. It is at the Parkside Hospital. The other four maintained by the League are at the North End Clinic on Holbrook Ave., the Neighborhood House at Fourth and Porter Sts., Woman's Hospital and Harper Hospital.

Mar 2, 1941 DFP

Aug 3, 1941 Sept 20, 1941 Aug 3, 1941

Like the rest of her family, Ferne admired FDR and his programs that helped people survive the Depression, and she liked working for the Grosse Pointe draft board, but she thought it wasn't fair the way rich boys' draft cards were shuffled to the back of the file. When Horace Dodge's son's card came, Mrs. Myers said, "Put it in the back!" Abe might have had a deferment if they had married before he had to register for the draft. But it was too late for that now. Ferne wondered how long before he would be called into the army; just this thought made both of them anxious to be together as much as possible.

As the summer progressed, Pa was strong enough to sit on the front porch and watch the traffic, but he couldn't walk more than a few feet at a time. One afternoon when the sun was low, Hattie helped him down the steps into the backyard so he could sit in a chair and listen to the birds.

That's where Ferne found him when she came home from work. "Hi Pa," she said, sitting down on the grass beside him. "I have really good news. Jeane and I went down to Briggs yesterday and applied for office work. They called today, and we landed jobs in the file room. I passed the shorthand and typing test, but all they need now are file clerks. I'll make more money than I do working for the army. And I'll be able to give Ma extra."

"Definitely good news, Fernie. I appreciate everything you can do."

"Briggs got a big contract from the government to make parts for aircraft."

"Soon Ma'll need even more help." He leaned his head back into the pillow and closed his eyes.

"The judge finally signed my divorce, Pa. Tomorrow Abe and I are going to the county clerk to get married."

"Good, very good, Fernie. I like him. Luke and Rose seem to have worked things out. I hope that lasts. Times aren't like they were for your ma and me. Everything is moving so quickly now in this country, another war, everything speeding up." He looked away and sighed.

Rose & Luke

September 1941

That night Abe and Ferne rented a small one-bedroom apartment above a flat on Phillip Street, a few blocks away from the Hostetter house. After the owner of the house went downstairs, they looked at each other.

Abe slowly pushed Ferne backwards until she fell into the bed, giggling. Then he took off her clothes slowly, one article at a time. He stood in front of her staring at her body with a big grin as he took off his clothes.

In the same way that they enjoyed dancing, ecstatically, they loved kissing each other and kissing every part of their bodies, from toe to forehead. Rhythmically and sexually they were very well suited.

That night they had to go back to the Hostetter flat, but after the next day, they would be able to sleep and live together every night in their own apartment.

When they went down to the county clerk's office the next day, what a surprise—they couldn't get married in Michigan until October 1st because the clerk wouldn't officiate the divorce until then. They didn't want to wait, so the next day they drove to Henry, Ohio where the laws were a little looser, and on September 20th, Ferne became Ferne Abriel.

A week later, Ferne took the streetcar from work to the last stop, in front of 3187 Alter Road. She wanted to check in on Pa. When she stepped down into the street, she saw that the yard and alleyway were full of cars. All her brothers and sisters were there. Immediately she knew that her father had died.

September 1941

September 1941

LUKE HOSTETTER

Services for Luke Hostetter, who died Monday after an illness of several months, will be held at his home, 3187 Alter road, Thursday at 2 p. m. Burial will be in Woodlawn Cemetery. Mr. Hostetter was born in Detroit 72 years ago and lived here all his life. He was a member of the Sons of the American Revolution, the Three Score and Ten Club, and the American Eagle Lodge, I.O.O.F. He leaves his wife, Hattie, four sons, Luke Jr., John, Ward and Lynn, and four daughters, Mrs. Catherine Spires, Mrs. Esther Wittenberg, Mrs. Fern Abriel and Jean Hostetter.

CHAPTER 7

John and Aggy had a potluck upstairs in their flat. Everyone in the family came except for Katie's husband and Luke and Rose, who were out of town. The table was full of dishes: tuna noodle salad, corn on the cob, leftover stew, fried chicken, sweet potatoes, salads, vegetables, rolls. After Hattie finished eating dinner with her children, she made a plate for her father and went back downstairs.

The upstairs flat was full of smoke from cigars and cigarettes. Everyone was laughing and telling stories and the children were running up and down the stairs to see Grandma and to get a nickel or a penny from Grandad. Then they'd run back upstairs to keep track of what their noisy parents were doing.

After the table was cleared, John rolled up the carpet and put on an Andrews Sisters record, "Boogie Woogie Bugle Boy," the top song that month. Everyone jumped up and started dancing like crazy. Even Dickie and Barbara were dancing. Terry, Johnny and Carol Lee were swaying at the sideline until they became tired, sat down on the rolled up carpet and fell asleep.

As Hattie and Helen were chatting downstairs, they looked up at the ceiling. "One day, dear, I'm afraid that ceiling is going to cave in," Hattie said.

A horn honked outside, and Katie called to her children, "Come on, Dickie and Barbara, let's go."

"Mom, we don't want to go," Dickie said. "We want to stay with Gramma."

"It's late, come on. Dad's outside in the car."

Reluctantly they followed her.

Then Esther's husband Jack picked up Carol Lee, and Esther took Johnny's hand. Out the door they went. Ward and Betty followed with little Terry. Then Helen and Lynn wrapped up their baby and followed suit. Jeane went downstairs to bed, and Abe and Ferne walked around the corner the three blocks to their apartment. It was cold enough to see their breath. With light flurries, the moon was barely visible and waning.

Are Women 'Sob-oteuring' Loved Ones in War Machine?

By Elsie Robinson

Blue letters from home are largely responsible for lowered soldier morale. Says Lieut Col. Walter M. Harrison, GSC Bureau of Public Relations: "Whining, crying, complaining letters from homefolk to men in the field do more to make grumblers than rain, heat, long marches and night alerts. "We can fight bullets and bombs but there is no way to combat the secret undermining effects of sabotouring love. "This country was not made by women who cried . . . or who encouraged their sons to cry." It was made by Spartan wives, mothers and maidens who gloried in the fighting independence of their men . . . who fought and suffered and often died beside them in the long trail they broke from ocean to ocean. Wherever American men went, their women followed . . . and whenever the man faltered or fell, the woman was there—not to weep over him but to reload his rifle and uplift his spirit. 'No braver human beings ever lived than the pioneering wives and mothers of America. Shall their modern daughters spoil their record now?' Walter M Harrison, Lieut, Col. GSC, Bureau of Pubic Relations

Shall they? The answer's up to YOU—wife, mother or sweetheart. Which are YOU sending that lonesome lad—GUMPTION or GOOSE PIMPLES? Distributed by King F. Byrd, Inc. Sept 29, 1941

SABOTAGE WAR MACHINES

FBI Aids Police Search for Clues; Feed Lines Stuffed

Thousands of dollars worth of machinery have been ruined by saboteurs at the Bendix Aviation plant, in Wayne, it was revealed today as FBI agents and local police began a dual investigation.

The machines have been ruined beyond repair, seriously delaying production of vital airplane parts being manufactured under national defense contracts.

Following the damage to machinery a score of workmen were discharged from the plant and additional plant protection men hired, it was learned.

The company is making airplane bomber struts and carburetors for large bombers.

Full extent of the damage has not been released by the investigating agencies, but the Times was informed that at least seven vital machines had been damaged. Two of these machines were newly shipped and damaged beyond repair while awaiting to be set up.

IN THE NEWS

A GREAT many correspondents ask:

"What will happen to us in case Germany wins the European conflict?"

It seems at the moment to be within the possibilities that the Germans might defeat the Russians and completely occupy European Russia, including the Ukraine.

And since the rest of Europe is already in the hands of the Axis powers, there is point to the query.

What would that complete control of Europe mean to us, and to the world?

Mitchell F. Hepburn, the distinguished premier of Ontario, Canada, is not dismayed by the prospect.

He predicts a triumph of Germany over Russia, but sees as a result closer relation and collaboration between the United States and Canada until "ultimately there will be no boundary line between us because of the need and necessity of national defense."

(Usually by Hearst)

Nazi Captors Foil Escape of Legless Flier

RAF Ace Slips From Germans' Party

Nazis List 12 Ships As Sunk

60,000 to Watch Louis Fight Nova

Sept 29, 1941

Report Cadillac Will Build Tanks

Preparations to convert part of the Cadillac automobile plant here into a tank arsenal for the production of 14-ton tanks were reported today by the Dow Jones news service.

The tanks would be powered with two 150-horsepower standard Cadillac engines, the service reported.

The General Motors Corporation is now negotiating for a contract to produce the tanks, it was stated.

The tanks would be produced by the mass production method on assembly lines.

TWO TYPES ALREADY

The corporation has already been alloted $26,000,000 by the Defense Plant Corporation to construct plants for the production of heavy and medium tanks. The production of the 14-ton light models by Cadillac would thus put General Motors into production of all three tank types.

The news service stated that those close to the contract negotiations forecast that all the GM tank contracts together would total between $250,000,000 and $400,000,000.

The total monthly output of all three types of tanks would be about 600, the report stated.

Nov 6, 1941

Roosevelt Talk On Air at 3 P.M.

Hint Draft of Boys, 18

Gen. Hershey Says Army Must Lower Age Limit or Stop Deferring Men Now on Lists

International News Service Wire

PHILADELPHIA, Nov. 6.— Faced by a shortage of military manpower, the government today must either lower the minimum draft age from 21 to 18 or end deferments granted to older men, in the opinion of Brig. Gen. Lewis B. Hershey, national selective service chief.

Present plans call for registration of an additional $1,700,000 men next July 1, General Hershey told Wharton School students, but Congress may nevertheless have to draft approximately 5,500,000 youths of 18, 19 and 20.

General Hershey said that he formerly opposed lowering the age minimum but had revised his stand in view of wholesale rejections and other factors.

Nov 6, 1941

111

On December 7th, Hattie was in the basement putting some coal into the furnace while Jeane was washing dishes and listening to the radio. Suddenly an emergency announcement. "Ma, Ma," Jeane hollered down the stairs. "Japan attacked the U.S.! Ma, come upstairs!"

One, two, three, four. Hello NBC. Hello NBC. This is KGU in Honolulu, Hawaii. I am speaking from the roof of the Advertiser Publishing Building. We have witnessed this morning a distant view of the battle of Pearl Harbor and the severe bombing of Pearl Harbor by enemy planes, undoubtedly Japanese. The city of Honolulu has also been attacked and considerable damage done. This battle has been going on for nearly three hours. It is no joke. It is a real war . . . We cannot yet estimate how much damage has been done, but it has been a very severe attack. The navy and army appear to now have the air and the sea under control.

Then the journalist was cut off. The Hostetters left the radio on all day. Outside, people walked quickly by, their heads down, occasionally looking up at the sky, perhaps expecting airplanes to appear and bomb as they had been doing in Europe, especially since Detroit was at the center of war manufacturing. Later that evening Eleanor Roosevelt made a broadcast. She explained that the president was meeting with Congress and the head of the military. She assured everyone that by the next day they would get a full report. In the calm honest voice that people had come to trust, she explained:

> For months now the knowledge that something of this kind might happen has been hanging over our heads and yet it seemed impossible to believe, impossible to drop the everyday things of life and feel that there was only one thing which was important — preparation to meet an enemy no matter where he struck. That is all over now and there is no more uncertainty.

Then she spoke directly to the women who had sons already serving and those who would be called upon soon. She explained that she too had "a boy at sea on a destroyer":

> You cannot escape anxiety. You cannot escape a clutch of fear at your heart and yet I hope that the certainty of what we have to meet will make you rise above these fears. We must go about our daily business more determined than ever to do the ordinary things as well as we can, and when we find a way to do anything more in our communities to help others, to build morale, to give a feeling of security, we must do it. Whatever is asked of us I am sure we can accomplish it.

Jeane started to cry after she heard Eleanor.

"Did you hear what she said, Jeane?" Ferne asked. "We have to stay calm and stick together. Let's help Ma with dinner." Ferne took Jeane by the arm back into the kitchen. Abe sat at the table peeling potatoes and Grandad hobbled into the sunroom, grumbling something about what had happened during World War One.

The next day FDR and the Congress declared war against Japan and its allies, Germany and Italy. While the country had previously agreed to give material support to the United Kingdom and other European allies, there had not yet been enough support by the people to send over American soldiers. After this attack, with only one dissenting vote in Congress, the country made the decision to fight back. After work, Ferne and Abe came over to the house to listen to the radio with Hattie, Grandad, Jeane and Eddy. Eddy and Abe started talking about enlisting, saying that it was their duty. The consensus in the house, however, was that they should wait a while. In the coming weeks, the draft offices were mobbed with volunteers.

Dec 8, 1941

The war was a force that was pulling apart family and friends, and everyone fiercely tried to resist. Couples were getting married quickly, not for deferment, that was off now, but for love and connection. They didn't know when the men would be called, but if they were, there would be very little time to prepare. In April, Ferne's friend Delores broke up with Jay and decided to marry Myron. Two weeks later, he enlisted. In July, Abe told Ferne he was also going to enlist instead of waiting to be drafted. "It's the right thing to do," he said. She was weepy, but she understood. Her brother Luke and Lynn had also volunteered. Everyone felt that the danger in Europe and Asia was spreading. Abe told her that before he left, he'd help her move back home with her mother. And she was not to worry; he was tough and would definitely be coming back. And the army would send her some money to help living while he was gone. At night even in deepest sleep, they clung to each other.

Ferne and Jeane's boyfriend, Eddie

The next morning when she was in the kitchen frying eggs and making toast, he came behind her at the counter and hugged her, kissing her neck. "Let's make a baby before I leave, Fernie," he said. Every day for the next month they diligently worked on that project. Then on July 21st, he went down to the draft office, and the next morning he boarded a bus to Camp Swift in Texas.

In his first letter to Ferne there was a silly photograph of him peeking behind a tree. What did they do to his hair? she wondered. And there was also a photograph of his new friend, Marv Bakke. "He's from Minnesota, a good-looking farm boy, don't you think?" he asked. "Maybe Jeane would like to write him? He needs a pen pal. Give her his photo and address. Can't say much now. They are working our butts off. I'm learning how to use a rifle. Austin is a fun town on our days off. Wish you were here, Love, Abe."

Jeane liked the photo, and she told Ferne it wouldn't matter that she was engaged to Eddy. She could write Marv, just to be a friend to a soldier. Now and again Ferne snapped their photos to include in the letters. Jeane always shyly drew back, but Ferne almost always stepped forward, sometimes acting silly, as if to say, *Look at me! I was here. I lived.*

Jeane   Me

May 1942

Me

august 1942

1942

Jeane

May 1942

1942 Feb 6 DFP

As Southerners migrated to Detroit for work in the defense industry, the demand for housing grew. Because of the war, there was very little home building. For the defense industry to work well, the housing problem had to be addressed. The Feds were aware that blacks had the most difficulties since they were segregated into crowded neighborhoods. Housing complexes were built for both black and white defense workers. The Sojourner Truth Project was planned in an area close to an already black neighborhood. Many whites were angry, not only because of their racism, but also because the Feds had redlined neighborhoods that touched on the project, and this meant that their houses would go down in value.

The day before the new tenants were scheduled to move in, on February 27, 1942, hundreds of whites showed up to protest; and blacks showed up to support those who were supposed to move in. 40 people were injured. Typical to the time, of the 220 people arrested, 217 were blacks and 3 were white.

(paraphrase) "Sojourner Truth Housing Project"

Rocks Hurt 2 In Melee at Home Project

Woman, Policeman Hit in Sojourner Truth Rioting

Fearing recurrence of a riot that earlier sent a white woman and policeman to the hospital, federal authorities today postponed the moving of Negro wamilies into the Sojourner Truth housing project.

A white woman and a white patrolman were injured by flying rocks today as rioting broke out at the Sojourner Truth defense housing project at Fenelon and Nevada avenues.

Twenty-four Negro families who signed leases for units in the project were to move in today and the riot started when a moving van, driven by a Negro, attempted to approach the project.

The van was preceded by two cars carrying several Negroes.

One hundred whites and 50 Negroes had gathered at Nevada avenue and Ryan road and stones started flying when the cars started down between the two groups.

Feb 27, 1942

118

Margaret Sanger Up in Arms
Over WAAC's 'No Babies' Rule

By the United Press

NEW YORK, June 9—Margaret Sanger, pioneer advocate of birth control, said today that the rule of no babies for members of the women's army will be a "Frankenstein which will turn and wreck the corps" unless it is mitigated by proper dissemination of birth-control information.

Mrs. Sanger, 59 years old, with the same snap and fire which has characterized her thirty-year fight for planned babies, pointed out what she considers the weakness of the Government's position.

"First of all," she said, "the Government owes it to women to give them preventive measures against pregnancy, just as it gives them protection against smallpox.

"Women should not be exposed to coming down with a baby any more than to coming down with yellow fever."

The WAAC expects to take 150,-000 women between the ages of 21 and 45, "the cream of womanhood." Proof of pregnancy will mean mandatory dismissal, under present regulations.

"Abortions and illegitimacy are bound to result if the Government doesn't recognize human nature," Mrs. Sanger said, "but lets dogma instead of facts control its attitude."

June 10, 1942 DFP

At the end of September, Jeane, Ferne and Delores were walking down Mack Avenue. They had just left the Uptown Theater where they had seen the new Sherlock Holmes film, *The Voice of Terror.*

"It was frightening, wasn't it?" Jeane asked, "with the radio announcer going on about the mighty wrath of the Führer and how they are coming to get the British, especially after that newsreel. I like the first Holmes movie better. It was more imaginative."

"I prefer comedy lately," Delores said. "I'm constantly worried about Myron. I need a break from the war."

"What I like," said Ferne, "is the way Holmes figured everything out and defeated the Nazis. But what an awful hairstyle he had with those curls on both sides of his forehead. Almost as bad as Abe's." She laughed.

"When Abe is sent to the Pacific or Europe and you watch those newsreels, it will seem more real to you," Delores said.

"We know, Delores," Jeane assured her. "We're just trying to look on the light side."

"We are all frightened about the war," Ferne said. "My father and mother taught us to be peaceful, and Pa was always helping people who were less fortunate. He would be shocked to see what is going on. Big factories building airplanes and tanks all over the world and everyone ferociously fighting with each other."

"There was a tinge of propaganda in the film, don't you think?" Delores asked.

"Yes," Ferne said. "Times will be difficult, but in the end, England will be greener and stronger."

"But we have to fight the Nazis and the Japanese," Jeane said. "They want to take over. We have no choice."

They all agreed.

When Jeane and Ferne got to their house, through the window they could see Hattie sitting in a chair under a yellow light reading the newspaper and waiting for them to come home.

THE WAR YEARS BROUGHT A number of hasty, impulsive marriages. . . . J. R. Woods and Sons, a large manufacturer of wedding rings, reported a 250 percent increase in sales after the Selective Service Act passed. In the three months after the military draft was initiated [September 1940], marriage rates climbed 25 percent over the preceding year and remained at the new higher level throughout 1941. Then came Pearl Harbor. In the month after the surprise attack, the marriage rate was 60 percent higher than in the same month one year before." Some married because of fear of being alone, of possible wartime death, for intimacy, to temporarily avoid the draft, to have quickly make a family, and some "married in order to receive the $50 monthly allotment checks and $10,000 life insurance policies given to the wife of each GI.
from Mintz & Kellog 153-154

Our Mailman

aug, 1942

Women Workers Win

Praised by Male Fellow Employes, Who Scoff
at Attitude of He Who Fled

Mack Mitchell can join the navy to get away from women workers at the Hudson naval arsenal at Center Line, but the women in the arsenal will not join the WAACs or the WAVES to get away from their male fellow employes. Nor will they let likes or dislikes of any disgruntled male scare them out of jobs they enjoy.

This was the consensus among the female workers in the same building at the arsenal where Mitchell was employed when he decided a ship would be a safe refuge from slacks. They enjoy working with men, they said yesterday, and strangely enough, most of the men working with them expressed a similar opinion.

The male workers as well as the female scoffed at Mitchell's uncharitable attitude toward women in the shops.

Nov 4, 1942

Salvages 2,500
Steel Hairpins

By CHARLES WEBER

Napoleon Fish has stooped 2,500 times in the last year to capitalize on milady's misfortune. Today Fish has a total of 2,500 steel hairpins he picked up in DSR buses. They're going off to war. An Employee of the DSR and old DUR for 23 of his 4 years. Fish started all his stooping merely as a hobby, which was a short jump to the war effort when it became evident scrap was the need of the day. For a year now, the hairpin Hawkshaw has been turning up seat cushions, peering up the floor for those little pieces of high-grade steel which keep milady's hair from doing a Veronica Lake. This is what Fish does during the stopover at the end of a bus-line run, impervious to the "kidding" some of the boys who would sooner spend the few minutes eating, smoking, or jawing. "The streetcars don't compare with searches for lost hairpins," he explains. "The coaches seem to shake them out of their hair more." Oct 24, 1942

me

The Wartime Cookbook

PREPARING MEALS for a family today is much more difficult than it was a year or even six months ago. Today homemakers are giving their time to Red Cross and civilian defense work so dishes that can be prepared in short order are much in demand.

Then, too, there is a need for new ways of packing lunches, and for foods that can be served at all hours of the day or night.

Meat substitutes are necessary to keep the budget down and the craving for something sweet requires the homemaker's cleverness in making desserts and candies that satisfy yet save on sugar.

"The Wartime Cookbook," offered by The Detroit Times Home Institute, is the answer to these and many more cooking problems. A meat loaf is a good way of stretching the budget, and here is a recipe for one taken from the cookbook:

Nov 4, 1942

WHERE'S THERE'S SMOKE, THERE'S BEAUTY

Exercise Program to Put Office Girls in Condition

By IDA JEAN KAIN

YOU HAVE to be in good condition to sit down and work all day. And that, so Gene Tunney says, it the reason the WAVES need a physical fitness program. They aren't expected to get tough, but they are going to have to get in shape to take over men's work.

They will have to work just as efficiently and for just as many hours as the men did. Besides taking daily calisthenics, they are drilling for that military bearing.

Everybody is working harder these days. If those girls need a daily dozen, certainly the average office worker does.

Nov 4, 1942

SECRET AGENT

Nov 4, 1942

CHAPTER 8

Jeane mom Agnes George me

5 Roads to Tokio All Long, Hard, Army Man Says

By MAJ. GEN. J N GREELY,
U. S. A.

Washington (INS). On Guadalcanal, on New Guinea, in Burma we have been killing Japanese and taking our losses in bloody and merciless fighting. In the Aleutians we have been making the Japs uncomfortable on their few remaining toeholds... Just as surely as we must end the European war in Berlin, we must dictate peace in the Far East from Tokyo. Japan has expanded beyond her strength... The road from India through Burma and China is likely to be the one we have to take and it is long and difficult... Fortunately India has great resources. There are nearly 400,000,000 Indians of all creeds and conditions... There is nothing easy about an island to island advance... Never-theless it can be done... Once we hold the Philippines again all Japanese shipping in the south is in danger. Mar 7, 1943

Abe came home on leave in March. He had good news for Ferne. His division was moving to Fort Sam Houston at San Antonio, and there was housing for families. She could come and they'd have an apartment together. The fort was right in the middle of town, he'd heard, so they'd have lots to do.

"How would I get there?" she asked as they sat on the back steps.

"On a train, of course."

"That's a long way for me to go alone, Abe. How long will you be stationed there?"

"I'm not sure, but I think a few months. Otherwise they wouldn't let us invite our wives."

"I'm afraid to tell Ma," Ferne said. "I don't like the idea of leaving her for that long."

"Come on, Fernie," he said. "Your mother will be okay. John is there with Aggy, and Kate is nearby, and Ward's down the block. They'll be sending me overseas soon enough." He kissed her on the neck. "Maybe you can bring Jeane with you. She'll like Marv."

Ferne looked at him, rolling her eyes. "She's engaged to Eddy!"

"Well, she's not married, right?"

"What about our jobs?"

"There are plenty of jobs in Detroit now. You'll find another when you come home."

Three days later, when Jeane and Ferne got off the train with their suitcases, Abe was standing on the platform with his friend, Marv.

They were off for the weekend, but maneuvers would start again on Monday morning. Then they'd be away for three days.

Ferne's first surprise was a large visitor from the insect world crawling around the edge of the front door. She screamed, and Abe laughed, stepped over it and grabbed a broom to shoo it away.

"Scorpions are quite common here. They won't hurt you unless you step on them. Be sure to check your shoes before you put them on."

That afternoon she made a list of groceries, and the men went to the commissary to buy supplies. Then they baked bread and cooked dinner. While eating, Marv told stories about his horses back home and the great cinnamon buns his mother made every week.

"Ferne's specialty is peanut butter–chocolate fudge," Abe said.

One night, Ferne and Abe were sitting in a cafe when a young woman walked by and stopped to say, "Hello, Abe." He smiled and she moved on.

"How do you know her?" Ferne asked. She crossed her legs and slid to the edge of the chair.

"She was here when I came with a couple of the guys a few weeks ago. That's all, Fernie. We talked. Nothing to be worried about."

She looked at him and he looked away. The girl was standing against a building next door, and she was staring at him.

Later that night in bed, Ferne turned over on her side, deeply disturbed.

"Come on, honey, I have no interest in anyone but you. She likes me. I talked to her. That's all. Nothing serious. I don't know why she was staring at me."

Ferne threw a pillow across the room, knocking a glass off the table. "Do you think I'm an idiot? How would you like it, George Abriel, if I went out and flirted with other men? I've been working and thinking only about *you*."

Abe got out of bed and started sweeping up the glass. "It's just a way of unwinding from the maneuvers, to just go out and talk to people. You're my wife, Ferne. Would I ask you to come here if I had something else going on?"

"You shit." She turned against the wall. "Remember, you took an oath."

"And I've kept it. I haven't done anything."

In the morning after the men left, Jeane told Ferne that she was going to marry Marv. They were getting married next week. "We're in love, Fernie."

"Are you kidding, Jeane? You just met him. What about Eddy?"

"I'll write him a letter, or maybe I'll wait and tell him when we get home."

"He's going to be heartbroken, Jeane."

"I know, but I can't help it, Ferne. I'm really in love with Marv. We can talk to each other. I like how he talks to me."

"Jeane, you better make a phone call home and talk to Ma first."

A week later Jeane and Marv were married. Hattie was concerned about how quickly Jeane had decided, but she knew her child well, so she said, "I'm so happy for you, Jeane. I hope he's a good man." Marv's mother was very upset when he called her with the news. She didn't like the idea of him marrying a city girl. He insisted that he loved her, so she, too, gave him her blessing and put an announcement in the Karlstad, Minnesota newspaper.

Marvel Bakke Married

On Palm Sunday, April 18, 1943 at the 377 Infantry Chapel at Fort Sam Houston, Texas, Miss Jean Hostetter of Detroit, Michigan became the bride of Col. Marvel Bakke, Mrs. George Abriel, sister of the bride, was matron of honor and Pvt. George Abriel, friend of the bridegroom, was best man. The ceremony was performed by Chaplain Donald F. Perron.

Miss Hostetter is the daughter of Mrs. Hattie Hostetter and the Late Mr. Luke Hostetter of Detroit. Cpl. Bakke is the son of Mr. and Mrs. Charles Bakke of Kennedy.

The bride wore a navy blue crepe afternoon dress trimmed in pink, with a pink carnation corsage. Her hat was navy blue straw with pink flowers and navy veiling The matron of honor also wore a navy blue costume with red carnation corsage.

When he returned from a four-day maneuver in the desert, Abe was covered with dust. After washing up, he sat down on a chair and started digging into his calf with a needle. "I have to get this damn tick out of my leg. Tomorrow we're on base and wrestling. I like wrestling."

"Wrestling?"

"They're using the sport to train us to fight."

"It sounds kind of disgusting to me."

"War is disgusting," he said, looking up at her. "Hon, let's go out for dinner or a movie. There's a comedy in town, *Swing It, Soldier*. Maybe Jeane and Marv will come with us."

"I think they're in for the night. They may be in for the night for a long time."

"They don't have that much time. We just found out today that we're being moved out of here in two weeks."

"What? Where are you going?"

"They won't say. We'll find out after we arrive. We need to get train tickets soon so you and Jeane can go back home."

Ferne kept brushing her hair. How could she bear it, she wondered, not just the separation, but now this new insecurity about his commitment.

He watched as she was looking in the mirror. "Let's forget the movie, Fernie. Even though I'm tired, let's go dancing. Okay, kiddo?"

The Floores store had a big cement outdoor dance space in back, and the music was country western with a jazzy twist. West Coast swing was not quite as wild as East Coast, but still great fun. When they were dancing slow, Abe whispered in her ear, "You know, Fernie, I love you, I love you inside out, outside in, all over."

So she forgave him his flirtation. After all, he was a flirt. That's what she liked about him, as long as he was flirting with her and nobody else.

George and Marv

One afternoon, Ferne was walking with Jeane along the river. "No matter what we do, my period starts just like clockwork," she said.

"Don't worry, Fernie, you'll have a baby soon. It's just not the right time, that's all."

"You're probably right. Will you do me a favor, Jeane? Will you ask Marv if Abe has been running around with other women?"

"What?"

"You heard me. When we go out, there's a girl. Once she said hello to Abe. Then she stood at a distance watching us. We had a terrible argument that night, but he assured me he wasn't seeing her."

"I don't think he is, Fernie. I really don't. But, of course, I'll ask Marv when the time is right."

Abe came home one night with the paper. "Jesus Christ," he said, "Detroit is exploding. There's been a big riot between blacks and whites, and the National Guard has been called in. You and Jeane can't go home until this is over. We've got to change your tickets. You can't leave tomorrow. They're turning over cars on the street, burning them and pulling people out of streetcars."

Ferne picked up the paper and started reading. "Give me some money, Abe. I have to call home." She scooped up some change off the table and ran out the door, letting it slam behind her.

Abe ran after her. "Wait for me, Fernie. Your mom will be fine! She has Ward and John there. And the fighting's mostly downtown in the black areas and on Belle Isle."

When she came out of the commissary, he was sitting on the bench.

"All is well. Everyone's staying inside. Ward's bringing her groceries. Everybody's okay, but she thinks we should stay another week until things calm down."

"I told you," he said. "We could have saved that dollar."

A few days later Abe and Marv left with their division, but Jeane and Ferne stayed behind for a few days until things calmed down in Detroit.

April 17, 1943

April 17, 1943

me *Jeane*

April 27, 1943

Troops Infiltrate City; Guns Cover Riot Areas

Bars Ordered Shut; Stores Close Early

Rioting Blamed On Youths; Kelly Eases Orders

10 KILLED, 261 INJURED, 434 JAILED IN RIOTS

Armored Crews Round Up Looters

June 22, 1943

Appeal to Reason

Dr. James J. McClendon, president of the Detroit branch of the National Association for the Advancement of Colored People, made this appeal today:

"We appeal to all citizens, white and colored, to refrain from taking the law into their own hands. Let us not fight among ourselves. Let us fight our enemies, the Axis powers. Remember the Axis method of dividing and conquering. We need to make guns, tanks and airplanes in Detroit. Let us do that. Let us not help our enemies."

The Rev. Horace A. White of the Plymouth Congregational Church, a Negro leader, made this statement:

"It is not the wishes of the colored people in Detroit that this riot continue, or even start. It is a hoodlum element of colored people who are carrying it out. We colored people have nothing to gain by such tactics and have so much to lose. I have requested of the mayor that if this continues that he deputize each colored minister in Detroit and give him permission to stand on street corners and try and stop the rioting."

Detroit Commanded to Halt Violence

In his executive order President Roosevelt commanded all Detroiters to halt violence.

Casualties, including those treated at neighborhood hospitals, totaled an estimated 600. More than 200 others were injured but did not require hospital treatment, police said. Receiving Hospital, which handled the bulk of the cases, registered 539 victims, of which 111 still were confined today.

A total of 1,300 men and boys, approximately 85 per cent Negroes, were under arrest. Under an agreement with courts, none will be released for 72 hours.

Up to noon today 35 of a long line of defendants facing court action as a result of the riots were sent to jail for 90-day terms.

Dozens of homes and buildings had been ripped by gunfire, including one that was besieged in warfare fashion, scarred by more than 1,000 rounds of ammunition.

Rioters Work For the Axis

THE rioting of last night and today is the most disastrous thing that has happened to Detroit since Pearl Harbor.

Unless it stops at once it may well become a disaster to the United States war effort, a disaster as grave as the loss of a major battle on one of the war fronts.

Because unless it stops immediately it is bound to interrupt war production in this war production center of the world.

If it continues, many war plants here will have to close because the rioting inevitably will spread to those plants.

Now is no time to argue the causes of the rioting, which is deplored alike by the great decent majority of Negro and white citizens of Detroit. The trouble obviously was fostered by unruly and irresponsible minorities of both groups.

NOW IS THE TIME FOR ALL PATRIOTIC DETROITERS, REGARDLESS OF RACE, TO CO-OPERATE IN A DETERMINED EFFORT TO STAMP-OUT THE DISORDERS.

Mayor Appeals To All for Order

"The whole trouble apparently had its inception in an isolated fist fight. There is absolutely no evidence at the present time of any organized effort to create trouble.

"The complete police department has been mobilized and law and order will be maintained."

"I appeal to all the citizens of Detroit to insist on maintaining our orderly routine. The nation needs our maximum resources — every minute counts. These fights accomplish nothing, except to upset our war efforts. Remember, your country needs you now.

"Edward J. Jeffries, Jr."

June 21-23 1943

Supreme Court Backs Reds, Hits Japs in Decisions

WASHINGTON, June 21 (UP)

The Supreme Court in a 5 to 3 split, ruled today that membership in the Communist Party is not sufficient reason for revoking a person's American citizenship. The decision came when the tribunal set aside lower court orders taking away the citizenship of William Schneiderman, Russian born California Communist earlier who admitted that he belonged to the Communist Party when he received his citizenship papers in 1927. The government contended that the party sought violent overturning of this government and therefore Schneiderman's oath of allegiance was fraudulent.

WASHINGTON, June 21 (INS)

The Supreme court today unanimously held constitutional military restrictions imposed on American citizens of Japanese descent on the Pacific Coast. Chief Justice Stone read the opinion in which the high court declared:

"We cannot close our eyes to the fact, demonstrated by experience that in times of war, residents holding ethnic affiliation with an invading army may be a greater source of danger than those of a different ancestry. Nor can we deny that Congress and the military authorities acting with its authorization, have constitutional power to appraise the danger." June 22, 1943

Yanks Smash Nazi Bases at Lorient, Brest

Raid Follows Quickly on Tremendous RAF Assault on Essen

LONDON, March 7 (Sunday) (INS).—American Flying Fortress and Liberator bombers hammered the Nazi U-boat base at Lorient and the naval and submarine harbor at Brest in France Saturday, it was announced officials today, only a few hours after the RAF pounded the German city of Essen.

The vital naval power station at Lorient was left in flames and a nearby railroad bridge was partly destroyed under the impact of several direct hits as the American planes heaped destruction on the enemy's fortified U-boat base. Three bombers and two fighters were missing.

U.S. Bombers Hit Factories In Ruhr Raid

LONDON, June 22 (UP)—Powerful formations of heavy American bombers successfully attacked the Ruhr and Belgium today, concentrating their bombs on a synthetic rubber plant in northwest Germany and the former General Motors plant near Antwerp.

Twenty bombers and four fighters are missing in today's United States and RAF attacks spearheading one of the most intense aerial offensives of the war.

May 7, 1943   June 23, 1943

When they arrived at the train depot in Detroit, John was waiting on the platform. "You two must be exhausted," he said, hugging his sisters and taking their luggage. "And now you're a married woman, Jeane. When will we meet your husband?"

"He'll have a furlough soon. What will Ma do with two couples in the flat?"

"Oh, she's used to us all driving her crazy," John said. "She'll love it."

"Why are we going this direction?" Ferne asked.

"I'm avoiding Black Bottom," John said. "It's not good there. Some places on Woodward, too. A lot of stores were looted and ruined. Brutal things going on. They were throwing people off the bridge at Belle Isle, mostly blacks."

"Is it going to be okay for us to go back to work?" Jeane asked. "We need to call the office to be sure our jobs are still there."

"I don't think it's safe for women to take the streetcars this week. Maybe wait another week or two. Your jobs will be there. They need you now... How did you girls like Texas?"

Jeane laughed. "You should have seen Fernie scream when she saw a tarantula."

"It wasn't a tarantula, Jeane, it was a scorpion. Nasty looking insect."

June 22, 1943

In August, Ferne received a letter from Abe. They were at Fort Polk in Louisiana and would be there for quite some time. It was blistering hot, he wrote, almost 120 degrees. "A few days ago they were marching us through a swampy area. It was burning hot. Suddenly we found ourselves in front of a watermelon patch. The guys went crazy. Out came our knives, and in an hour's time we had devoured all of the melons."

Jeane laughed. "Marv told a story, too, about a sergeant who made them stand in pouring monsoon rain for four hours straight. Then he said to the men, *That's just a touch of what you may experience. Instead of standing still, you'll be soaking wet, fighting off mosquitos and marching through jungle turf.* I guess that's not funny."

While listening to his aunts talk, little Terry was running an army truck around the corner of the table. He watched them as they mixed dye into a sink full of water and painted their legs a light shade of brown, then drew a straight line up the back of their calves.

"Why are you drawing on your legs, Auntie Jeane?" he asked.

"We can't get stockings so this is the best we can do."

POPULAR

Dorothy Donnegan is the sensational new boogie pianist who will be featured in the new show opening Friday at the Paradise.

Volunteers Escort Women War Workers

PHILADELPHIA, Nov. 4 (INS)—The old cry of "lady, there's a man following you," has taken on a new meaning in the Quaker City, since auxiliary policemen and air raid wardens have undertaken the job of escorting feminine war workers to their homes at night.

From sundown until midnight, and sometimes later, these uniformed volunteers patrol their neighborhoods, meeting trains, trolleys and busses, and seeing that women who work late get home safely.

Order War Stamps delivered to your home by your Detroit Times carrier.

Homemakers Can Avoid Monotony

MANY A WOMAN who waits hand and foot on every member of the family gets to feel like a drudge and to look it. She is beset with complexes, no matter how happy she is to serve in the domestic cause. She loses contact with what is going on in the world.

Nothing wrecks good looks like monotony. One day the same as another. It is better for the homemaker to lay off the floor mop and duster and look after herself, so she will keep within longer touch of her youth.

She should read interesting books, see interesting movies, find time to call in her neighbor for a cup of tea and a nice little hour of gossip. That can be done without neglecting the job.

Nov 4, 1943

Cossacks Slaughter Germans

40 JAP SHIPS BLASTED
UAW Joins Soldier-Santa Drive

Nazis Lose Town In Slav Battle

Nov 4, 1943

November 25, 1943

Ferne looked out the back window and saw Jeane rushing across the yard to take down some laundry. She darted out to catch a photo of her. "No! Don't you dare take my photo!" Jeane yelled, but it was too late.

Then Ferne spotted Hattie walking through the alley heading home from the Piggly Wiggly on Mack Avenue. She stopped her for a photograph.

"Can't I put down the grocery bags?" Hattie asked.

"No, Ma, I want you just as you are." Behind her there were some heaps of dirt from repaving the alley.

When Ferne picked up the photos from the drugstore, she showed them to Jeane.

"Jeanie, you look so beautiful. Look at your little belly."

"Ugh!" She grabbed the photo out of Ferne's hand and with a green pen she drew an arrow and the words: True Ugly Duckling!

"Jeanie, damn, you ruined the photo."

In the winter, when Ferne heard from Abe that they were in the desert in California, she was worried they were going to send him into the war in the Pacific. She didn't mention her fear to him. Instead she sent a photo of herself ice skating at a rink near Esther and Jack's house. "Skate to me!" Esther's husband Jack yelled to Ferne. Then he snapped her photo, and she turned and continued gliding around the pond. The wind was cold and her toes were a little numb but around and around she went chasing the children.

"Whenever Esther needs me," she wrote Abe, "I take the streetcar over to babysit for Johnnie and Bicky. I love those kids. You may be freezing in the desert at night, love, but my fingers are tingling here, too. Tingling for you. Love, Ferne."

me   Bicky

Jan 2, 1944

Ferne with Esther's daughter Carolee (Bicky)

PENICILLIN TO BE PLENTIFUL

Firms Speed Output of Wonder Drug

Penicillin, medicine's m o d e r n wonder drug, will be available for civilian and military use in sufficient quantities to meet the demand before the end of 1944, it was predicted Tuesday night by Miles Bruno, head of bacteriological research for Frederick Stearns & Co.

Bruno, who spoke at the first winter conference of the Michigan Academy of Pharmacy at the Rackham Memorial Building, said that concentration on the production of penicillin by major pharmaceutical firms had resulted in improvements in technique which assured a supply sufficient to treat patients whose infections could not be treated by other agents.

In the interim, it was explained by Dr. John W. Hirshfeld, of Wayne University and Receiving Hospital, victims of certain infections could obtain the drug in some cases on application by their physician to the Office of Scientific Research and Development, which is headed by Dr. Chester Keefer, of Boston.

Dr. Hirshfeld said that only physicians trained in the use of penicillin in a special field and registered with the research bureau could administer it.

"As the Government at present controls the distribution of even small quantities of penicillin, ap-plications for the drug are carefully scrutinized," he said. "If it is believed that it is the only curative agent, it can be granted for civilian use, but the administering physician must keep complete records of dosage and results to be turned into the bureau for statistical compilation."

The doctor, who is one of the few Detroit physicians qualified and authorized to administer the drug, emphasized that much resentment had been aroused among laymen who gained the impression from published articles that they could obtain it to treat almost any ailment.

Dec 29, 1943 DFP

Enemy Doomed, Roosevelt Tells Nation

WASHINGTON, Jan. 1 (INS)—President Roosevelt said today the "walls are closing in remorselessly on our enemies."

In a New Year's message to the American people, the President added that the armed forces of the United Nations were "gathering for new and greater assaults which will bring about the downfall of the Axis aggressors."

Looking ahead to the postwar world, he appealed to the people to pledge themselves to support in peacetime the co-operation among the United Nations that is bringing victory to the Allied cause.

"To make all of us secure against future aggression and to open the way for enhanced well being of nations and individuals everywhere." the President's statement continued, "we must maintain in the peace to come the mutually beneficial co-operation we have achieved in war.

On the threshold of the new year, as we look toward the tremendous tasks ahead, let us pledge ourselves that this co-operation shall continue, both for winning the final victory on the battlefield and for establishing an international organization of all peace-loving nations to maintain peace and security in generations to come."

Detroit's War Record For Year Reviewed
See Page 2, Column 1

Largest Circulation of Any Michigan Newspaper

DETROIT TIMES

Only Detroit Newspaper Carrying Both International News and United Press

FINAL

44TH YEAR, NO. 92   PART ONE   DETROIT 31, MICHIGAN, SUNDAY, JANUARY 2, 1944   ISSUED EVERY SUNDAY   TWELVE CENTS

Beaten Nazis In Disorderly Flight West

Germans Abandon Korosten Positions In Headlong Retreat

MOSCOW, Jan. 1 (INS)—Red Army troops raced to within 27 miles of the old Polish border today on the heels of routed Nazi forces fleeing in disorder before a Soviet juggernaut rolling westward along a 200-mile front in the central Ukraine.

New Year Firsts

Stork Takes a Bow in GP Hospital

("First Baby" picture, Page 3)

Following is a list of "firsts" for 1944 in Detroit where the populace took only a brief interlude to welcome the New Year before returning to the job of helping to win the war.

First birth: An eight-pound, three ounce baby girl born at midnight in Grosse Pointe Hospital to Mr. and Mrs. Harvey E. Kuffert of 15822 Faircrest. The physician was Dr. A. J. Neumann.

First marriage: Alfred A. Rahy and Retha Sagg, married at 12:01 a. m. at the home of the Rev. John Shuring, 1442 Maryland. They both work at the U. S. Marine Hospital.

FIRST HOLDUP

First holdup: At 12:05 a. m. an armed man took $72 from Louis Stavros, an attendant in a filling station at 11530 Wyoming, and three friends who were waiting for him to lock up.

Cash Speeded To Wounded

Immediate Payment of Benefits O.K'd

By DAVID CAMELON
Detroit Times Washington Bureau

WASHINGTON, Jan. 1 — No more red tape delay, no more months of hunger for the boys who have lost legs or arms in the war.

The veterans' administration has sent orders to its rating boards that in amputation cases they shall not wait for medical records, but shall award disability compensation immediately.

Jan 2, 1944

138

Town Talk---by Stark

By GEORGE W. STARK

APRIL 1 portends and with it the birthday of Joseph Grundy, who will be 90 years old on that day. He will celebrate by following the day's routine, which means that he will be up early and about his tasks at the River Rouge plant of the Ford Motor Co. There he is the oldest employe, and while Town Talk has no statistics available it would not be surprising to learn that he is the oldest employe in point of years in the entire huge Ford industrial domain.

Joe Grundy went to work at the Rouge plant in 1922, when he was a mere youth of 70 years. He still gets a smile out of an incident that happened when he was hired. His son was just ahead of him in the employment line and when they came to Joe, the man said, "Well, Mr. Grundy, we just hired your brother and I guess we can use you, too."

Ninety-year-old Joe Grundy was hired as a railroad car inspector. He still does a good job of inspecting, which requires sharp ears, good eyes. "In fact," says Joe, "you got to keep your eyes peeled all the time. I carry a little kit of tools around with me and I fix all the little things that can be fixed right on the spot. The bigger jobs I turn over to the shopmen."

Joe was working for a railroad when he came 70. The railroad told him he was too old to work and had to quit. That made him mad so he went right out to Ford's, got himself a job, and there he's been ever since.

He has an A1 attendance rating. He's never been late a day. He gets up every day at the crack of dawn (war time dawn) and one of the boys drives him to the plant. Once in a while he takes a bus.

Ordinarily a man would hesitate on his ninetieth birthday and call it a holiday. Not Joe. He aims to be at the plant on time and put in a full day.

"This is no time for April Fool jokes, birthday parties or any other shenanigans," says Joe. "We're in a war!"

*   *   *

JOSEPH GRUNDY
—Henry Ford's oldest

Apr 1, 1944

When Grandad turned 90 years old, George Stark wrote an article about him in his column in *The Detroit News* celebrating the fact that Joseph was the oldest employee at Ford. Grandad explains why he was so diligent. "This is no time for April Fool's jokes, birthday parties or any other shenanigans," said Joe. "We're in a war." Still he would have been disappointed if the Hostetters and Grundys had not shown up to celebrate, and that Sunday was a bigger celebration than a wedding. He sat in his chair in the sunroom waiting for all the grandchildren to pass through, each paying respects and receiving a nickel in exchange. Ferne sat at the dining room table with a stack of newspapers, clipping one for each person. Abe liked Grandad a lot, so she sent him a clipping, too.

Abe wrote that they had just arrived at a base near Harrisburg, Pennsylvania. He begged Ferne to come to Pennsylvania. They would be stationed there for a while, he thought. It was a 500-mile trip, part by train, part by bus. In the beginning of April she and Jeane packed up again and went to join their husbands. They had adjoining rooms in an apartment building, nothing quite as charming as their housing in San Antonio. When the boys were gone, the girls would play cards and try to entertain themselves. They had hardly any money, but Ferne had brought a secret stash of coins, so they could go to the canteen and split a sweet roll or a hamburger.

In May, the two wives were sent home, and the men were given a short leave. Both couples boarded a train to celebrate Mother's Day with Hattie. Jeane was already three months pregnant.

After the men left to return to the base, Jeane told Ferne that when she tried to ask Marv about Abe and other women, he wouldn't say anything. He said that Abe was his friend and he didn't want to say anything that might be misunderstood.

"Huh? What does that mean? His unwillingness to say something makes me even more suspicious," Ferne said. "Otherwise, he would have said— absolutely not. Wouldn't he? I'm going to try to block this thought out of my mind. With the war, and now they're going—Jeane let's not talk about it anymore."

On D Day, June 6th, the Battle of Normandy began, and the allied troops began pushing Nazi Germany back. Ferne and Jeane hoped that this meant the war would be over soon. Then in the middle of July, Abe and Marv got orders to ship out. No one knew exactly where they were going, but surely somewhere in Europe.

Marv and Jeane   Ferne and George

Abe, Barbara, Ed, Katie, Jeane, Dickie and Marv

Women Rap Strike Call

Two women MESA strikers, interviewed today outside the Parker Wolverine plant at Milwaukee and St. Aubin, admitted they were not in sympathy with those who ordered them to quit work on war materials.

"I am a member of the union and I have always felt it is a good thing," one of the women said. "Today, however, I have a guilty conscience. I feel as though I have pulled a low trick."

The other woman said:

"I cannot understand why labor trouble in Ohio should affect our jobs here."

Five men in another group agreed with a spokesman who said:

"So long as the union called us out it is O. K. It's not up to us to explain why the strike in Toledo was called."

Its Treason, Army Says

WASHINGTON, Nov. 3 (UP)—Undersecretary of war Patterson today telegraphed Matthew Smith, secretary of the Mechanics Educational Society of America, Cleveland, charging that strikes sponsored by Smith's organization were "equivalent to treason" because they were stopping the flow of vitally needed munitions and supplies to the fighting front.

The strike in 21 Detroit area war plants controlled by the Mechanics Educational Society of America started today at 10 a. m. as scheduled, with plant after plant closing as the men walked out in sympathy over a jurisdictional dispute with the UAW-CIO in Toledo.

Why Girls Use 'Miss'

By HELEN ROWLAND

"THE 'MRS.' before the name of any novelist, playwright, actress or woman in business," writes my confrere E. V. Durling, "packs more of a punch than 'Miss,' does."

Well, I wouldn't argue with you, Mr. E. V. But I can explain why a career woman so often insists on calling herself "Miss" when she is really a wife and mother and would just love to use her husband's name and the title "Mrs."

If the career-girl has made her name of commercial value before she marries, it would be a very expensive experiment for her to change it from "Jane Smith" to "Mrs. Johnny Jones." So she just goes right on being "Miss Jane Smith" or Fannie Hurst or Billie Burke or whoever she was when she became famous.

Nov 4, 1944

More Typists Needed for War Work

By PHILOMENE EZACK

THE RAT-A-TAT of a typewriter manned by you, Sue Smith of Detroit, may prove to be just as deadly to the Japs or Nazis as the similar sounding, death-dealing clatter of a machine gun!

You may have the satisfaction of knowing you're hurling a blast at the enemy and getting paid for it!

Authority for this statement is Col. F. L. Devereux, administrative officer of the Office of the Chief of Ordnance, Detroit, whose job it is to keep the implements of war rolling to the battle fronts.

Start Them Rolling

Everything on wheels: tanks, jeeps, trucks, gun motor carriages, transport and combat vehicles, all rolling stock that goes to the various theaters of war are issued through this ordnance office. Yet before they can be sent on their way, it takes many, many Sue Smiths to do the paper work that starts them rolling.

So important is this work that Col. Devereux maintains the war depends right now upon typists.

"If our girls, who work with codes and handle all addressing, make a mistake, Gen. MacArthur will get a shipment of screw drivers instead of the tanks he needs," is the way he explains it.

To keep supplies moving to the front, more typists and stenographers are needed right now. If you are 18 years of age and a high school graduate you may qualify for one of these jobs.

Full time employment consists of a 48-hour week. Salaries start at $1,260 per year for a 40 hour week, with time and a half for all over time work.

Personal Service

A specialized training unit enables employes to learn while earning. If you can type but need more speed, you will be given the chance to acquire it during working hours. Or if you need to brush up on your stenography, the training unit will help you.

Even your personal problems are considered and this is handled by the employe-relations bureau that aids employes in everything from financial troubles to finding a place to live. Help with personal shopping, a vacation service, securing tickets for various plays and concerts, a Christmas shopping aid and organized social activities are just a few of the services offered by this bureau.

All employes of OCOD enjoy the rights and privileges of civil service employes, but it is not necessary to pass a civil service examination.

Those interested are asked to contact Miss Mildred Downend, U. S. Civil Service Commission representative, room 402, Federal Building, Detroit 33, Mich.

Nov 4, 1944

Let All Off to Vote, FDR Tells Industry

WASHINGTON, Nov. 3 (UP)—President Roosevelt requested today that any employe who is not allowed sufficient voting time away from his job next Tuesday "inform me of the circumstances, together with the name of his company and any pertinent facts."

Nov 4, 1944

After Abe was sent overseas, Ferne rarely heard from him, but she wrote him almost every day. When his letters arrived, anything indicating where they were was blacked out. But he did mention at one point that there were so many casualties that almost half his platoon had been taken prisoner, wounded or killed. Fighting was fierce, nothing like he had ever expected. He mentioned having a lot of trouble with his feet because of the flooding. Ferne wrote him on November 20th asking him to tell Marv if he saw him that Jeane just had a beautiful little boy, little Marvel Lynn. "He's got red hair! And he looks like a baby picture of Marv. We're waiting for both of you to come home. Lots of love, Ferne."

In early December, a Western Union messenger knocked on the door. Jeane walked into the room with Marvel Lynn in her arms. Hattie handed her the envelope and took the baby. Jeane was crying even before she could tear it open.

"Oh my god, Ma, he's missing in action. Missing . . ."

Hattie followed her into the bedroom. "I'm very sorry, dear. Maybe he will be found. Let's pray for him, Jeanie. Let's pray for him."

When Ferne came home from Briggs, she found her sister locked in her room and her mother was taking care of the baby.

That night Hattie wrote a letter to Marv's mother in Minnesota, a woman neither she nor Jeane had ever met.

> Dear Mrs. Bakke,
> I don't know if I should tell you this or not, but I think you must have had word by now. Jeane got a telegram from the War Department saying Marvel has been missing since Nov. 13th. I do hope they find out more about the real facts, as Jeane and all of

us will feel better about it. He is possibly a prisoner of war or in some hospital. Please let us hear from you. Our phone is under the name of Ferne Abriel. Tuxedo 1-2609. So if you would rather call Jeane, you will be able to do so. The baby is doing nicely, but I hope he doesn't get a setback, because Jeane is surely taking this awful hard.

Mrs. Bakke, I do wish I were able to talk with you. I might be able to help you, but God knows best if this has to be. I hope and pray we will be able to bear up. Let us hear from you.

With Sympathy, Mrs. Hostetter

A few days later, Ferne heard from Abe. "Thank you so much for all your letters, Fernie. They mean a lot to me. I got a stack of them today. It's great about the baby. Give Jeane a kiss for me. I haven't seen Marv in a while. We aren't in the same platoon and we've been out on different actions."

After writing three letters to the War Department, Jeane received a letter from the adjutant general explaining that "The term missing-in-action is said only to indicate that the whereabouts or status of an individual is not immediately known. I wish to assure you, Mrs. Bakke, that at any time additional information is received, it will be transmitted to you without delay. Experience has shown that many persons missing in action are subsequently reported as prisoners of war."

CHAPTER 9

After taking off so much time, Ferne was at the bottom of the list for seniority at Briggs. In March when the production started declining, she was laid off. She had only a small monthly stipend from the army for wives ($28 plus $22 a month from Abe's allotment). She gave half of this to Hattie to help with the bills for the house. She also made money by making drapes and clothes for friends and neighbors. They would buy the fabric, and she'd make the dress or coat. Today she was working on making a little jumpsuit for Marvel Lynn out of scraps left from a neighbor's blue-stripped dress. She went into Jeane's room to measure him.

"Gosh, he's bigger than he was three days ago! Jeane, I can't believe it. I'll have to extend this pattern." She picked him up and laid him on the bed. He giggled and rolled over, watching Ferne with his eyes as she wiggled the yellow measuring tape around him like a dancing snake. "What a head full of red hair he has! Where did that come from, buddy?"

"I hope his father comes home. What will we do without him?" Jeane was folding diapers and putting them into a big basket in the corner.

In his last letter, Abe had written that they had lost so many guys that his platoon looked entirely different from when they started. He mentioned that they were crossing over into Holland soon and this time not one line in his letter was censored.

While Ferne was sewing the pieces together, Marvel Lynn was asleep and Jeane was on the porch with Hattie. The house was quiet except for the sound of Ferne's foot pumping the pedal on the machine.

After several days of rain, the clouds moved over the horizon. Ferne and Jeane took the baby in the carriage over to the children's playground on Nottingham. Whenever Jeane stopped pushing the swing, Marvel would cry. Then she'd push him again. Then she'd stop and he'd start to whine. Then she'd push him again.

Suddenly Jeane started crying. "What have they done to him, Fernie?"

"There's a good chance he's alive and in a prison, Jeanie."

"Look what the Nazis did to the Jewish people. The Soviets found thousands in a concentration camp, millions killed, millions of children. Even if he is a prisoner, we don't know that Marv's okay. I'm sick of this war. Nothing will ever be the same."

"I think we will still love each other, and if we keep that alive, maybe that's all we can do. Abe thinks the war'll be over soon," Ferne took the baby out of the swing. His cheeks were bright red from the cold. She adjusted his hat to cover his ears, kissed his cheek, and set him in the carriage. Then they walked home, crossing over the borderline between Grosse Pointe into Detroit. As they were waiting for the light to change, Jeane noticed Ward's son Terry on the porch. "Stay there, Terry!" she yelled. "Don't come down the stairs!" The streetcar horn blew a warning, and little Terry held on tight to the railing, waiting for them to arrive. Then he came running down the front steps toward them. "Next time, Auntie Ferne, take me to the park, too," he said.

After dinner Hattie turned on the radio for the news; they were stunned. President Roosevelt had died from a stroke. Hattie started to cry, then Jeane and Ferne, too. Terry looked around with concern. "Gramma," he said, "what's wrong? Why is everyone crying?"

Good evening Ladies and Gentlemen, this is Fulton Lewis Junior speaking from the Mutual Studios in New York City. This nation has suffered this day a staggering loss. At this moment, in Warm Springs, Georgia, the President Franklin D. Roosevelt lies with the problems of the nation finally lifted from his shoulders. Stricken late this afternoon with cerebral hemorrhage, he passed away before his physicians could be of any assistance, if assistance in such a case is possible at all at all. Vice President Harry Truman, who from here on will be President Truman, went immediately to the White House. A special cabinet meeting was called, and we should know more about what is going to happen in Washington as the evening wears on. But Franklin D. Roosevelt, the first president to be elected for four terms in the white house has passed away. And that is the overshadowing of all news events that have happened or could happen for quite a while.

The beginning of Fulton Lewis Jr.'s regular Mutual Network newscast, 7 P.M. Eastern time, April 12, 1945.

Roosevelt's Body on Way Home

FDR's Death Stuns Detroit

In the home and factory and office and on the street in Detroit today, there was but one topic of conversation—President Roosevelt's death.

The atmosphere was of awe and reverence of the stature of the mighty man who had fallen in action as truly as any soldier. The city moved quickly to honor his memory.

Common council directed that municipal memorial services be held at 4 p. m. Sunday in Cadillac square.

April 14, 1945

Eisenhower Pledges No Letup by Armies

SUPREME HQ. ALLIED-EXPEDITIONARY FORCE, April 13 (INS)—Gen. Eisenhower today promised President Truman and, through him, the Allied world, that the death of President Roosevelt will not deter American armies in their final dash for victory.

Speaking in his capacity as head of the American—and Allied—forces in Europe, Eisenhower said:

"Although we are grieved and shocked by the death of President Roosevelt, the American armies in Europe pledge you, our new commander in chief, our unremittent efforts for the achievement of final victory."

Eisenhower also sent a message of condolence to Mrs. Roosevelt.

April 14, 1945 DFP

From Hattie's Scrapbook posted in their window
Detroit Times Apr 16, 1945

147

Nazi Radio Announces:
WAR ENDS IN EUROPE

May 9, 1945

Murder of 5 Million in Nazi Camp Charged

BY ROBERT RICHARDS

NEAR ERFURT, Germany—(UP)—Dr. Bela Fabian, one-time president of the Hungarian Independent Democratic Party and prisoner of the Nazis, charged Wednesday that German elite-guard troops had slaughtered five million men, women and children at the Auschwitz concentration camp in Upper Silesia.

Fabian, who said he was a close friend of New York Rep. Sol Bloom and had once dined with President Roosevelt, was freed by United States Third Army troops who overran the Ohrdruf work camp just south of Gotha.

He had been transferred here from Auschwitz where he and some half-million Hungarian Jews were imprisoned last October because of the approach of the Red Army.

* * *

DECLARING that he owed his life to the fact that he was able to speak French, German and Hungarian, Fabian said as many as 10,000 Jews were gassed at Auschwitz each day and cremated.

"The officer in charge at Auschwitz met us at the gate," he said. "All children were murdered instantly. All men over 50 were killed. All women who refused to leave their babies were killed, but if they were healthy and good-looking and would let their children die alone, some were allowed to live."

A man's life, Fabian said, hung by the slim thread of the SS officer's whim.

* * *

"HE WOULD just look at you when you walked past—flipping his finger," he said. "If he motioned one way, you lived—until you were worked to death. If he motioned in another direction, you went immediately to the gas house and death."

Fabian, who is 56, lied about his age and that, plus the fact that the Germans needed his services as an interpreter, saved him.

Apr 15, 1945 DFP

148

When news came on May 7th that the Germans had surrendered, the celebration in the city was subdued. Some stores had closed expecting possible damage from the crowds, but it was difficult for everyone to get excited with half the soldiers still in the Pacific fighting Japan.

Every afternoon Jeane waited on the porch for the mailman with news about Marv. Three weeks after V day, a telegram was delivered stating that he had been returned to Military Control. Just one sentence, and Jeane was bouncing Marvel Lynn on her foot and singing *The Saints Come Marching Home*. Marvel Lynn always giggled when his mom was happy like this. A week later, Marv called from France; he was in a hospital recovering, and they were going to keep him there for another month, feeding him and helping him put on weight. "I love you" was said back and forth. "I love you, too. So much." Ferne was washing dishes and listening. Hattie was reading the paper. Luke Jr. would be coming home soon too. He'd been sent to Europe. He had written that he was fine. Lynn was recently sent from Europe to the Philippines, playing the trumpet in a military band. Hattie wasn't sure when he'd come back.

One afternoon when Ferne came into the house, she found Hattie scrubbing the floor in the kitchen and weeping. "What are you doing, Ma? What's wrong?"

"How could Christians do this?" She pointed to the paper. Ferne had read about it before, but this article about the Nazi methods and about the children was devastating. Ferne put the paper down and went outside for a walk. One must go on, she thought. How would the world ever recover from this war that had killed so many people? That was a question in many people's minds. How could you go on living in the same way?

Military Munitions Shipments Shut Off

WASHINGTON, May 8 (INS) —The last thin trickle of military equipment which has lately been moving to Europe was shut off today.

The war department announced that only supplies now authorized for shipment to Europe include food, clothing, post exchange goods and other subsistence items.

May 9, 1945

EXTRA DETROIT TIMES **RED LINE**

Only Detroit Newspaper Carrying Both International News Service and United Press

45th Year, No. 220 C Detroit 31, Mich., Wednesday, May 9, 1945 5 Cents COMPLETE MARKETS PAGE 13

Official! Peace in Europe

VICTORY!

Truman, Churchill Say So

WASHINGTON, May 8 (INS)—President Truman, speaking to a victorious nation, today told the American people that the hour of complete victory had come in Europe and that Germany had surrendered unconditionally to the Allied forces. At the same time the President directed a grim warning to Japan that now that the war is over in Europe the greatest military machine in all the world's history would be unloosed upon the Japanese homeland to bring about its utter destruction and unconditional surrender.

Full Blow On Japan

WASHINGTON, May 8 (INS)—President Truman declared today that the greatest war machine in history will now be turned upon the Japanese as he warned Nippon to surrender and spare itself further agony.

Along with his proclamation of victory in Europe, the President issued a statement asserting that the power and intensity of the blows against Japan will steadily increase until the utter destruction of the Japs.

(At London, Prime Minister Churchill also announced Germany's unconditional surrender and said that it would be "ratified and confirmed" today in Berlin by the western Allies and Russia.

(Monitors listening to Moscow radio said Stalin did not broadcast simultaneously with Mr. Truman and Churchill, and that no mention of V-E Day had been heard from Moscow today. Russian broadcasts reported continued fighting in Czecho-Slovakia and at other points. See Page 2.)

"This is a solemn but a glorious hour," the President told the nation in his victory broadcast which began at 9 a. m. EWT.

"Gen. Eisenhower informs me that the forces of Germany have surrendered to the United Nations. The flags of freedom fly over all Europe."

(Continued on Page 2, Col. 6)

106,000 Quit To Celebrate

(Other local V-E Day stories, Pages 2, 3 and 10)

Approximately 106,000 Detroit area war workers left their jobs today to celebrate the victory over Germany.

But workers employed on highly essential work remained on the job, factory officials reported.

Requested by the U. S. navy to continue production of rocket shells for Pacific invasion forces, the entire personnel of the Pontiac Motor plant, Pontiac, remained at their jobs throughout the day.

Departments in the Rouge and Highland Park plants of the Ford Motor Co. manufacturing Pratt & Whitney engines, also remained in full operation, a Ford spokesman said.

A mass tooting of trumpet let off the celebration at the Ford Lincoln plant shortly after President Truman's declaration of V-E Day. The bands played through the plant tooting "Deep in the Heart of Texas," and was joined

(Continued on Page 2, Col. 4)

THE WEATHER

FORECAST:
Fair tonight and tomorrow; slightly cooler tonight about 55.

The first picture of the German capitulation in Allied Headquarters, Reims, France. Col. Gen. Gustav Jodl (center), chief of staff under the new German fuehrer Adm. Doenitz, signing the document by which all Germans forces are bound to lay down arms in unconditional surrender. Other members of the German surrender party flank Jodl. They are Maj. Wilhelm Oxenius (left) and Gen. Adm. von Friedeburg of the navy.

Nazi Fleet to Britain

LONDON, May 8 (INS)—The remnants of the German navy will be brought to British anchorages, it was understood today. The vessels probably will be brought to Rosyth or Scapa Flow.

Pope to Broadcast

ROME, May 8 (UP)—The Pope plans to broadcast a message to the world on the end of the war in Europe at 8 a. m. EWT tomorrow.

North Norway Occupied

LONDON, May 8 (INS)—The Norwegian high command, in a broadcast heard in London, reported today that Norwegian and Russian forces have now occupied the whole of northern Norway.

Get 2 Shoe Stamps

WASHINGTON, May 8 (UP)—The OPA adds substance to its contention. It said today it will issue two valid shoe stamps to American civilians (free) from enemy prison camps.

Nazi Chiefs Together

LONDON, May 8 (INS)—The London Evening News said today that it believed Gestapo Chief Heinrich Himmler and Reich Marshal Goering were with Adm. Doenitz's government.

Detroit Stores Close To Mark End of War

Downtown retail stores and most large mercantile establishments in outlying districts of Detroit closed today, to reopen for their regular hours of business tomorrow.

The Retail Merchants Association explained that the closing was "in the public interest as a result of cessation of hostilities in Europe."

Notice

The Detroit Times' advertisers have voluntarily omitted their advertising from this edition so that all readers may receive complete Victory news without exceeding today's allotment of rationed newsprint. The Times expresses appreciation for this wartime co-operation.

May 9, 1945

Abe Me Marvel

July 1945

Marvel Sr + Jr.

July 1945

151

MARVEL Sr & Jr.

July 1945

GRAMP MARVEL LYNN

JULY 1945

MARVEL - JEANE

Full-Page Picture: Page 1, Part 3

Underground AGAINST The Japs PAGE 6, PART 1

DETROIT TIMES

Largest Circulation of Any Michigan Newspaper

Only Detroit Newspaper Carrying Both International News and United Press

48th Year, No. 310 6* 6 DETROIT 31, MICH., Aug. 12, 1945 Part 1 18 60s.

FINAL

Allies Decide to Let Hirohito Stay On Throne

JAPS CEASE FIRE, TOKYO SAYS

Aug 12, 1945

Jobs to Fade For 8 Million

WASHINGTON, Aug. 11 (UP) —The army and navy, reacting swiftly to the Japanese surrender offer, today ordered war contract cancellations totaling almost $4,-000,000,000.

That is only a fraction of the orders that will be canceled when the war officially is ended.

A high ranking official estimated that 8,000,000 persons would be jobless within the next six months. He said that only the swift reconversion of industry can alleviate this situation.

The overnight contract cancellations by the war and navy departments constituted but a small portion of outstanding contracts.

Additional cancellations will be ordered in the next few days.

Contracts for experimental development and for food and clothing for the army and navy will be continued. The navy also was expected to permit completion of a few contracts for planes.

The master reconversion plan approved by OWMR Director Synder probably will be revealed today or Monday.

Aug 14, 1945

U.S. Reveals Atom Bomb Perils World

WASHINGTON, Aug. 11 (UP)—The atomic bombs which wrought cataclysmic destruction upon Hiroshima and Nagasaki were relatively harmless— a slight improvement would have made them weapons of such unimaginable power as to threaten the end of the world.

The war department revealed the mind-numbing potentialities of the atomic bomb tonight in a technical report on the five years of experimentation which produced it. The report was written by Dr. H. D. Smyth, head of the Princeton University physics department and one of the atom bomb's progenitors.

300,000 Facing V-J Layoffs Here

Army, Navy to Cancel 90 Per Cent of Orders

Between 250,000 and 300,000 Detroit war workers will be jobless within a week after official V-J Day, it was estimated Saturday by R. J. Thomas, president of the UAW-CIO.

Aug 12, 1945

House Hints End Of Induction

WASHINGTON, Aug. 11 (UP) —Legislation to halt the drafting of men for the armed services was being held in readiness today by House military affairs committee members for introduction as soon as Japan is defeated and Congress returns.

They said there was no reason to continue inductions after the Jap surrender, as it would mean only additional tax burdens.

Most members of the committee were irked by Selective Service Director Hershey's recent statement that inductions of 100,-000 a month would continue after V-J Day.

They said drafting should stop with the end of the Pacific war. One member said he would introduce a bill as soon as Congress reconvenes to halt inductions Nov. 1.

Aug 12, 1945

Ferne and Abe rented a small frame house in Roseville, a suburb on the east side of Detroit. They needed a car if they were going to live in a place that didn't yet have streetcars or buses (parking lots were abundant), so Ferne and Abe used their savings to buy John's old car.

As soon as they moved in, Ferne started putting the house in order, making drapes and buying kitchen things from the dime store and a resale shop a few blocks from their house on 12 Mile Road. But why couldn't Abe find work? Marv was lucky. He found work right away as a bus driver in Detroit, driving the Chalmer Street bus. On weekdays Abe took the car and went out looking for work in the factories, but when the soldiers came home from the war, work was hard to come by. The women had been laid off from their jobs, and the factories weren't pumping out war machinery like they had been before. On top of that, the thousands of southerners who had migrated for defense work were still living in Detroit, trying to hold on to their jobs. Every night Abe came home without success. He sat in the chair in the corner, smoking and drinking beer.

Ferne was tense. How would they pay their rent? They both had saved some money during the war, and the army was giving him $80 a month unemployment for one year. Just barely enough to scrape by on.

After being in ground combat and before that traveling from one base to another for two and a half years, the transition was difficult. Ferne understood that, but she didn't know what exactly he had gone through. She knew that a lot of men in his platoon had been killed, and she'd heard the stories of what had happened to Marv when he was captured, nearly starved, marched hundreds of miles, crammed into railroad cars with no air or light and stood beside other prisoners who were shot for simply asking a question. Abe, on the other hand, had fought his way across Germany. He was used to living in dangerous situations. He had a bronze star for heroism. But he came home a different person from the young man she had married. At first, he was joyful and happy to be home, but as time passed he became somber. And he started drinking too much. She tried to get him to tell her what he did for the medal, but he just said, "I helped another soldier. You wouldn't understand."

Marv and Jeane found a house just a block away from the Abriels. In the afternoon, Ferne would often walk down the street to visit: Jeane now had two children, Marvel Lynn and a new baby, Karen.

"Why don't I ever get pregnant?" Ferne asked. "You get pregnant every time Marv looks at you."

"Do you think it has something to do with the operation?"

"Maybe I won't be able to have children. That just breaks my heart, Jeane. It doesn't seem fair. And on top of that, Abe isn't getting a job and I don't think he's really trying. He's gone all day and then he comes home with no good news."

"Marv told him he knows a place where he could get some day labor, but he wants to find something better."

"You're lucky with Marv. Even after everything he went through, he's still optimistic, and he loves the children. I wish I could have a baby. That might help us. If something doesn't happen soon with Abe, I'm going to have to find work."

"What could you do out here?"

"Maybe a waitress job. Maybe if I get to know people around here, I could start sewing again."

Marriage Certificate Discovered in Papers

Nuerenberg (INS)—"Discovery of Hitler's will and a political statement." The documents were found in a suitcase 30 miles south of Munich." Hitler's political testament blamed the war on those international statesmen who were either of Jewish origin or who worked in the Jewish interest. "It is my wish that I and Eva Braun, who married me when she volunteered to share my fate in besieged Berlin, should be cremated immediately... he and his bride Eva Braun preferred death to "the disgrace of being forced to surrender... German eyewitnesses previously had testified that the 56-year-old Hitler and his 35-year-old bride committed suicide after a macabre wedding supper but their remains never have been found. Hitler said he had "enjoyed many years of true friendship with Eva, whose recently uncovered diary showed she was tormented with fear she was losing him to other women and that she once contemplated suicide... The suitcase also contained three photographs, two of which were believed to be of Eva and the other of an unidentified boy about 12 years old. Dec 30, 1945

155

Me

July 1946

Bakke's

February 1946

Text from ad: Beautiful women keep youthful slenderness these days by smoking Luckies... there's real health in Lucky Strike. That's why folks say: "It's good to smoke Luckies." For years this has been no secret to those men who keep fit and trim. They knew that Luckies steady their nerves and do not harm their physical condition. They know that Lucky Strike is the favorite cigarette of many prominent athletes who must keep in good shape. They respect the opinions of 20, 679 physicians who maintain that Luckies are less irritating to their throat than other cigarettes.

Future Gloomy, Von Wiegand Says

By KARL H. VON WIEGAND

At Havana, aboard Spanish Motor ship Magallanes en route to New York, Dec 29—Eight months after the end of war in Europe there is no peace. There is civil war in China and continuing hostilities in Java. It is the year of "great hunger" in Europe and Asia. Perhaps never before in history... so dark and gloomy an outlook into the future.... America enters the year 1946 of epochal developments as world power number one.... Not since the Roman Empire under Augustus has any country been so completely world power number one in all domains—military, political, economic, financial, scientific and commerce—as is America at the dawn of 1946.... Russia is our one formidable rival and will not cease to strive to occupy one day the position now held by America. Dec 30, 1945

Fannie Hurst Sees Grave Danger in Laxity of Teen-Agers

By Fanny Hurst. New York (INS). Juvenile delinquency... Wars are fertile soil for it... Millions of our youth will muddle through this period into the normal and good life. Others will succumb.... Do you remember the flapper? She was that controversial girl of the twenties. She was jazz-mad, drank cocktails, slapped on the lipstick, and was allegedly on her way to the dogs. But apparently she never received that limbo of baying canines supposed to lie in wait for young generations. Instead she married her returning dough boy who was the GI of World War I and they became the parents of the bobby soxers. And so we have that slim young stick of 1920 dynamite developing into the not-so-slim mother of 1945.   Dec 30, 1945

When Ferne finished eating the dinner she had prepared for both of them, she sat in the armchair by the window and lit a cigarette. She was smoking far too many cigarettes lately, and she was starting to lose weight again. In the morning when she was sorting their laundry, she found a small piece of folded-up paper in Abe's pocket with a woman's name on it: Marian. Marian. So that's what has been going on. All those days looking for work, and now this. For three years she had waited for him. She wrote him letter after letter, gave up her job, moved out of her mother's house and here she was now alone in a little house in Roseville. It was becoming more difficult to imagine having a family with him.

She put out the cigarette, put on her coat and walked over to Jeane's. They had just finished eating dinner, and their new baby was asleep in the bedroom. Marvel Lynn jumped up and down when he saw Ferne. He climbed up on her lap and showed her a little wooden horse Marv had made for him.

"See my horsey, Auntie Fernie."

She hugged him and sat down at the dining room table with Jeane. She tried to hold back the tears.

"Marvie," Jeane said. "Take your horsie and go play with daddy, okay?" Off he went.

"What's wrong, Fernie?"

"That shit . . .," she started sobbing.

Jeane put her arm around her. "What now?"

"He didn't come home for dinner, and I found this in his pants pocket." She put the paper in Jeane's hand.

"Maybe it's the number of someone for work."

"Come on Jeane, come on."

Marv walked into the room. "What's wrong, Ferne?"

She folded her arms on the table and laid her head down on her arms, weeping.

When Jeane explained the situation, Marv said, "I'm sorry, Ferne, very sorry."

That night Abe didn't come home until ten o'clock. When Ferne laid the note in front of him, he looked down at the floor. He didn't deny it. He said, "It doesn't mean anything. It was just something in the moment."

"Something *in the moment*? Did you sleep with her, Abe? I can't do this. We made a promise to each other. But you didn't mean it, did you? Have you been sleeping with women all the time you've been gone? Have you? Have you?"

He put his coat back on and went out the door.

She yelled behind him, "That's my car, too, buddy!"

After he drove off, she lit a cigarette and sat on the porch looking at the moon, barely visible behind a blanket of clouds.

The next morning, when he didn't come home, she dialed the number.

A woman answered and Ferne hung up.

She put on her coat and went over to Jeane's. Jeane had pumped Marv for more information. Finally, he gave in and told her that when they were in the service in the States, Abe was always trying to get him to go out with other women. Marv wouldn't though. Abe used to say, "Oh come on. They aren't here. It won't matter."

Ferne stood up, clenched her fists closed and moaned, trying to hold back the tears. "I want him out of the house," she said. "This can't work. I can't have children with someone I don't trust. And I'll never trust him again. I'm going home and packing up his things."

"If I were you, Fernie, I'd do the same thing," Jeane said. "Do you want me to come with you?"

"No, I'll do this myself."

When he came home, she didn't shed a tear. She looked at him and said, "Leave the car keys and the car and get your stuff out of here."

He looked at the two small boxes of his clothes sitting in the middle of the living room. Then he threw the keys on the table, turned around and walked out the door.

Of course, where else could he go but to Marv and Jeane's. Later that night Marv came by and picked up Abe's things. Ferne wasn't there.

While the divorce was in process, Abe was frequently over at the Bakke house. To avoid encountering him, Ferne had to stop visiting with her sister. It seemed like she'd lost not only her husband, but also her sister. At the end of the month, she emptied out the house, turned it back over to the landlord and moved back in with her mother.

Later in the summer, Jeane phoned to say that she and Marv were going to visit Marv's family in Minnesota for a few weeks. She wondered if Fernie might want to go along with them. Ferne didn't hesitate. "Yes, yes, Jeane, I want to go."

July 1946 Ferne and Marvel Lynn in Minnesota

Divorce -- It's Fast and Easy

BY ARTHUR JUNTUNEN
Free Press Staff Writer

IF YOU'VE BEEN at odds with the little lady, don't frown over your morning coffee unless you're the type that likes the self-brewed kind.

Michigan laws are such that she may not only ask for a divorce, but she may get it under a dozen classifications which could label you for life as a heel, a wife-beater and a form of monster they'd call a "mental cruelist."

In fact, say Judge Joseph A. Moynihan, Friend of Court Edward Pokorny, Recorder's Court Domestic Relations Chief Ralph Doherty and others in the know, the sanctity of the home is practically a myth under present Michigan divorce statutes.

The divorce rate in Wayne County almost doubled since Pearl Harbor and the number filed in January alone—2,068—was a new high, yet spouse can shed spouse almost for the sake of a change.

* * *

"**IN ONE DESERTION** case recently, no one even bothered to make an appearance, so a decree was granted in less time than it takes to snap your fingers," Judge Moynihan said.

Feb 10, 1946 DFP

160

> For many returning GI's and their wives, the stresses of adjustment were barely manageable, and as the war ended, these strains were reflected in a startling upsurge in the nation's divorce rate.... In early 1946, when only half the GIs had returned home, 200,000 were already involved in divorce proceedings. by 1950 as many as a milion GIs were divorced.... Whereas, in 1940, one marriage in six had ended in divorce, by 1946 the figure had worsened to one in four.
>
> There was no single explanation for this dramatic rise in the number of broken marriages. Contributing factors include the haste with which couples had wed; the strains of wartime separation; and the shock of strangeness and disillusionment on being reunited... (Mintz and Kellog, 171)

Ferne wanted to believe that love was a force that could heal, but here she was, unable to love Abe. She felt deserted and yet she wondered if perhaps she was deserting him. What she wanted most in life was to have a family, and she wanted to do this with someone who was as steady as her father had been. Abe was definitely too immature. He had always been immature, she thought. Maybe she had, too, but now it was different. The war was over, and she wanted to get on with her life.

—⚬⚬⚬—

When I was ten years old, my mother told me that she had been married twice before she met my father. She was very young with the first one and it was annulled, she said (although that isn't in the historical record). But the other was a marriage with no children. After she died, that conversation stayed in my mind. I'm sure she never could have imagined that fifty-five years later her poet daughter would still be searching for the story of her marriage to George Abriel, sorting through negatives to make photos, developing and replacing prints that her mother had earlier destroyed, trying to discover who he was and what really happened. Ferne probably would have skimmed over the article in the *Detroit Times* about Gertrude Stein dying, possibly not even knowing who she was, but it called out to me. Gertrude and her circle and my mother and her circle were alive at the same time and lived through the same war.

Novelist Gertrude Stein Dies in French Hospital

PARIS, July 27 (UP)—Gertrude Stein, the novelist, died in American Hospital tonight, hospital officials announced.

Cause of Miss Stein's death was reported to have been a tumor. Her life-long friend, Alice Toklas, was at the bedside. The famed expatriate writer set a distinctive style of writing all her own.

Miss Stein lived for many years in the Latin Quarter of Paris until the Germans forced her to move south.

STILL AN AMERICAN

In December, 1944, the first winter of liberation, she declared her years of voluntary exile had not altered her outlook as an American.

"You bet your life we welcomed the Americans when they came up with the Seventh Army," Miss Stein declared.

"For one thing, for all the time I've been in France, I have never been called an expatriate and that is the thing I am proud of," she added. "I proved you could be a good American anywhere in the world."

FIRST BOOK IN 1900

Miss Stein and Alice Toklas endured many difficulties during the first post-liberation winter in Paris.

Miss Stein's first published book was "Three Lives," rated highly by critics who reviewed it in 1909. Her publications were many, most of them causes of literary controversy.

J. C. TOOLE, DENTIST
110 W. Lafayette, at Michigan, opposite City Hall. Hours 9 to 9. Tel. CA 6689.—Adv.

Byrnes Urges Haste to Halt War Threat

Says Big Powers Must Remove Friction Causes

WASHINGTON, July 27 (INS)—Secretary of State James F. Byrnes declared tonight that "the hope of avoiding some new and terrible war" greatly depends upon how quickly sources of friction left over from the last war can be removed.

The secretary cited the Italian-Yugoslav border dispute as an example of the dangers which must be eliminated.

President Truman led high-ranking government officials and congressional leaders today in an unprecedented farewell ceremony for Byrnes.

More than 3,000 persons at the national airport heard the President wish Byrnes' Godspeed and continued success.

July 28, 1946

On October 29, 1946, Ferne and Abe's divorce was final. Three months later, on January 18, 1947, he married Donna Mae. They had four children, and then she divorced him. A cousin of his wrote, telling me that he had died from alcoholism on September 6, 1972, in Riverside, California. When Donna died, she was living just outside Detroit, in East Detroit, the small city where Ferne and my father began raising their family.

CHAPTER 10

Ferne was holding baby Karen in one arm and chasing little Marvel around their backyard. "Watch out, I'm gonna get you," she yelled.

He laughed hysterically.

"Look at me, Marvie, I'm a princess with a baby girl," Ferne said, twirling the baby around, her dress catching in the wind.

Marvie stood still, staring at her, his eyes widening as he anticipated what would come next.

"Now I'm an evil princess and I'm going to get you." She started chasing him. He ran around in circles and then rolled around on the ground. Their dog, Cookie dashed over and started putting her nose into Marvie's belly.

Jeane opened the back window. "Fernie, can you come in and help me move this box?"

Fernie put the baby in the playpen. "Where's Marv?"

"He just went to the supermarket to get a few more boxes. We don't have much room in this little trailer. If there's anything you want or you think Ma wants, we're piling the giveaways into the bedroom."

"I just gave away so many things. . . . Have you heard from Abe?"

"Do you really want to talk about him, Fernie? Hasn't he caused you enough grief? I wish I wasn't in the middle of this."

"Well you won't be in the middle for long. You'll be in Minnesota and I'll be at Ma's, and Abe will be wherever he'll be. Maybe he'll marry that woman. Our divorce is final. Just got the papers yesterday."

"Take this box out to the front porch, will you? Marv will put them into the trailer when he gets back."

"What will I do without you, Jeanie, hundreds of miles away?"

They stopped and hugged each other. Marvie kept pulling on Ferne's skirt. "Pick me up Auntie Ferne, pick me up."

The two sisters sat down on the stoop, looking down the block at the row of little identical houses, not a tree or a person on the block.

"The Bayview Yacht Club," Ferne said, "is much livelier than working in an office. As a hostess I meet all kinds of people. Met a couple of interesting men already. Maybe I'll never get married."

"You'll definitely get married, Fernie, and you'll have children, too. You're so beautiful. Don't worry, just look for the right guy."

"Maybe you won't like farming. Maybe you won't like his family. Maybe you won't like living in the sticks."

"Maybe we *will* like it," Jeane smiled. "Sor-ry. Marv really wants to live in the country, Fernie, near his family. And the cost of living is much cheaper."

"Maybe you *won't* like it. I was telling this girl at work how sad I was about you leaving and she had an idea. There's a country club in Minneapolis where I might be able to get seasonal work in the summer."

"Oh Fernie. What a great idea! *Please*. Try it. You can come and stay with us. . . I'm gonna miss you and Ma so much."

"I think they'd give me a leave at the yacht club. I like working there and they like me. Oops, it's already 4:30. I have to go. Right now, Jeanie. I have to go! I'll be late as it is. Love you, love your babies and I love Marv, too. Drive safely. Write me."

Police Seek Help to Fight Crime Wave

Assignment of 50 additional detectives to the detective bureau was requested by Chief of Detectives William Dresden today to combat a record breaking wave of 35 holdups and robberies.

In a letter to Supt. Edwin Morgan, Dresden pointed out that the bureau is operating with 71 less men than it had in 1935.

Total crimes during the first nine months of 1935 were 18,815 and during the same period of 1946 had grown to 24,780.

Dresden said the city's population has grown by 300,000 in the intervening 11 years.

37 HELD IN ROBBERIES

Use More Potatoes

By FRUDENCE PENNY

"Quantity huge, quality high" is the potato picture this fall. Retail markets will offer huge supplies of potatoes during the first two weeks of November. Nov. 7 to 16 has been set aside for a "Use Potato" drive as the crop is so large and as a result is one of the least expensive vegetables on the market.

These late potatoes are good keepers, so the homemaker can be sure that even if she buys a bushel they will always be in good condition. The ideal storage temperature is 40 to 50 degrees, which is well above freezing. If they are stored below 40 degrees they take on a sweetish taste because some of their starch turns to sugar.

There are many ways to prepare potatoes so that one dish need not be repeated.

Nov 4, 1946

164

On Mother's Day, May 11, 1947, Ferne was passing from the kitchen to the bathroom when she saw her mother reading the paper. The morning light was passing through the window and falling on Hattie's hair and shoulders. Soon this quiet hour would be over and her brothers and sisters with their families would be arriving, everyone but Jeane. How Ferne missed having her sister close by. As she stood undetected in the corner looking at her mother, she felt her childhood and her own life passing. Ducking into the bedroom, she took her Brownie camera out of the dresser and out of the box. Then she peeked around the corner and snapped her mother's photo.

Barbara Spires, Ferne, Grandad, Grandad's friend
from the Alter Road Bar, Hattie, on Grandad's 93rd birthday.

Ferne did land a summer job at the Auto Country Club in Minneapolis. Working as a hostess four days a week, she was able to spend the rest of the time with her sister on their farm in Stephens, Minnesota. Besides their two children, the Bakkes had a couple of sheep, a chicken house, a bull, a cow, a dog, a big garden, a field of oats and Jeane was already eight months pregnant with her third child. When Ferne came barreling down the dirt road and turned into their farm, Jeane ran out the door with Karen and Marv trailing after her. The two sisters embraced. They were like twins who had been separated and then found each other again.

The girls and Ferne at the Minneapolis Auto Country Club

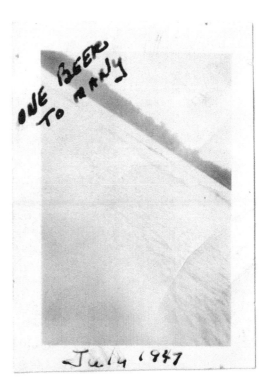

Ferne holds up her bottle of beer, as if saying to the photographer, "To you!"

One Monday when Ferne returned to the farm, Jeane was feeling weak. She asked Ferne to call Hattie and try to talk her into coming for the rest of the summer.

"Ma, it's me, Ferne. Can't talk for long. Too expensive. We're wondering if you can come and stay with Jeanie for a while. She's kind of isolated out here. I'm only here a few days a week, and she misses you terribly. In less than a month, she'll have the baby."

"Is she okay?"

"Yes, she's fine, just tired, but she wishes you could be here when the baby's born."

"I have to talk to John. Maybe he could drive me up there. How's your job, Fernie?"

"Good, very good. I'm saving money. You'd like it up here Ma. It's nice for the summer. The kids would like to see you, too."

"Let me talk to John. I'll call you back tomorrow."

"If you can come, I'll drive you home when my job's over at the end of August."

Woolie   John   Mom   Marvel

JUNE 1947

Marvel   Karen

JUNE 1947

1947

Marvel Lynn and Karen
with their dog, Cookie

MARVEL LYNN   ME

Aug 18, 1947

MARVEL   ME   KAREN

August 18, 1947

Shortly after Hattie arrived, Jeane started experiencing cramps in her lower belly. Ferne stayed with the children while Marv and Hattie took Jeane to the doctor. The doctor put her in the hospital. Later that day he broke the amniotic sac and the labor started instantly. Patty Helen was born a few hours later, but she was small and premature.

Jeane couldn't breastfeed because she had a cold in her breast. When they brought the baby home from the hospital, she was instructed to feed her a formula, but Patty wasn't interested in eating. She wasn't gaining weight or energy. No one, not even the doctors, could figure out what was wrong with her. In mid-August, Ferne resigned from her summer job to stay with Jeane. One morning, with everyone surrounding the baby, Hattie baptized her, and a few hours later Patty Helen died.

Ferne had to leave a few days after the funeral because she had promised the club manager that she'd be back in the beginning of September. She needed the job.

When they turned onto the highway, she said to her mother. "That was the saddest thing I've ever experienced." Just saying it made her start crying again. "When you had to pry Jeane's hands off the baby, Ma, I almost fainted. Then when you cleaned her little body, wrapped her in that lace blanket and laid her in the box Marv made, it was heartbreaking, Ma, heartbreaking . . . I'm very worried about Jeanie."

"Maybe you should pull over until you get yourself together, dear. Let's not add a car accident to our list of losses."

"I'm okay, Ma."

"Jeane will be ok. Marv is there for her and Jeane loves the little ones. She'll get over it. We have to go on. That's our task in life. Help each other and be strong for each other."

"Was it hard for you, Ma, when you lost Helen Ruth?"

"It was very sad, but she never took a breath. She died in the birth canal. Still I had known her. She'd moved around inside my body. I used to sing to her. I sang to all of you. Jeane has two children, and I already had four running around the house. We go on."

"I hope I have a family." Ferne lit a cigarette and cracked the window.

"Fernie, you smoke too many cigarettes. No matter what *they* say, or what *you* say, you *know* they're not good for you. Look how thin you are."

Ferne laughed. "I'm fine. I like smoking. It gives me energy and calms me down." She looked at Hattie out of the corner of her eye, then slowly turned her head toward the side window and blew out a long stream of smoke. "I think smoking is kind of glamorous, don't you?"

"Oh, come on, don't be silly. Glamour isn't everything."

"That's all I have going for me now, a divorced woman twice over," Ferne said, laughing.

"What about health and a long life?"

"What about grandad? He smokes those pipes one after another, and he's 93 years old. Look up there, Ma! A flock of seagulls. We must be close to the ferry."

"There's the sign. Turn here."

"Got it . . . Let's not stop anywhere. Let's drive right through now. I can do it. We'll have a break on the ferry."

"Jeanie was telling me she wants to move back to the city," Hattie said. "I think the well water might have been too strong for the baby. Maybe that's why she died."

"That and the doctor who broke her waters. She wasn't ready to be born." Ferne turned into the lot, paid the man and they boarded the ferry.

Me

Sept 2, 1947

Karen Marvel Jeane Marvell.

Sept 2, 1947

Fair and Warmer After Storm Here

Fair skies with slightly warmer temperatures were forecast for Detroit today after another heavy thunderstorm caused considerable damage in the city and county.

The mercury, which reached a low of 63 at 7 a. m., will rise to a high of 82 for the day, then drop back to a low of 63 for tonight, the weather bureau forecast.

Last night's storm plunged three districts into darkness as lightning hit high tension wires.

Without lights for periods ranging from minutes to two hours were districts bounded by Bewick, McClellan, Mack and E. Jefferson; Continental, Lakewood, East Jefferson and the River, and Green-

Sept 2, 1947

⎯⎯⎯∞⎯⎯⎯

When I left home in 1966, I took Ferne's Bible with me. One night when I was flipping through the pages, I saw some underlining. John 4: 17: "I have no husband," the Samaritan woman says to Jesus. He looks at her, a woman, a foreign woman to boot—he is not supposed to even speak with her—and he tells her that he knows she has had five husbands and is now living with a man. He tells her he is the Son of God, and she becomes his first evangelist. Inside the cover, there is an inscription "from Mother" and the date, Ferne's birthday, Nov 4, 1947.

CHAPTER 11

Labor Act War Unites CIO, AFL

Holiday Rallies Center on Taft-Hartley Law

(Pictures on Page 17)

The AFL and CIO today girded for a new fight against the Taft-Hartley bill after the legislation was blistered in speeches and caricatures during the city's biggest Labor Day celebration.

Featuring the day-long observance were mammoth parades by both unions, which attracted about 300,000 spectators and participants, and speeches by former Vice President Henry Wallace and Senator William Langer, (R) of North Dakota.

Wallace, who marched at the head of the CIO parade and spoke later in Cadillac Square, deplored the Taft-Hartley legislation and added:

"The liberals in this country will never get anywhere until there is a unified labor movement, and there can't be any such unified movement until there is a unification of labor here in Detroit."

Sept 2, 1947

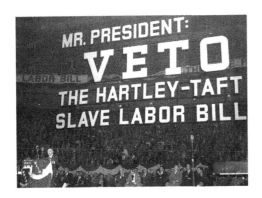

The Taft-Hartley Act pushed for changes on three fronts. In an early manifestation of McCarthyism, the law required union officers under the National Labor Relations Board's jurisdiction to submit anti-communist affidavits. It tipped the scales in labor disputes by dispensing with the expectation of management neutrality and prohibiting a range of "unfair labor practices"—including jurisdictional strikes, secondary boycotts or pickets, and wildcat strikes. And it opened the door for individual states to outlaw "union security" provisions (which required workers in unionized shops to join and pay dues to the union) through the passage of what became known as "right-to-work" (RTW) laws.... Truman vetoed the bill, but it was a gesture seen as little more than a "grandstand play for labor support" given his willingness to quash strikes in steel and coal the previous year. And Congress had the votes to easily override Truman's veto. On June 23, 1947, Taft-Hartley became the law of the land.

...Within months, most Deep South states had RTW laws on the books. Ardent segregationists and civil rights leaders alike recognized that RTW was a way to maintain the color line in Jim Crow labor markets —"a whip to preserve the sharecropper wages," as Martin Luther King put it.... "This high-sounding label," as Martin Luther King observed in 1961 "does not mean what it says. It is a dishonest twisting of words with the aim of making a vicious law sound like a good law. It is a travesty on the true meaning of 'right.' This so-called 'right-to-work' law provides no 'rights' and it provides no 'work.' It is instead a law to rob us of our civil rights and job rights." (Colin Gordon, 2017).

The Federal Government Must Censor Movies

IN THE "cold war" which Soviet Russia has declared and is waging against the United States, any form of collusion with Communists in this country comes perilously close to being AN ACT OF TREASON as that crime is defined in the Constitution.

"Treason against the United States," the Constitution says, "shall consist ONLY in LEVYING WAR AGAINST THEM, or in ADHERING TO THEIR ENEMIES, GIVING THEM AID AND COMFORT."

Because the "cold war" has not become a "shooting war"—for which Soviet Russia is unquestionably preparing—the stark realities may not be apparent to all but the protected dissemination of pro-Communist, anti-American propaganda in a great medium of public entertainment, information and education is unquestionably a MORAL BETRAYAL of the American people.

* * *

NOT only does it endanger our nation abroad, where our armies of occupation are holding thin lines of defense against Communist aggressions and trying to save some degree of liberty for other people.

Worse than that, it imperils our freedom at home, for the constant intent and endeavor of the Communists in this country is to SUBVERT OUR INSTITUTIONS and to OVERTHROW OUR SYSTEM OF REPRESENTATIVE GOVERNMENT.

The congressional committee on un-American activities has made alarming revelations of a veritable multitude of Communists in the film industry.

The evidence indicates that there may have been, and probably was, a working liaison between some of the Hollywood Reds and secret agents of the Soviet government engaged here in wartime espionage.

But even if this were not the case, the enormous evil and the domestic danger of sheltering and richly rewarding Communist propagandists

Nov 4, 1947 Hearst

On March 12, 1947, . . . President Harry S. Truman asked Congress to grant economic and military aid to Greece and Turkey to help those countries resist Communism. The speech established what became known as the Truman Doctrine, a policy "to support free peoples who are resisting attempted subjugation by armed minorities or by outside pressures." . . . Truman's announcement marked a distinct shift in U.S. foreign policy. . . . pledging to intercede in conflicts all over the globe to contain the growth of Communism. . . . The Truman Doctrine would form the basis of U.S. policy during the cold war with the Soviet Union — in fact, many historians argue that the cold war began with the Truman Doctrine. Over the next several years, the United States would strengthen its policy of containment through the Marshall Plan to provide economic aid to Europe, the formation of the North Atlantic Treaty Organization (NATO) to protect against the Soviet Union, and the National Security Council's top-secret NSC-68 paper, which supported a military build-up to combat the Soviets. The containment policy presented in the Truman Doctrine would lead the U.S. into conflicts like the Korean and Vietnam wars. New York Times (March 12, 2012)

After the war, Hearst's newspaper articles continued to rail against unions and communism (the Soviet Union), as well as advancing a fear of working-class people having too much power. In the 40s, Hearst blamed academics and public schools for anti-American teaching. Many consider him responsible for the adoption of loyalty oaths in public schools and universities. With editorials like the one to the left, he helped set the ground for "McCarthyism." Anyone who had an affiliation, even unofficial, with the Communist Party or ideology could be blacklisted. Many people lost jobs and turned on their neighbors and colleagues.

After their experiences during the war, the Hostetters and many other ordinary people went along with Truman's ideas about the Soviets. They were less supportive, however, of his stance against the unions. Many of the men in the family had worked in factories building automobiles, defense equipment and manufacturing adding machines for Burroughs. They knew how necessary unions were, but by the late 1940s, the World War II generation did not want their country to get into a war with the Soviets. Communism, to many of them, meant the possibility of another war. The men had been away for four years fighting. Now they wanted to raise families and live a peaceful life away from the Depression, wars and conflict, away from bad news.

OCT. 24 TO NOV. 22
Scorpio—By giving your brain a rest, refusing to worry or undertake too much, you can easier cope with existing problems. Smile kindly on suggestions that may be worth your using.

Nov 4, 1947

December 5, 1947

Dear Jeane,

I am so happy to know you will be coming home on Christmas, and for a whole month. That's wonderful. I'm looking forward to seeing you, Marvie and Karen. How tall is little Marvie now? Has he reached the doorknob yet? I'm sorry to hear that the Bakke farm didn't do well this past season, but I'm glad this is a family venture, and you and Marv aren't in it alone.

Ma is doing well, her normal in-charge, but ever-loving self. I'm enclosing a few photos for you. Bad news for us, but good for John and Aggy (I suppose); they are looking for a house on the West side, probably in a suburb. Burroughs is moving out there and so are they. It will be such a change for Ma not to have John here all the time. Katie finally got her divorce a few weeks ago, and she and her fiancé Art are going to get married later this year. Everyone is ok. Ward and Betty are doing fine. They are staying in their place on Alter Road for the time being unless Ward can find another job and he is looking.

Terry just this minute ran into the house. He wants to play cards with Grandad and he's all excited about the Joe Louis fight tonight. Everyone's going upstairs to watch it on John's new television. Oops. Grandad just sent Terry across the street to get a pitcher of beer. Bang, he lets the door slam behind him. This house is crazy as usual.

The news is that I have a new beau, and when you come, you will meet him. Don't worry, I'm being cautious. Last month, I ran into Ginny Henning. I was coming home from the yacht club on the Jefferson bus. You remember her, don't you? When I was working at the draft office in Grosse Pointe, she was a friend of Loretta's, Rob's sister. Remember—we all went out to the Vanity together a few times. I think you were with us once, weren't you? She married a barber in Brooklyn. Can you imagine? And she moved there and got a job working for a coffee company. Anyhow she was on the bus coming home from shopping at Hudson's, and we made a date to meet at the Drop In, and surprise, she brought along her brother. Do you remember Bob? When he was young, he used to come by to pick up papers out back. If you saw him, you'd remember him. He was the cute boy with the big ears. And when we were talking, I learned that my high school flame, George Bixler, once rented a room from his mother. They used to pass each other on the way to the bathroom. Ha ha.

Anyhow, things go as things go. He and I hit it off right away. He's funny. He talks a lot, tells stories and he likes to dance. Hurray for that.

He's got a job working in the warehouse at Briggs on Plymouth Avenue, and he's been attending meetings to try to force the owners to pay them better. They were on strike, but now that's over, and he's back to work. He was in the army in the Philippines (a radio operator repair man). When he came home, he immediately found work. That's a good sign, right? He's smart, too, and funny.

Don't worry. Again, I am being cautious this time. But, Jeane, he's a serious person, and he wants to have a family. And he likes me, a lot. He grew up just a few blocks away from us on Nottingham. He went to Grosse Pointe High instead of Southeastern. He had a better education, I think. You know how Grosse Pointers draw a line and set themselves off from Detroit. When we look out our window, it's like we are looking across a class line (if we could see over the trees and houses).

177

That's not to say that the Hennings have a lot of money. Well more money than our family; there are so many of us. There were a lot of them, too, back in the day, but his half-sisters and brothers were all grown before his mother even married his father and got him to build their house. His father does plaster work; he did the molding and sculptures in the Ford mansion. His mother, I haven't met her yet, but she sounds like a feisty lady. She came over alone on a boat from Switzerland when she was sixteen and worked in the kitchen at the Ford place. Now she has a gift shop on Grand River. When I told Bob I was divorced, he said that it didn't matter to him—his mother had been divorced twice. I'm enclosing a photo Ginny took of him a few years ago when he was on furlough. He looks the same. Maybe you'll remember him. Please send this photo back (or bring it when you come).

And so, dear, I'm excited, but staying calm and cautious--except when I think of you coming home to visit. I'm so excited. I want <u>so much</u> to see you, Jeanie.

Your loving sister, Ferne

The Bakke's.

Christmas 1947

Me Dick Marvel Karen Marvel Jeane

January 1948

Dick is Katie's son.

The Bakkes, Dick Spires and Bob Henning sat at a table on the porch of the yacht club overlooking the Detroit River and the rows of boats covered with tarps and snow. Even though the sailing season was over, members still came to the club to fraternize and to eat dinner. The next day Jeane and Marv and the children would be driving back to Minnesota and Ferne wanted to introduce Bob. While Ferne was closing out the cash register, Bob picked her camera up off the table and stood at a distance taking a photo of everyone framed by the lighted windows. When he sat back down, he asked, "Marv, are you planning to stay in Minnesota permanently?"

Jeane raised her eyebrows.

"Well, Bob, it depends on how the next season goes. And it depends on how happy Jeanie is. Sometimes life on the farm is kind of rough." He looked at Jeane and smiled at her. "I think my wife likes city living better, but we're giving it a try."

"Yes she does," Jeane said as she lifted Karen up onto her lap. "I'm glad we could come and meet you, Bob. Fernie is very special and she wrote me all about you."

"I hope it was good," he said. "Can I buy anyone another drink?"

Marv waved him off, but Dick wanted another beer and Karen had spilled her orange juice.

When Bob opened his wallet, Ferne approached the table. "No need, Bob, it's on me."

When she turned to walk away, she heard Dick say to Bob, "My Aunt Fernie is a wonderful person. I love her dearly. She and Jeane used to take care of me when I was a boy. I was a lucky boy."

Everyone at the table turned to look at Bob. It was almost as if in their silence and expressions, they were saying, "We hope you'll be good to her."

On the way home from the club, as they passed through downtown Detroit, Bob asked Ferne if she had to work the next day.

"No, I'm off on Monday. Do you?"

"Seven to four every day. I could pick you up after work on Wednesday and we could go downtown to Greenfield's for dinner. Would you like that?"

"Maybe. I have to check my schedule. Do you like my sister and her husband?" she asked.

"Oh, yes. Jeane's a lot like you. Very sweet."

"I was curious because you and Marv didn't say much to each other."

"Well, we just met. I'd like to get to know him. You didn't introduce me until now and they're leaving tomorrow."

"Marv is very devoted to his family."

"If you marry me, we'll have children, too. I want to have children, with you. I love children."

"I might not be able to have any. I want to. I really want to. Do you have a light?"

They sat in front of the house talking and smoking.

"We could get a house with the GI bill and have our own place."

"I'll have to think about it," she said. "I like you a lot, Bob. But I just want to be sure. I don't want to make any more mistakes." She put her hand on his shoulder.

"Why don't we go away for the weekend? I'll rent a place in Algonac. It's cold but we can spend some time together." He pulled her over beside him.

"That sounds good," she kissed him lightly on the cheek. Bob stroked her hair. Then, "Sorry, I have to go in now. I want to spend some time with Jeane before she leaves. Call me tomorrow afternoon, and I'll let you know what they say at work about taking off for the weekend. I have to find someone to fill in for me."

Postcard from the Algonac Inn

Bob   ME   JEANE KAREN DICK

JANUARY 1948

February 29, 1948

Dearest Jeanie,

I have good news. I just left the doctor's, and he confirmed that I am definitely six weeks pregnant. Bob and I are going to get married next week. Did you like him? I hope so. For the time being, we'll stay here with Ma. I'm going to keep working as long as I can, and we're going to try to save a down payment to buy a house.

Bob wanted us to move in with his mother and stepfather. They definitely have a bigger house than we have, but I want to stay with Ma. I want her to be there when I have the baby. His family is very different from ours. I usually give in to what he wants, but I was firm about this. I wish you could be here, Jeane. How I miss you.

I've gotten to know Bob's mother better. Last week Ginny was in with her husband Al and we all played poker together. You should see his mother, Virginia, shuffle cards. They fly through the air and land into her other hand.

She's an ace at playing cards. And when she gets a winning hand, she slams the cards on the table. "A pair of deuces!" When they play for money, she almost always wins. I like her husband, George, too. He's kind of quiet, a real estate broker, and she's also studying real estate. She plans to close her gift shop as soon as she passes the exams. I guess they'll work together. A very different woman than Ma, very keen on making money.

Last Sunday we went to Bob's church (Grosse Pointe Memorial) with Ma and afterwards we talked to the pastor. I wanted to get married at Knox, but he insisted. It's a more beautiful church, he said, and they are both Presbyterian, so I went along with him. We told the pastor the truth, that I am pregnant. That was uncomfortable (for me because I don't know him). He asked us a lot of questions, and then agreed to marry us on March 6th. Ginny can't come. Darn. She can't take off work anymore, but Ma is planning a shindig after the church affair in a little hall. I'll send you photos in my next letter.

I'm including a few photos Bob took last Sunday. Take a look at Grandad. He's definitely getting up there.

Everyone's ok in the family, the same as when you were here. No new news. I hope I'm alright with this pregnancy. Pray for me, will you? And please write and tell me what's going on with you and the children. Your letters are so short, Jeane. I know you don't like to write, but please tell me more about what's going on at the farm. I'm saving some money so I can call you soon.

Love,
Ferne

Ginny and Bob Henning and Bob's mother, Virginia

George Marx and Virginia Dubois Henning Marx

Nottingham House

Mom   Mé

February 1978

Mom   Bob

February 1978

ME

February 1978

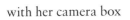

with her camera box

Gramp   Mé

February 1978

April 15, 1948

Dear Jeane,

Wow one page and that's all. Come on, dear. I want to know about your life. You are planting oats already? I guess it is the time of year, isn't it? Thanks for that tidbit, sister. Isn't it still cold up there? It's slightly warmer today, about 40 degrees.

I'm three months pregnant, and I can't eat much. Nausea, especially in the morning. I'm glad I'm with Ma, though. She knows all the right teas to drink. I wish you were here to give me advice. I'm going to quit working in two weeks. Then Bob and I will be on our way up north and over to Minnesota to see you. We'll stop by and see Esther and Katie at their cottage, and we're planning to spend the night with Rush in his place in West Branch. Soon he'll be giving up his room in our house and moving up there permanently. Ma says she's going to make his room into the baby's room. I hope I can handle all the driving and boating. Ma tells me the nausea should pass by then.

I'm attaching some snapshots we took after the wedding. When you look at me, imagine my suit as a light green color. I spent a week making that suit and covering the buttons. Bob rented a black double-breasted suit from the tailor. There was a good crowd at the wedding. Lots of our friends were there. I met some of Bob's half-brothers and sisters. I guess we are going to have a very big family now, all combined. When we came home, Bob's dad stopped by and Katie was here with Art, too. We had a party after the party. We were missing one important person: YOU!

So take care. I can't wait to see you.

Love,
Ferne

Me

MARCH 28, 1948

Bob

MARCH 28, 1948

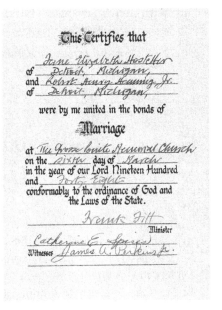

Ferne, Bob, Hattie, Katie,
Art, Grandad, wedding dinner

This Certifies that

Jane Elizabeth Hostetter
of *Detroit, Michigan,*
and *Robert Henry Henning, Jr.*
of *Detroit, Michigan,*

were by me united in the bonds of

Marriage

at *The Grosse Pointe Memorial Church*
on the *sixth* day of *March*
in the year of our Lord Nineteen Hundred
and *Forty-Eight*
conformably to the ordinance of God and
the Laws of the State.

Frank Fitt
Minister

Catherine E. Spragg
Witnesses *James A. Perkins Jr.*

Sixty-eight years later, on August 6, 2016, I was in Detroit spending a few nights helping my stepmother. At the time, she was 90 years old. Late at night, as we were talking, she said, "Barbara, one day I was looking for something in the garage, and I found some papers your Dad had hidden, wrapped in old newspapers."

"Where are they?" I asked.

"In the cabinet, inside Dad's funeral book."

I unfolded an old yellowed crumbling paper (Oct 23, 1974, *The Macomb Daily*. "Be the Envy of your block in Spring"). Inside, I found the invitations Gramma had sent out for the wedding, an announcement in the newspaper of their wedding, a record of the marriage service, what they said to each other, their oaths and Ferne's death certificate.

"There was a pornographic photograph in there, too," she said.

"Where is it?"

"I threw it away."

"You threw it away?" I cried.

"She was sitting in a chair, naked. I don't think it was your mother."

"That's just naked," I said, "not pornographic. Why would it be anyone else?"

I thought to myself: folded away on a tool shelf, next to an oilcan, wrapped up with their marriage certificate, why would it be anyone else?

Even though Ferne had written March 28, 1948 on the photographs, the date on their marriage certificate was March 6th.

Border Alerted For Alien Reds

Movement of known Communists between Detroit and Windsor were restricted today as Canada joined with the United States in a general crack down on the agents of Soviet Russia. . . . Since enactment of the Taft-Hartley law, numerous Communist leaders in this country, and particularly Detroit, have resigned from union positions rather than sign anti-Communist affidavits. ..."We already have authority to deal with the situation," Adams said, "Under Canadian immigration law, aliens who advocate the overthrow of organized government through violence are prohibited from entering the country." Mar 6, 1948

JELLYBEAN JONES

"I'll ask them to play you a lullaby, dear . . ."

The Detroit Times

Mar 6, 1948

BULLFIGHTER . . .
Conchita Cintron, 25, who
says she is the world's only
lady bullfighter, arriving at
LaGuardia Field, N. Y., on
her return from Portugal to
her home in Lima, Peru.
Senorita Cintron claims she
killed 828 bulls in 10 years.

Mar 6, 1948

Detroit Symphony Fights Concert Ban in South

By Jack Pickering. The Detroit Symphony Orchestra 'went to war' today as a religious group of Chattanooga Tenn. tried to prevent the orchestra from playing a concert there. . . . "It is going to cost us a great deal of money but it is worth it to fight bigotry. It is hypocrisy, and it is un-American. Every church has music on Easter. . . We will play only religious and established classical music—but we are going to play, whether any one is in the hall or not." Mar 28, 1948

July Roundup Likely to Rout Out Millions

Numerous Reds Still in Country on Visitor Basis

By DAN MARKEL

Immigration authorities have proposed a July registration roundup of all aliens in the United States, it was learned today.. . . If enacted, every alien beginning July 1 would be required to report his present address to Immigration officials within a month.. . . The last alien registration was in 1940 when 5,000,000 aliens registered. Since then 1,131,244 aliens have been admitted on non-immigrant visas which means they entered with permission to remain only three to six months. Many were natives of Russia or Soviet satellite countries. The total departures during the same period totaled 843,957. These 267,287 are unaccounted for. Mar 28, 1948

. Strikes in Violation of Taft Law Barred

INDIANAPOLIS, March 27 (AP)—Federal Judge Luther M. Swygert today issued an injunction restraining the AFL International Typographical Union from causing printers' strikes which violate the Taft-Hartley law.

They are restrained from authorizing or encouraging "subordinate local unions and members of * * * International Typographical Union * * * to engage in or to continue to engage in any strikes, slowdowns, walkouts or other disruptions of any kinds to the business operations of employers in the newspaper publishing industry" in maintaining contracts which violate the Taft-Hartley law.

Of course, Hearst—owner of twenty plus newspapers, radio stations, film studios etc—does not want strikes. March 28, 1948

Billion Fags a Day Go Up in Smoke

BY ALEXANDER R. GEORGE

WASHINGTON—(AP)—American smokers are now consuming nearly a billion cigarets a day.

The wartime business boom gave a terrific boost to cigaret smoking, especially among teen-agers and women with good-paying jobs. Sales of factory-made cigarets jumped from 172 billion in 1939 to 352 billion, more than double, in 1946.

Thirty-five years ago the respectable cigar-smoking business man regarded the smoker of a factory-made cigaret as a sort of social outcast.

Back in the spiffy spitoon era many members of Congress were tobacco chewers and proud of it. A typical newspaper advertisement of the period pictured Speaker Joseph Cannon, of Illinois, with the caption: "The thinking men of America chew —— twist."

Today the factory-made cigaret not only has wide social acceptance but is a sizable item in the national economy.

* * *

IT IS ESTIMATED that the cigaret tax increases the United States Labor Department's consumer price index by nearly 1 per cent.

In 1946 American consumers paid a total of $3,400,000,000 for tobacco products and smoking supplies. The 1929 expenditure for tobacco products was $1,700,000,000.

Treasury tax experts, who recently made a study of tobacco use, report that cigarets in 1946 accounted for 77 per cent of the total tobacco used in production. Back in 1915 cigarets accounted for only 10 per cent.

* * *

THE USE OF cigars and smoking tobacco (pipe and roll-your-own cigarets) has had a big drop in the past 30 years. The biggest slump has been in tobacco chewing. Consumption recently was less than one-third that of 1918.

Cigar smoking in this country reached a peak of 8,100,000,000 cigars in 1920, the silk shirt year. It dropped to 4,592,000,000 in depression 1933, picked up some in the years immediately before and during the war.

Government research experts say there has been "a significant decline" in cigar consumption since February, 1947. They explain that recent increases in the cost of living may have affected the demand for cigars.

March 21, 1948 DFP

TO SKATE HERE. Yvonne Sherman, who finished in sixth place in the Olympic figure skating championships this winter at Switzerland, will be among the prominent figure skating stars to appear at the North American speed championships, sponsored by The Detroit Times, at Olympia, April 12. She will skate with Dick Button, national world and Olympic men's figure skating champion.   Caption Mar 28, 1948

Bob's mother Virginia with her Swiss Chalet.
She grew up in Biel, Switzerland.

On Sundays after church and before the Hostetter children would arrive at the flat, Ferne and Bob would visit with his family. Sometimes they'd play cards. After dinner, his mother would sometimes play the organ. In the corner of her crowded living room a model Swiss chalet was on display. "I built this to be exactly the same as the chalet where I grew up in Biel," she said, "on a farm and we had cows. I kept my bicycle right here." She pointed to the side of the house. "And in the morning, I would pedal to the market to sell cheese."

"Do you have to leave so soon, Bobby?" she asked.

George was sitting at the dining room table reading the paper.

"Mother," Bob said, "the Hostetters are gathering today, too. We want to be there to see Ferne's brothers and sisters. Can I help you with anything before I leave?"

"Some of the tiles are lifting on the kitchen floor. Can you look at them? Maybe you could put down some tar later in the week after you get off work."

One weekend in the spring, Bob talked Ferne into going fishing with him. She wasn't especially excited about fishing, but she wanted to go out on the water, and it was important to Bob so she went along. It was damp outside, so she wore her coat and a scarf.

When they were in the middle of the bay, he turned off the engine and asked her, "Are you sure you don't want a fishing pole?"

"No, I'll just watch," she said.

Then they sat there and sat there. When she would say something, he would shush her. "The fish go away when they hear us talk, Fernie," he whispered.

"Bob, I don't feel comfortable sitting here like this for this long."

"Humm…," he smiled at her. "I guess you won't be my fishing partner. That's okay, honey." He rolled in the line and laid the pole back in the bottom of the boat. Then he started up the motor. "Let's go for a ride around the lake."

As the boat glided over the lake, the breeze blew Ferne's head scarf down around her neck.

"It's so quiet out here," he said. "That's what I like. I can hear myself thinking." Then he turned the boat around and headed for the shore. "Let's stop for dinner at the Algonac Inn."

Me

Lexington

MAY 15, 1948

Dicky + ME

MAY 16, 1948

Dicky + Bob

MAY 16, 1948

194

June 24, 1948

Dear Jeane,

We are on our way. We just arrived last night at Rush's place on Peach Lake. A very secluded cabin, very small with an outhouse. Rush is in the process of bringing in plumbing. Bob and I put up our tent. He brought along a cot for me so I'm more comfortable than sleeping on the ground. Bob can sleep anywhere. I usually have to push him around in the morning to wake him up, but he was up and about very early this morning. He and Rush went out fishing and came back with a bunch of perch. We're going to cook them for dinner. At the window of his tiny kitchen, Rush set up a board that goes out to a tree branch. He sits at the table and the squirrels come up and eat out of his hand. Very funny. I wouldn't let a squirrel eat out of my hand. Tomorrow morning we'll be driving to Burt Lake where Bob's sister Elna has a summer cottage.

I didn't tell you how wonderful our weekend was at the cottage with Katie and Esther's families. Bob is a storyteller and he entertained everyone at night with his stories about his years in the Philippines. I'm glad he didn't tell any of the more violent stories. The Japanese were very cruel to the native people who lived there, and they retaliated. I won't give you the details. I'm glad he didn't tell many of those stories. During the day, Jack, Bob and young Johnnie went out fishing. Katie's new husband Art's not much into fishing. He stayed back in the cabin with us women and Bicky. She's already ten years old.

We're cooking now, so I'll finish this letter in the morning.

Ok, here I am again. We just arrived at Bob's sister's place at Burt Lake, near Cheboygan. Elna and her husband, Norm, are a little chilly with us, especially Norm. He doesn't seem to like Bob much. I don't know why. Maybe he's just a snob. Just because you own a plumbing business and have a big house in Grosse Pointe doesn't mean you are better than others. Maybe there's some old hostility because Elna and Bob are half siblings. I can imagine Bob's mother being difficult with the older teenagers when she married their father. And then when she divorced him, all the children were angry with her. But his sister Florence and her husband Earl are very warm and friendly. I'm glad we're not spending the night here. At first, I was surprised when we rented a cabin because Elna and Norm have a very large cottage, but now that I've met them, it will be much more comfortable to go to our own place.

Tomorrow morning we're taking the ferry at Mackinaw City, and it won't be long before we arrive at your place. I'm going to close this letter, put it in an envelope and mail it from the first post office we pass. I hope you receive it before we arrive.

Much love, your sister,
Ferne

Elna, Chris, Florence, Mo, Dick

June 27, 1948

Bob's step sisters Elna and Florence
and their children.

Ferne and Bob

Mo

June 27, 1948

the PONTIAC waiting for the BOAT

JUNE 28, 1948

IN the FERRY

JUNE 28, 1948

July 5, 1948

Dear Ma,

We made it up to Jeane's. What a long trip. I wish you could have come with us, but I'm sure you wouldn't like sleeping in a tent. Even at Jeane's, we decided to sleep in our tent. Their place is very small and noisy in the morning with the children. Bob wants to sleep in since he's usually up early and off to work. The cot I'm sleeping on is fairly comfortable, although I have to shift around with my belly to get on my side. Everyone seems healthy here, and Jeane just found out that she's pregnant, too. We'll have our babies almost at the same time. There's a little carnival here in Stephen, and today we're taking the children there. We're taking a lot of photos, so you'll get to see the children.

We saw Rush in West Branch. He's looking wonderful, and his place is small but well organized. He said he's planning to come to Detroit for a week in December to see the baby. He's hoping we have room for him. Maybe he can stay upstairs with John and Aggy.

I hope you like these postcards. I wanted you to see where we've been. Please save them for me. The one with the picture of Peach Lake is very close to Rush's place. Burt Lake is the lake where Bob's sister has a cottage. We stopped at Vin's Rustic Bar on I-29 and had lunch there. And the boat is the same ferry you and I took to the Upper Peninsula last year. North Shore Drive in Superior, Wisconsin—we drove along this cliff and over the bridge into Duluth. Then we had breakfast at the Paul Bunyan Restaurant in Duluth.

Sorry for not writing as I went along. Things got away from me. Got to go now. I need to shower, and we do it outside here in the summer. Plumbing issues.

Lots of Love Always, Ferne
     (hugs and kisses for everyone)

PS—We'll be here 5 days then heading home. I'll phone you before we leave.

July 4, 1948

ME & MARVEL

July 1, 1948

Put-in-Bay - ME

July 28, 1948

The government guaranteed loans for veterans who borrowed money to purchase a home, business or farm. These loans enabled hordes of people to abandon city life and move to mass-produced, "cookie cutter" homes in suburbia. This exodus from major cities would help shape America's socioeconomic and political landscape for years to come. https://www.history.com/topics/world-war-ii/gi-bill

The Federal Housing Administration that FDR had set up in the 1930s guaranteed mortgages for low and middle class people. As part of their guidelines they made maps coding areas according to market stability. It is clear now, according to Mike Dugan, mayor of Detroit, that these maps were drawn to reinforce segregation, denying most African Americans access to mortgages and home loans. And this led to the deterioration of housing and the destruction of most of the neighborhoods in Detroit.
Paraphrase of Mike Dugan, Utube, May 17, 2017.

Nov 10, 1949 SMN

For several years, the second generation of the Hostetter family had been settling around their mother's house on the far east side of Detroit. Because of migration and other factors, real estate prices in the city were high. After the war and into the mid 1950s Ferne's brothers and sisters slowly relocated to the suburbs where prices were lower, taxes were lower and where many of the factories and businesses were already relocating. At the time the east side of Detroit was still segregated and mostly white. The Hostetters were not moving because of white flight. That came later. They were lucky, however, that they were not black and therefore forced to live in areas that didn't qualify for a mortgage. When Bob and Ferne started looking for a house, he had his job at Briggs, he had the GI mortgage and a car and there were many inexpensive houses being built in the suburbs. On the weekends they would drive to the various models, look at the houses and draw up budgets, trying to figure out what they could afford.

Finally, near the end of August, they found a house that seemed promising in a small developing suburb: East Detroit. The house would be built using cinderblocks. They couldn't afford a brick house, and it was important to Bob to have a strong structure. His father had built their house from cement; cinderblocks would be fine. Their lot would be on the edge of town, with fields and forest behind them. They talked about planting apple trees, a garden and a strawberry patch. There were two small bedrooms and a big attic that Bob could refinish into bedrooms. The builder said the house would be ready by the middle of the summer of 1949. They put $200 down and stayed with Hattie while waiting for their house to be finished.

Chester + Bob

August 1948

September 30, 1948

Dearest Jeane,

I am stumbling around the house today with my big belly and wondering how you are. I'm writing this letter while lying on the couch. Oh, the baby is turning over now. Is that an elbow? Ow. I'm eight months and counting the days. Dr. Bedell thinks everything is fine. I just have to try not to overexert because of that little flutter organ in the middle of my chest. I'm ok. Thank the lord. How are you feeling? Are you as big as I am? I have gained 15 pounds. I hope you have some help with the children, and I hope you are not working too hard with the animals.

When are you moving back home? Ma has asked the renters upstairs to find another place so you can stay here until Marv gets work and you find a house. We all want you here. If your baby is due in December, you probably couldn't get here until January. I'll bet Marvie and Karen are excited about the new baby and moving to Detroit. One thing you'll like—the winters will be less severe. Just think, dear, in a month I won't be pregnant anymore. And a month after that, you won't be either.

Bob's very excited about the baby, but I think he's working too hard. After working all week putting trim on airplane lights, he's spending the weekend fixing his mother's roof. He's also taking a class during the week to finish his GED. Some days he has such a hard time waking up in the morning.

This morning Bob's mother showed me some photos of Bob as a child. Oh my god, she used to dress him as if he was little Lord Fauntleroy in knickers, a tie and a white shirt, as if they were a wealthy family. They aren't, but she likes to pretend. Now he's wearing his old factory work clothes and climbing on her roof.

Let me stand up and put this letter in an envelope with a stamp. Jack (he's still our mailman) will be here soon. He'll take this letter and start its journey toward you. Three days from now in your hands.

Love, your sister,
Ferne

Hattie and Ferne, October 24, 1948

Universal Military Training is advocated by members of the Blue Star Mothers, Inc. who are holding their national convention in the Book-Cadillac Hotel. . . . "We favor the Universal Military Training Program as it was first set up, to give every boy of 18 who is physically fit, a year's military training. . . . We saw the mis-trained boy go out to die in World War II when it was unnecessary. . . . Also we want to see every American boy, his wife and children properly housed before displaced persons are admitted to this country."

Oct 26, 1948

Dad Works, So Family Of Four Is Homeless

By FLOYD THOMS

A family of four living in an automobile in Palmer Park since last Saturday, today gave up almost all hope of finding a home.

Richard Wladek, 58; his wife, Jennie, 38, and their children, John 11, and Henry, 4, have been without a real home since last May.

But they had managed to shelter with relatives until last Saturday, when they had to leave a relative's home in a Hamtramck housing project.

Wladek, employed steadily as an auto plant grinder, said he has tried every means of finding a home, but met with failure.

"We have applied to every project in the city," Wladek said, "but have been turned down every time.

"You see I am employed and I make about 11 cents an hour over the limit for a housing project. Even the welfare can't help because I am employed.

"I explained that we needed a place for the children to stay but they told me they couldn't take care of me."

Mrs. Wladek said that the children have been living on sandwiches and milk and an occasional bowl of soup.

"My little boy, Henry, cried for the first three nights wanting to go home," Mrs. Wladek said. "I finally convinced him that we have no home and can only stay in the park.

"It is quite cold for the children and my husband is working days and needs his sleep but there is nothing we can do about it. We have made a bed in the back seat for the children and we cover them with all the blankets. My husband and I sit in the front seat and try to sleep but it isn't very successful."

Wladek said that he could afford to pay about $50 a month rent but that would be tops.

"I only bring home about $55 a week after everything is taken out of my pay," he said, "and we couldn't afford to go over $50 a month because we have the children to clothe and feed."

Wladek explained that because they have no permanent address his son John has not been to school this year.

Under a state law, a parent is subject to prosecution if a child is kept out of school.

Home to Be Career Of 14-year-old Bride

NIAGARA FALLS, N. Y., Oct. 26 (AP)—A 14-year-old bride says she's "going to stay home and be a housewife."

The former Marlene Thompson, eighth grader a week ago, and Martin Adams Jr., 17, went to Atlanta and were married Saturday under a Georgia law which permitted their marrying with parental consent. They returned here yesterday.

Oct 26, 1948

According to Leah Platt Boustan and Kenneth Jackson after the influx of 400,000 migrants into the city during the early forties, the cost of housing went up in the inner city and remained lower in the periphery of the city. Then as more and more whites left the inner city, the prices started to rise in the suburbs and fall in the inner city, driving even more migrants to Detroit. In the meantime, there was still a shortage of housing for people like Wladek. "No homes for sale or apartments for rent at war's end . . . six million families were doubling up with relatives or friends by 1947" (Kenneth Jackson 233).

1948 Presidential Election

The Progressive Party candidates [Henry A. Wallace and Glen Taylor] and campaign called for a complete end to segregation in the South and to all forms of social discrimination. In the South, the Progressives faced terroristic violence when they held integrated meetings. . . . While early optimistic polls . . . the Truman administration's sharp shift to the Left during the campaign brought millions of working-class and liberal voters back to the Democrats.. . . [After the Progressives lost the election] Domestically, the red scare intensified as purges of trade unions and blacklists of radicals and noncommunist liberals in the arts, sciences, and professions were institutionalized, both by private bodies, . . . and by state and federal laws . . . This domestic cold war peaked in the early 1950s, as Senator Joseph McCarthy both fomented and scavanged in an atmosphere of anticommunist political hysteria.
(Dictionary of American History)

Oct 26, 1948

War Orphans on Their Way to America

SIXTY-THREE ORPHANS waving from the bow of the US Army transport Gen William M. Black as they sail from Bremerhaven, Germany for the United States. The ship carried 813 displaced persons—the first shipment of the 205,000 DP's expected to find homes and jobs in the United States before July 15, 1950. The DP's are being admitted into this country through an act of Congress.
Caption. Oct 26, 1948

Dictator Perils
Seen by Truman

Last night Mr. Truman implied that a dictatorial form of government might result from a Republican victory in the Nov 2 election.. . . Truman . . . told his Chicago audience the campaign is more than a battle between two parties. "It is a fight for the very soul of the American government, "he said. "This countries freedom and democracy," he said are seriously threatened by powerful forces of reaction 'working through the Republican party. In our own time, he added, we have seen the tragedy of the Italian and German peoples who lost their freedom to men who made promises of ...efficiency and security. And it could happen here.
Oct 26, 1948

Salute to Women Voters

THE LEAGUE OF WOMEN VOTERS, a comparatively new force in American politics, is increasing in power and stature.

It is a nonpartisan group, designed only to obtain and present facts about political candidates together with what statements on current issues the candidate chooses to make.

But, by question and answer procedure, the league attempts to extract true beliefs from candidates, scorning political evasions.

Able men running for public office welcome this inquisition.

Others fear it.

The face-to-face encounter with intelligent, well-informed women has been dodged by those candidates who have no concrete opinions or have opinions they wish to hide.

A SECOND service performed by the League of Women Voters is the study of amendments, charter changes or other similar issues to appear upon the ballot.

In most cases, as with candidates, the league makes no recommendation; simply brings out the facts for the voters.

In a rare exception, the league this year is urging that a state constitutional convention be called to study revisions of Michigan's 1908 constitution. But, basically, the league's position remains unchanged since calling of the convention forces no specific alterations.

In its questioning of candidates and open discussion of issues the League of Women Voters performs a service for both men and women.

Further, it operates in the finest tradition of American politics—presenting the facts for the individual to make his own decision.

Oct 26, 1948

205

Red Probe Files Looted, Says Thomas

By DAVID SENTNER

WASHINGTON, Oct. 26—Rep. J. Parnell Thomas, chairman of the House committee on un-American activities, today charged that the committee files, including his personal and official correspondence, had been systematically rifled during the last nine months. He will demand an investigation.

The New Jersey Republican, engaged in a bitter feud with Atty. Gen. Clark over the latter's failure to prosecute members of the Soviet-Communist spy ring, attributed the current grand jury investigation of the conduct of his office to matter purloined from his files.

Thomas labeled the probe of his office pay roll as smear tactics and political persecution intended to detract public attention away from the justice department's failure "to prosecute the Communist enemy."

Oct 26, 1948

November 15, 1948

Dear Jeane,

Thanks for your phone call last week. I'm so glad to be here with Ma. She's helping me with the baby. We are waiting patiently for you to arrive. Mr. Rannell and his wife found another place over on Wayburn, and they'll be moving out at the end of December. We are going to clean it up for you and put some new sheets and blankets up there.

My body is very tired, to say the least. Sis, why didn't you warn me how difficult birthing can be? All night long I was crying and moaning, and finally Barbie was born at 3 a.m. So here we are. Survivors. I was in the hospital for two nights. Now I'm trying to regain my strength. We'll be taking the baby with us to see Dr. Bedell later this week. She was 6 pounds 12 ounces at birth, not a bad size the doctor said for a girl. I'm trying to nurse her a little, maybe for a month.

Katie's Barbara stayed over this weekend to help out. When we baptize the baby, she'll be the godmother. I'm hoping with my next child you and Marv will be godparents. Katie's Barbara (now I'll have to call her that) is in love. All she can talk about is a young man she recently met, Robert Criss. We've yet to meet him, but she's definitely in love. I hope she'll be ok. We know how that young love goes—I certainly made enough mistakes.

Our house is being built. The land has been cleared and they've laid a foundation. There's a beautiful big oak tree across the street. The city is planning to make a park there.

I send lots of love to you and Marv and Karen and Marvie.

Your sister,
Ferne

Nov 4, 1948

Nov 4, 1948

American Women Do Home Sewing

THE GENTLE WHIR of sewing machines in American homes grows louder.

Latest figures from the National Needlecraft Bureau show 34,500,000 or 96 per cent of the homemakers in the United States today do home sewing. They report that 52½ per cent are creative sewers who make clothing and household items, while 43 per cent confine their activity to mending and darning.

Augmenting this activity are 60,991 sewing classes being taught weekly by 5,335 teachers of home economics.

A breakdown of income groups reveals that 45 per cent of this home sewing is done by the middle class, 20 per cent by the upper middle class, 30 per cent by the lowest income groups and 5 per cent by the well-to-do.

Nov 4, 1948

Barbie   M&

DECEMBER 8, 1948

208

Barbie Bob Gramp

NOVEMBER 21, 1948

Me Barbie

November 7, 1948

Me

Dec. 11, 1948

ME

DEC. 11 1948

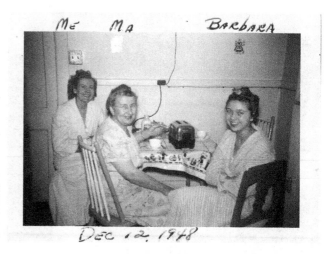

ME   MA   BARBARA

DEC 12, 1948

The doctor's receptionist called Ferne to the window. "The doctor will see you first, Mrs. Henning, and then the baby."

Ferne sat nervously on the edge of the table, a white sheet over her knees.

When the doctor came into the room, she was relieved. He was a soft spoken, calm man in his fifties with greying hair. He shook hands with her. "I'm glad to meet you Mrs. Henning. I see from your chart that you just had a baby on October 26th, just a bit over seven weeks ago. And you had rheumatic fever as a child. And you had one of your fallopian tubes removed. How are you feeling now?"

"I'm tired, doctor. The baby wakes me up a lot, but I'm so happy to have her. I was worried I wouldn't have a child."

"I hear the flutter in your heart that Dr. Bedell noted. We think you have some heart damage. There's a new heart specialist on the staff at St. Joseph's Hospital in Mt. Clemens. Later I might send you to him for an examination. In the meantime, I want you to be very careful that you avoid getting throat infections and colds. If you start coming down with something, see me immediately."

"Doctor, I've had this murmur for several years, but I'm strong. It never bothers me."

"Well, we know more now. Sometimes the damage caused by rheumatic fever reoccurs and starts getting worse as an adult. You must be careful."

After he examined her cervix, he said, "Everything seems fine. Are you still abstaining from sexual activity?"

She smiled. "That's kind of difficult."

"Mrs. Henning, this is important. You are young and relatively healthy, but it will not be in your best interest to get pregnant immediately. As I'm sure you are aware, your body takes a beating from pregnancy."

"I know doctor, but. . . ."

"If you can't hold off, try using a diaphragm. Have you ever used one before?"

"No."

"I hope you aren't pregnant already. You are not breastfeeding and your body will be very fertile."

He went back into his office and came back with a box, opened it and took out a round rubbery cup. "You have to fill this with spermicidal jelly and fold it like this and put it deeply into your vagina so that it covers your cervix. Put it in an hour before sex. Then leave it in for six hours after sex. It's not 100% for sure, but it works pretty good. Don't leave it in longer than eight hours."

Ferne went out to the waiting room to get the baby. She unwrapped her and undressed her on the examination table. Barbie was quietly looking around until the doctor came into the room. Then she started screaming.

"Very good," he said. "Now we know you are here with us!"

He checked her heart, measured her and weighed her.

"She's fine. Keep her on the formula and let me see both of you again in two months."

Art is Katie's husband

In January, Jeane and Marv arrived from Minnesota with a trailer full of boxes, Karen, Marvie and their new baby, Linda. They moved into the flat upstairs, temporarily until Marv could find work.

One day while the babies and children were sleeping, Ferne and Jeane sat on the front porch. Ferne was smoking, but Jeane never liked cigarettes.

"The doctor's gonna to be mad at me, Jeane."

"Why? Did you do something wrong?"

"I tried to use that thing he gave me, but I forgot once, and now I'm pregnant again." She laughed. "I'm going to have a family."

"That's my idea, too," Jeane said. "It might kill me, but I want one more. Three doesn't seem big enough to be a family."

Karen and Jeane, 1949

Feb 13, 1949

212

Me + Barbie   Jeane + Linda

Febuary 5, 1949

CHAPTER 13

The single-family tract house—post World war II style—whatever its aesthetic failings, offered growing families a private haven in a heartless world. If the dream did not include minorities, or the elderly, if it was accompanied by the isolation of nuclear families, by the decline of public transportation, and by the deterioration of urban neighborhoods, the creation of good, inexpensive suburban housing on an unprecedented scale was a unique achievement in the world. (244)

As early as 1963, industrial employment in the United States was more than half suburban based, and by 1981 ... about two-thirds of all manufacturing activity took place in "industrial parks" and new physical plants of the suburbs. (267)
Kenneth T Jackson, *Crabgrass Frontier*

22858 Almond, East Detroit

me & Barbie   *Barbie & Gramma*

august 6, 1949   *august 6, 1949*

Bob's Mother,
Virginia (Henning) Marx

When Ferne and Bob moved into their new house, she was 27 years old. To Dr. Singer's dismay, she was pregnant again and due in November. For several years she had been deeply worried about her ability to have children. Like her mother, now she would have a family, but she was a modern woman, so she would have no more than four. And she wouldn't need to work as hard as her mother did because their house was clean, new and modernized. It was heated with natural gas rather than smelly coal, and she had a new stove, refrigerator and an automatic washing machine. What she really enjoyed were the fields outside the back door, and a more densely wooded area close by where she could walk down paths and find wild raspberries. Just a few blocks away there was a big horse barn where people rented horses. She wasn't interested in riding, but she liked seeing the occasional person heading into the woods on a horse. She knew more houses were planned, but for now, she had a bit of country.

Halfway between Mt. Clemens and downtown Detroit, East Detroit was a developing suburban city. In 1837 it was called Orange Township, then in 1924 it was named the village of Halfway, where the stagecoach would stop. My father, Bob, once told me that gangsters hung out there during the Prohibition era. In the 50s and 60s, it was all white, mostly Roman Catholic. Eventually in 1993 the name was changed to Eastpointe, to create a distance from Detroit, and perhaps to make some kind of connection with Grosse Pointe. The city is now more diverse. The 2010 census lists 65.6% White, 29.5% African American, .4% Native American, 1.1% Asian and 2.1% Hispanic or Latino. In 2018 when I was visiting Detroit, I drove by the house and stopped to talk to the two African American women who were living there. They loved the house and told me that they never locked their doors. My father always locked the doors.

In 1949, while Bob was at work from seven a.m. to five p.m. trimming aircraft parts for Briggs at the Connor Plant, Ferne cooked, cleaned and took care of the baby. Most of the women in the neighborhood stayed home with their young children. While their children were in school, some of the women took part-time jobs in supermarkets and offices. Ferne was happy to stay home. But she wanted money of her own, so as she met the new neighbors, she started taking orders for drapes and for reupholstering furniture. She insisted to Bob that she needed a car to shop for food and fabric, and also to visit with her family. There was no reliable bus service. Even though Bob wanted to save money, he relented and bought an old Ford from his mother. Several times a week, she would put the baby into the car and off they'd go to Jeane's house.

"Where did she go?" Ferne ran down the hall, following the baby as she scooted into Karen's bedroom where toys were scattered in every corner. Karen was busy putting a blonde doll into her little cradle.

"That's okay, Auntie Fernie, she can stay in here with me." She handed Barbie a little doll that squeaked whenever she pushed its belly.

"Karen, don't let her put anything tiny in her mouth, ok?"

Jeane and Ferne sat in the living room so Ferne could have a clear view into the bedroom. Jeane's youngest child, Linda, was busy in the middle of the living room playing with a set of blocks.

Ferne picked up the newspaper from the table. "I thought Truman was going to be good for us, but here we are sending more men to Korea. I think Eisenhower will be a better president. What do you think, Jeanie?"

"Why are you asking me, Fernie? You know I don't care about politics."

"Politics is what put Marv in war prison and what brought him home, too. If Eisenhower hadn't taken the troops to D-Day, who knows what could have happened?"

"I don't want to talk about it, please, Fernie, let's talk about something else. . . Did you meet the couple who moved into the house next door to you?"

"Yes, a very nice woman, Marie. She came over for coffee and she liked the way I had reupholstered that old armchair Ma gave me, so she's paying me to redo two chairs for her. And she wants me to make drapes for their living room. She works at Hudson's so she gets a discount on fabric. Finally I'll have some money."

"I don't understand why you don't handle the money. Then you could have what you need."

"Well, Jeanie, Bob likes to take care of the bills and the bank account. He's working very hard. What can I say?"

"Give me some money. That's what you can say."

"He buys the groceries and everything I need, and he gives me money for the bread and milkman. Now I can work at home. It'll be fine."

"While Marv's doing carpentry work for people, I'm home with the children. I like taking care of the bills and the bank account, and he doesn't mind."

"Well, they're two very different men. Marv grew up on a farm with brothers and sisters, but Bob was the apple of his mother's eye, her little boy. From what Ginny told me, she gave him pretty much whatever he wanted. Now he wants to be the head of the household, to provide for me. How can I complain? . . . I wish you would learn how to drive so you could come and visit with me. Why don't you have Marv take you to the shopping center parking lot at night and try spinning around."

"I'm terrified, that's why," Jeane said, "and I don't need to drive. I walk up the block to the grocery store and Marv takes me to see Ma on the weekend. Then you come here." She smiled at Ferne.

"You got it made: the purse strings, the driver, your sister." Ferne stepped across the room and hugged her. "Love you, Jeanie. I have to go now. I want to pick up some thread at the dime store and then I have to cook dinner. I'll see you at church on Sunday."

Ferne scooped up the baby and off she went. At home she put her down for a nap, took some diapers out of the washer, hung them on the line and then she started to make meatballs and spaghetti for dinner.

She sat on the couch, lit a cigarette and looked across the dirt road at the house across the way. She could hear the baby in her crib gurgling. Sometimes it seemed like she was playing house. But then she agreed with what her mother said on the phone. She had to meet more neighbors and in time she'd get used to living out here.

When Bob's car passed by the house and turned right, Ferne picked up the baby and went out the back door to greet him.

On Saturday morning, Bob painted the house a blue-gray and then he planted shrubs in the front. Every paycheck he bought another small tree to plant in the yard. Ferne hung endless diapers on the line and planted strawberries along the fence. After four years at war, couples all over the country were moving out of the cities and trying to put their lives together.

Ferne with Virginia and her neighbors

Ferne was resting in bed when Bob came into the room after taking his bath. "Bob, my fingers are aching."

He sat on the side of the bed and massaged her hands.

"I'm worried. I have an ache in my lower back. Maybe I'm going into labor."

"You're a month early, Ferne. Maybe you just pulled a muscle when you were working in the yard."

"No, something else is going on," she moaned. "That felt like a contraction."

"I'm calling the doctor."

"No, wait, don't call yet. I want to take a bath first."

"Ferne, I don't think that's a good idea.".

"Can you fill the tub, please? Just use lukewarm water. I want to be clean if I'm going into the hospital."

While she was in the bath, she had another contraction. They were about an hour apart. Bob called Hattie. Hattie said she would get Ward or Marv to bring her over to watch the baby, and Bob should call the doctor immediately.

When Ferne was on the couch dressed and ready to leave, she gripped her belly and started moaning. Bob ran across the street and pounded on the door to ask their neighbor Willa if she could stay with the baby until Ferne's mother arrived.

At 6 a.m. in the morning, Robert Bruce was born, 5 pounds and 11 ounces. "He will be fine," Dr. Singer assured her, "but because in the last month of pregnancy the baby's lungs are not yet completely formed and he can't yet digest food properly, he will need to stay in the hospital for a week or two. We'll keep him in an incubator where he won't be around germs, and we can give him oxygen. He just needs to put on a little more weight."

Ferne stayed in the hospital for three days. She visited the incubator room several times a day to hold the baby. When Bob arrived on the day she was to be discharged, he found her standing and staring at the baby. "I don't want to leave him here," she said, crying.

"Everything will be okay, Fernie. He just needs to stay a few more days. Barbie misses you. I'll bring you back every night until we bring him home. In the afternoon, Katie and Esther will take turns driving you here."

A month later when the doctor put the stethoscope to her heart, he could hear the murmur. It was on the left side, her mitral valve. "Pregnancy is very demanding on the heart, Mrs. Henning, and your heart is already damaged. Perhaps you should learn to enjoy a smaller family. You have two healthy children."

She looked at him and said, "I may have a heart murmur. A lot of people have heart murmurs, but I am strong, and I want a bigger family. Two is kind of a lonely little family."

"Well, give your body some time to recover this time, okay?"

"Don't worry, doctor. We're using the diaphragm."

Von Wiegand Says:

A-Bomb Revelation Boosts Soviet Stock

By KARL H. VON WIEGAND

Dean of American Foreign Correspondents
Written Expressly for Hearst Newspapers

ROME, Oct. 1—The American, British and Canadian governments are considered in many quarters to have done a great service for Generalissimo Joseph Stalin, his Communist Soviet regime, the Russian Communist party, the cominform and Communists throughout the world when President Truman, himself, made the sensational announcement that "Russia has the atomic bomb" simultaneously with statements in London and Ottawa.

The President's statement was accorded one of the biggest front page newspaper displays around the globe since the end of the war.

Communist throughout the world felt a thrill they have not had in years and Communist stock rose as it has not gone up since the beginning of the "cold war" between the East and West.

"We have the atomic bomb," the refrain in Communist circles. The President's announcement was like a powerful "shot in the arm" to communism.

Now that both the East and the West have "the bomb," the world is marching with stepped up tempo on the rocky, torturous road to another global conflict.

UAW Pension Drive Will Start in Toledo

TOLEDO, Oct. 1 (INS)—The Toledo area has been selected by the UAW-CIO for the first area-wide drive for the adoption of a pension plan modeled after the Ford settlement.

Richard Gosser, international vice president of the UAW, said the drive would begin next week and involve some 33,500 workers in 65 Toledo area plants.

Hurt in Fall Off Roof

Joseph Usannoz, 61, was criti-

Oct 2, 1949

OCTOBER 26, 1949   28

The Eisenhower Proposal

Welfare Studies

GEN. EISENHOWER proposes that leaders in every field of activity meet with the faculties of some of our great universities and determine how social and economic welfare can be promoted "without jeopardy to individual freedom and rights."

The coincidence of two devastating strikes over welfare issues in this Country with retrenchment in Great Britain's welfare state spotlights the need of some such convocation of the best minds of the Nation to deal with this fundamental problem.

Whether they could permanently lift it out of the domain of partisan politics and self-interest may well be doubted.

Yet by subjecting the trend to welfarism "to logical analysis and enlightened judgment" they could give authoritative and sadly needed guidance to people groping for the answer in a jungle of strife, greed and bitterness.

Oct 26, 1949 DFP

Barefoot Trend In Shoes

By JOE RAITI

By International News Service

CHICAGO, Nov. 4. SPOKESMEN FOR the nation's shoe industry said today they would come up with a topper of the fashion world's recent new look with introduction of a naked look in footwear.

Examples of the naked look—nylon fabrics, a two-way stretch job for men and llama skin slippers—are just a few of the novelties on display in more than 1,300 exhibits at the national shoe fair in Chicago.

Nov 14, 1949

Mother Gravely Ill with Throat Polio

A 20-year-old mother is in critical condition, is among the four South Macomb victims of polio reported this week by the County Health Department, bringing the County total to 42 this year.

Mrs. Yvonne St. Mary of 27360 Edward avenue, Roseville, the young mother, was seriously stricken with a throat infection last week and taken to Herman Keifer Hospital. She is the wife of Willis St. Mary. The couple have one daughter, Sherry, nearly two years old.

Others hospitalized were Louise Doan, 13, of 37180 Curwood avenue, Warren Township; Charlotte Miles, 8, of 18370 Hazelwood avenue, Roseville, and Patrick Murphy, 14, of 3238 Thirteen Mile road, Warren Township.

The first polio fatality in Mount Clemens this year occurred was William Anderson, Jr., 17, who suffered a three-day illness. The County's six other polio deaths were centered in the East Detroit area.

Nov 2, 1949 SMN

To the left, the original building from All Saints Lutheran Church,
later a Baptist church and in 2019 "For Sale"

GRAMPA HERRING - DADDY - BOBBY

NOVEMBER 13, 1947

On Sunday, they put Barbie into the back seat and Ferne held six-week-old Bobby on her lap. Off they went to All Saints Lutheran Church on Kelly Road where Bobby was to be baptized. Jeane and Marv were there with their children, Ferne's mother, Great-Grandad, as well as Bob's father, his mother and stepfather (Virginia and George) and Bob's Aunt Aline, who was visiting from Long Island. After the ceremony they gathered at his mother's house. She called everyone into the vestibule one at a time to have their photos taken. Ginny couldn't get back to Michigan until her vacation in the summer, and she had begged her mother to send photos of the new baby. On the wall behind them was Virginia's crocheted and quilted flag celebrating the formation of the United Nations.

"Did I ever tell you, Ferne, how I was in the *Free Press* in 43 for crocheting this flag? President Roosevelt sent me a letter thanking me, but I haven't been able to find that letter." Then she passed the clipping around the room for everyone to see.

On the way home, Bob and Ferne drove along Lake St. Clair on Jefferson Avenue, passing the magnificent Grosse Point mansions; the last on the right was the entrance to the Ford Mansion, hidden from sight by trees and fields.

"How lucky we are," Bob said, looking over at Ferne and the baby.

She unwrapped the blanket around Bobby's face. "We have to be careful. A child in the newspaper, only half a mile from where we live, has polio. I'm so worried. Little children can't breathe, and then they are crippled. We have to keep them away from crowds. They have temporarily stopped gym and swimming classes in the city."

Parents all over the country were terrified of polio. A second wave of the disease had hit the country and the baby boomers were at risk, especially in the summer months.

Monday, June 14, 1943

United Nations Flags Symbolize Spirit of the Home and Fighting Fronts

Mrs. Virginia Marx, of 4600 Grand River, has worked every evening since February to crochet this fifty-four-by-forty-one-inch United Nations' flag. She estimates that working the liberty head and designs for the 33 nations has required over 5,000 yards of crocheting cotton.

DFP

Almond Blvd

April 3, 1950

When the rain came down, the dirt road in front of our house would flood.
Bob and some neighbor men dug into the mess trying to encourage the water
to sink into the earth. It was a hopeless task until a few years later when
drains and sewers were installed and the street was paved. I remember waking
up from a nap once when I was a toddler. Bobby was in the room with me
in his own crib. We yelled for Mama, but there was no answer, so I climbed
out of my crib and pulled the rail on his down. Then we went into the living
room. No one was there. I took Bobby's hand and we went out the front door.
We stood on the front porch, then went down the one step. There was a river
of water in front of the house. I heard Ferne screaming as she ran down the
block, holding her pregnant belly. She caught up to us just before we went into
the water. She had been at a neighbor's borrowing a cup of sugar. This is one
of my earliest memories

Almond Blvd

April 4, 1950

Karen + Maev

Easter - 1950

Jeane's two oldest children beside their new television

Barbara Criss (Spires),
Hattie and Ferne

Barbara   Dad   Bobby

Peace at Briggs; Contract Settled

Pensions to Pay $100 a Month

Picture on Page 3

Briggs Manufacturing Co. and the UAW-CIO Saturday reached a contract agreement averting a strike that would have affected 30,000 workers and threatened a large segment of the auto industry.

In a joint announcement, Briggs and the UAW summoned all employes to report for their regular shifts Monday. The strike had been set for Monday.

Terms of the new three-year contract, which was still subject to ratification by the union membership, include a union shop, dues checkoff, $100 pensions, hospital-medical plan and a 5-cent an hour pay boost.

June 25, 1950

Reds Invade South Korea

Report North Korean Forces Capture City

SEOUL. Korea. Sunday June 25 (UP)—North Korean forces launched a general attack across the border into South Korea Sunday morning, fragmentary reports from the frontier said.

Bell Building Slated to Cost $6,000,000

Will Be Addition to Main Telephone Offices in Loop

(See Picture, Page 18)

Plans for an eight-story building, to cost $6,000,000, were announced Saturday by the Michigan Bell Telephone Co.

The new structure will rise at First and State streets and will connect with the company's main building at 1365 Cass.

Into the building will go $7,000,000 of new equipment, an important part of which will permit operators in other parts of the country to dial straight through to Detroit. Detroit operators now dial certain cities across the nation.

Detroit operators may dial carrier cities across the nation.

June 25, 1950

Bing and His 4 Boys Vacation at Ranch

HOLLYWOOD, June 24 (INS) —Bing Crosby and his four boys left for their usual vacation trip to the Crosby ranch near Elko, Nev., today after an intimate family dinner last night at the Crosby household in Hollywood. But Bing's wife, Dixie Lee, remained at home.

A studio spokesman said he attached "no significance" to the fact Dixie remained behind. He said it is no secret that she does not care for rough ranch life but visits the boys occasionally.

June 25, 1950

Colder Tonight After City Gets 1st Snow

Old Man Winter gave Detroit and southeastern Michigan a preview of things to come today with a blanket of light snow and a promise of below freezing temperatures tonight.

The snow, first of the season, fell generally in the Detroit area and outstate around Battle Creek, Lansing and Flint. For the main, the snow melted as it hit the ground, but it covered car tops.

Lowest temperature was 33 degrees.

The weather bureau said the mercury would drop to 30 degrees tonight, first below freezing prediction of the season. The temperatures will climb to 48 degrees tomorrow.

Subfreezing readings were reported this morning at many outstate points. Lowest was 23 reported at Sault Ste. Marie.

Nov 4, 1950

Ribbons for Fall

RIBBON, RIBBON everywhere is the cry for fall and winter. You'll see ribbons put to many uses. There are ribbon ascots that will give just the right touch of color needed for that fall and winter outfit. Ribbon belts are also a fashionable accessory for any costume as are ribbon ties. Place a "chunky" piece of jewelry on the ribbon tie and it will give an outfit sparkle as well as give it color.

Nov 4, 1950

Shortly after we moved to the suburbs, William Randolph Hearst died. *The Detroit Times* still had a station for paperboys behind the Hostetter house. The Detroit paper would continue to publish as did many other Hearst papers, but now they were under the direction of his son. Many people called Hearst a patriot. In Hearst Jr.'s book about his father, he catalogued the ways in which his father had championed concerns of working people, and there were many. But labor unions and educators did not mourn Hearst's death or the end of his over-the-top anti-communist reporting. After Hearst died, his son, William Randolph Hearst, Jr., followed in his father's footsteps, supporting Senator Joseph McCarthy and his Communist witch hunts.

William R. Hearst Dies in Coma at 88

Was Active Almost to the End; Sons to Carry On with Papers

BEVERLY HILLS, Calif.—(*P*)—William Randolph Hearst, 88-year-old patriarch of publishing, died in his Beverly Hills mansion Tuesday after a series of strokes.

The controversial "chief" of the vast newspaper and magazine empire had been a working newspaperman almost to the very last. He thus was able to realize a wish he expressed a score of years ago—to die a newspaperman.

W. R. HEARST
Dies a newspaperman

ALTHOUGH reduced to near-invalidism in recent years, he still actively directed the editorial policy of the Hearst newspapers until he sank into a coma Monday.

At the bedside when the end came were the five Hearst sons, William Randolph, Jr., George, John, David and Randolph. Also there were Martin F. Huberth, chairman of the board of the Hearst Corp., and Richard E. Berlin, president of the Hearst Corp.

Hearst, armed with a $25,000,000 mining fortune left him by his father, entered the newspaper business when he was 23.

* * *

HE SOON became—and stayed —the most spectacular publisher of the modern era in journalism.

Dr. Myron Prinzmetal, his physician, said Hearst enjoyed "robust health" until four years ago.

"Then," the doctor's statement continued, "he became subject to the ailments of advanced age."

But although Hearst spent much of his time in a wheelchair in a bedroom of his mansion here, he still gave the orders to his editors.

* * *

WHEN President Truman fired Gen. Douglas MacArthur, a great Hearst favorite, this spring, the lead editorial denouncing the act was dictated personally by Hearst.

Titled "Made in England," and decrying the United States foreign policy, the editorial was on front pages of all Hearst newspapers.

The big question—who will run the publishing empire now?—was

City Flags to Fly at Half Staff

Flags on all City buildings will fly at half staff Wednesday in memory of William Randolph Hearst.

Mayor Cobo ordered the honor to the famous publisher.

partially answered in a statement by William Randolph Hearst, Jr., publisher of the New York Journal American.

* * *

IT PLEDGED the intention of the sons "to continue to operate our father's publications as he guided us, and our determination to carry on in the tradition of his life which was dedicated to the service of America and the best interests of the American people."

Aug 15, 1951 DFP
Hearst owner of *The Detroit Times*

When I was about three years old, my father came home from work one day and he chased me into the bedroom and spanked me. I have no idea what I was punished for, but he frightened me. Trauma is what stands out when you might have had hundreds of wonderful moments as well. Ferne kept Benjamin Spock's book on top of her dresser and consulted it frequently to learn how to feed her babies and how to make potty training work. Spock did not recommend physical punishment, but my parents wanted us to grow up to be decent human beings, so they were afraid to follow Spock's advice. They practiced a milder form of discipline than their parents had practiced, spanking us, rather than using a strap. "Wait until I tell your father" was probably not the best way for children to develop a relationship with their father. Spock understood that parents have their own troubles and are not perfect, but he disagreed with a parent "who seriously believes that punishment is a good regular method of controlling a child" (270). My father disliked spanking us. Sometimes he cried while spanking us.

Bread Sent Here From Outside

Fleets of trucks from other cities today rushed bread to Detroit's dining room tables to avert a bread shortage threatened by the shut down of 10 large bakeries which normally supply half this city's baked goods.

Other bakeries, large and small, unaffected by the strike which closed the 10 plants, have stepped up their production to keep Detroit's bread supply as near normal as possible.

Sept 17, 1951

U.S. to Offer Peace Plan

World Disarmament Program Is Ready

Nov 4, 1951

Peace in Near East To Test U. S. Tact

Largest Circulation of Any Michigan Newspaper

Detroit Times

The City's 26th Year, The Times' 62d

FINAL

Eisenhower Denies Political Aspirations

RECORD COLD, MORE SNOW ON WAY

Two Became Ill on Same Day; Victims Get Aid From Pontiac Center

By MARGARET DALY

Polio struck a little home on crescent Lake, near Pontiac, four times. It hit the children, all four children of Helen and Raymond Sneed who live at 5533 Eldridge. . . . It all happened so quickly we just couldn't believe it. First Roger. He was so terribly sick. Then Judy just wanted to sleep all the time. She got up one day and her leg just gave away under her. . . . The children's father, a plant protection man at the General Motors plant in Pontiac, said: "You just can't believe that this could happen to you. Nov 4, 1951

Eva Peron Readied For Serious Operation

BUENOS AIRES, Nov. 3 (UP) —Mrs. Eva Peron, wife of President Peron, was taken to a hospital today to undergo an operation within the next 24 hours.

Mrs. Peron has been reported seriously ill from anemia in the past several weeks. She was said to have undergone several blood transfusions.

New Mothers' Club Meets in Pershing High

Nov 4, 1951

Nurse School Project O.K'd

Opening of the Mercy School of Practical Nursing next February, with headquarters of the central school at Mercy Hospital, Cadillac, has been approved by the Michigan Board of Registration of Nurses.

Affiliating hospitals besides Cadillac are the Mercy hospital in Manistee and Grayling.

Aims of the school are to pre-pare the practical nurse to care for the convalescent, the chronically and the subacutely ill, either in a hospital or in the home.

Students must be between 18 and 65 and must have at least an eighth grade education or its equivalent.

Nov 4, 1951

When Ferne went into labor on September 17, 1951, Bob put the children into the back seat of the car. Ferne tried to sing a few lines from *When the Saints Come Marching In* because she didn't want to moan and scare the children. "Bob, hurry up, the contractions are just half an hour apart." When he pulled in front of Jeane's, Marv ran out to the car and collected the children. Then Bob sped down Gratiot Avenue to the hospital. When they arrived, the orderlies rushed her into the delivery room. Virginia was born a few hours later, full term and with a head of black hair.

She was named Virginia after Bob's mother and "Linne" after Ferne's brother Lynn. We called her Ginny. After Ginny's baptism, the family gathered at our house. Ferne was still beautiful then, wearing wire-rimmed glasses. I used to love the rocking chair she would sit in. She had reupholstered the cushion several times and painted it different colors. Once I bought a chair like hers and painted it turquoise, one of her favorite colors. In this photo, she and my father appear at ease and happy with their family. Once when I was working with a therapist on a deep depression, he took me back into my childhood and helped me realize that I felt so much loss because I actually had had a lot of love in my early childhood, even from my father.

CHAPTER 14

"Hello Jeanie, I thought you'd never answer. What took so long? Diapers? Oh diapers, diapers and more diapers. That's our life now, no more movies or dancing, just diapers. Are the twins keeping you awake all night long? They're adorable, but yeah, a lot of work. I'll be over there tomorrow if I can get Bessie moving. Well, something's wrong with her. When I pull up to a light, she peters out, and I rev her up and say a prayer. The kids start laughing. The new couple who moved next door, well finally she came over for coffee. Just left. She's pregnant with her first. I couldn't believe it when she told me she was the youngest of 21. Yes, *twenty-one*. That's what I said. Yeah, I saw the doctor yesterday. Not only did I see him, but when I pulled into the parking lot with all three kids in back, I saw him out there, and he saw me, too. Guess what he was doing? No, he wasn't peeing! Smoking, he was smoking. Damn, he tells me not to smoke, but there he is smoking. Okay, you don't like a smoke now and again, but I do. Why shouldn't I be able to smoke a few a day? It's one of the pleasures in my life. The doctor said that's okay. Just a minute. *Barbara, I'm on the phone with Aunt Jeanie. Go play with Bobby. Go on, go on. See what Ginny's crying about. Go on.* Anyhow the doctor went on again about birth control. We're trying, I tell him. I don't like the diaphragm, sticking a rubber thing up there. I'm counting the days instead. I didn't tell him that last week we slipped up. Don't yell at me. I know. Yes, I won't forget. I gotta go. I've got a pile of dishes here and everyone's crying. I'm gonna put them all out in the yard while I hang a load of laundry. Talk to you tomorrow. Bye bye."

Ferne stubbed out her cigarette in the glass ashtray beside the phone. Then she swiveled around on the stool, stood up and moved toward the weeping sounds in the living room. "Hey everybody, let's go outside. Barbara, you can help me hang clothes. Bobby, you're in charge of pushing Ginny around the yard in the wagon. Then after that Daddy will be home."

Ferne was tired of hearing about the Cold War with the Soviets and the war in Korea, tired of hearing news of more American boys killed in wartime. When would this ever stop? She switched the radio to NBC to listen to the new *Barrie Craig Show*. The announcer's deep voice boomed, "Barrie Craig, confidential investigator, starring William Gargen." Then the trumpet made a jazzy cry, and while frying a chicken, Ferne swung her hips dancing in the kitchen. Barbara and Bobby came into the room laughing and dancing with her. "Barry Craig speaking. Detectives come in three sizes: city cops, big offices and guys like me with a small office and an insurance retainer to help pay the rent. Cops don't have to worry about getting cases and the big agencies have branches from here to Shanghai. . . but from where I sit you never have to worry about where your next case will come from."

"Go on now, go play in the living room. I've gotta cook now." She shooed them out of the kitchen.

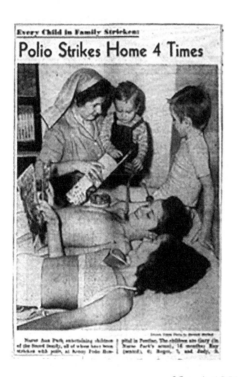

Every Child in Family Stricken:

Polio Strikes Home 4 Times

Narcotics Violations Tighter in New Law

WASHINGTON, Nov. 3 (AP)—President Truman has signed legislation tightening the penalties for violations of narcotics laws, and set up a government committee to study other ways of controlling the drug problem.

Among other things, the new law sets a minimum prison term of two years, and a maximum of five, for the first violation of the narcotics and marijuana laws.

Nov 4, 1951   Nov 4, 1951

U. S. Accuses Russians of Plane Attack

UN Told Reds Fired On Bomber Over Free Area of Japan Sea

(AP) — The United States charged today that a missing navy Neptune bomber was attacked without warning by Soviet fighter planes over the free international waters off the Sea of Japn. Nov 6. The plane with 10 men aboard is presumed to have been shot down.

The United States rejected as untrue a Russian complaint that the American aircraft had "violated the Soviet state frontier" before it was approached by two Russian fighter planes. The Russians also alleged that the American plane opened fire first." Nov 25, 1951

Eisenhower, President To Confer

General Says NATO More Important Than Partisanship

WASHINGTON, Nov 3—Gen. Eisenhower flew back to America today with a fresh disclaimer of political ambitions, and amid indications he may step swinging into a Washington clash over the speed of rearmament. Eisenhower told newsmen:

"I have never had any political aspirations—period.

"I am on a job in which the United States has invested worlds and worlds of treasure, time and thought, and for me to imply any political or partisan leanings would be a disservice to the country."

Asked "Can we say specifically, come what may, that you will not be a candidate for the presidency next year?" Eisenhower replied:

"Of course you can't say that. I will not indicate political leanings of any kid. I'm doing a job. That's my statement."

HOLDS CONFERENCE

Then he was asked: "Are you a Democrat or a Republican?"

Grinning, Eisenhower answered: "Just because it's the football season, don't pull a quarterback sneak."

All four of Ferne's sisters had worked during the Depression and war years when their families needed their help, but after their children were born, they were at-home moms. By 1952, Hattie had eight children and eighteen grand-children. The two older girls each had two children, but the two younger ones, Jeane and Ferne, had nine between them. In their own families, Jeane and Ferne had been the happy recipients of their older sisters' care. The older girls, however, had already had their share of mothering. Two was enough.

Jeane Esther Ona Kay me

22 March 1952

me

March 22 1952

Barbie George me

22 March 1952

On March 21st, Bob turned thirty. They celebrated at his mother's house. After the birthday cake and a few drinks, everyone sat in a circle. When Dad picked up the camera, Ferne slid down on the floor, tipsy, laughing, her legs crossed, a black slip under her dress, posing like a movie star. Those beautiful legs and high heels.

On Easter morning, Ferne hid eggs around the house and in the yard for the children to hunt. Little baskets were waiting with fake grass, jellybeans and chocolate bunnies. This same celebration of spring and the rebirth of Jesus was happening in houses all along the block. While the children ate their jelly-beans and cereal, Bob was in the garage at his workbench, drawing a diagram of an addition he wanted to put on the house. Sometime in the future, his father or his mother might need to stay with them. He had recently applied to the bank to remortgage the house so they could pay for the addition. Ferne called out to him, "Bob, you have to get dressed. We'll be late for church. He was never big on church, so he stalled. He changed into a suit, brought out the camera and photographed Ferne with each of the children in new spring coats she had made. He loved her, and he liked saying, "I'm a family man." The wind ruffled through her hair. She was wearing heels, a ring, a bracelet and she was dressed in a new suit. She stood in front of the garage in their back-yard. The frame around the garage window was newly painted and detailed.

In a reoccurring dream, my father is at the workbench in the garage, red plaid flannel shirtsleeves rolled up, the muscles in his arms, a gold band on his finger, the darkness of the garage, hammering, cool damp air. I'm hiding in the darkness, behind the clutter of tools and boxes, his arm flexed on the worktable, the gold band, shiny opening over the maple tree, lightning strikes, the hole in the trunk, a glimmer of blue sky, on the stool reciting my ABCs, the sound of pounding, diapers on the line, the station wagon in the drive, the gate won't open, on the floor babbling, a b c d e f g h i—

Every summer Ward and Betty would host a family reunion for the Hostetters at their place in Clinton Township. While the men played horseshoes and drank beer, the women gathered in circles. They turned to look at the pho-tographer, probably Bob, based on the symmetry of the photo. He liked symmetry. They are all laughing. He liked to be funny and make others laugh. In the middle of the four, little Ginny is in her stroller looking straight at him with her mouth open.

Ginny

17 August 1952

17 Aug 1952

August 7, 1952 Jean, Ferne and Ginny

My brother, sisters and cousins would sit together on Gramma Hattie's front porch in the city and watch the trolley, cars, neighbors and strangers passing by. "With a much used front porch one could live on Andy Hardy's street, where doors need not be locked, where everybody was like family, and where the iceman would forever make deliveries" (280). Kenneth Jackson describes the passing of the front porch as a sign of the decline of community. We had only a small slab of cement in front of our house; it served as a step to go into the front door. Our lives took place in the backyard. The fence posts in the above photo marked the border of the yard. I remember my father pouring the cement into the ground and then anchoring the posts and painting them green and the tops white. The side gate opened into a small lot with five trees. Our old Plymouth was parked on the side street, another car passed along from Bob's mother. Jeane stands slightly behind her sister with a shy flirty look. It is her A-line skirt with swishy trees that holds my attention. Then my eye moves toward the baby's legs and on to those white fence posts.

Aly, Rita Hold Hands; Mum on Reconciling

By BARNEY COHAN

HOLLYWOOD. Aug. 16 (INS)—Aly Khan and flame-haired Rita Hayworth laughed and joked and held hands throughout a press conference today but said that, while they were "very happy," they did not have a word to say about a possible reconciliation.

Aug 17, 1952

Ginny, Bob, Bobby, Marvel Lynn, Barbara, Ferne, Karen, Linda, Jeane
in front of the Bakke house. Photo by Marv

Detroit Vote Stuns Experts

Balloting Heavy Across Nation

By BOB CONSIDINE

WASHINGTON, Nov. 4 (INS) — Balloting records in the nation's history apparently were being swept into discards today as American voters, somewhere between 55 and 60 million strong, went abotu choosing between Gen. Eisenhower and Gov. Stevenson for president.

Nov 4, 1952

Detroit Schools Pick Democrats

Straw vote returns from 15 of 21 Detroit public high schools today gave an overwhelming majority to Democratic candidates.

In the presidential race, it was nearly 2 to 1 and in state races virtually 3 to 1.

Here was the vote:

For president: Stevenson, 16,055; Eisenhower, 8,725.

Governor: Williams, 18,159; Alger, 6,577.

U. S. Senator: Moody, 18,893; Potter, 5,941.

Nov 4, 1952

Flares to Glow on E. Detroit's Armistice Day

EAST DETROIT—This year's "Flare Night" sponsored by the East Detroit Rotary Club, is slated to start at 8 p. m. Tuesday, Nov. 11. Members of the Rotary Club have expressed a desire that everyone in the city be "lit up," for a few minutes next Tuesday.

The flares are on sale at local business places, and members of the Rotary Club will station themselves on various corners in the city to sell flares from tonight until Saturday from 6 to 9 p. m.

The price of the flares is fifty cents each, or three for a dollar. All of the funds collected from the flare sale will go to aid the crippled children of this city.

All residents of East Detroit are urged to buy a flare and upon signal of the local fire siren —at 8 p. m.—light the flares to commemorate both Armistice Day and Flare Night.

Nov 6, 1952 SMD

THE DETROIT TIMES
Tues., Nov. 4, 1952

Silent Voters Baffle Pollsters

By WILLIAM K. HUTCHINSON

WASHINGTON, Nov. 4 (INS) —The "silent" American voter, who refused to participate in any poll, determines the fate of Gov. Stevenson and Gen. Eisenhower today in the most baffling presidential election of modern times.

These four or five million Americans hold the "balance of power" in a contest that has "stumped the experts" and puzzled top strategists in both Democratic and Republican parties.

Top leaders in both parties are confused over the terrific increase in voter registration clear across the nation.

WOMEN'S VOTE

But more than being confused over total registration figures, they are in a total blackout over how the women of America are going to vote.

All things considered, the women may well hold the fate of the election in the way they mark their ballots

Nov 4, 1952

243

Ferne and Bob, like many Americans, voted for Eisenhower. He was already a hero before he ran for president, the commanding general of the Allied Forces who had brought the war in Europe to an end. Both parties had asked Eisenhower to run. He chose the Republicans, so many Democrats migrated over to the GOP. Ferne and Bob liked that he talked about keeping the country safe and at peace. Eisenhower's mother was a Mennonite and a devout pacifist. He had been against dropping the atom bomb on Japan, and he wasn't going to take away Social Security; in fact, he was going to improve it. His voice was calm and serene, and he didn't seem worried about the Soviets and all the talk about communism. When the scandal broke out about Nixon taking funds from wealthy donors for his private use, Nixon made a television appearance. He seemed to be on the verge of weeping. Bob felt sorry for him, but Ferne thought he was whiny and seemed dishonest. Despite Nixon's behavior, Eisenhower won with a landslide, but he never trusted his vice president, Nixon.

I remember one evening when my mother was watching television. "Bob," she yelled. "Come on. Hurry up! President Eisenhower is on the television." It was as if he was almost a god. Recently when reading Ibram X. Kendi's *Stamped from the Beginning* (2016), I learned that many of Eisenhower's decisions were destructive for civil rights; for example, he discontinued the Truman Doctrine on civil rights and he refused to endorse *Brown v. Board of Education.* When I was scanning the Hearst newspapers, I never saw an article criticizing Eisenhower's stance on civil rights. I'm not surprised.

Mayor Louis C. Miriani presents a replica of the *Spirit of Detroit*
to President Eisenhower. At far left is Councilwoman Blanche Parent Wise
and council president Eugene Van Antwerp (1958)

Heavy Voting in S. Macomb Returns Slate

An unprecedented 82,000 voters all but clogged Macomb County's balloting machinery Tuesday in the most amazing election turnout in all history.

They represented approximately 75 per cent of the county's 109,000 registered voters.

On the basis of incompleted unofficial returns — with one precinct still being counted late Wednesday — the electors wove a strange, Republican-Democratic pattern.

They followed the national swing toward Eisenhower — but kept Stevenson closely trailing the GOP victor.

Eisenhower—34,281; Stevenson—32,134.

Nov 6, 1952 SMN

Ballot Boxes Running Short

By early afternoon, Elections Director Louis Urban was getting calls for additional ballot boxes from precinct workers who were worried because the boxes first alloted them were becoming crammed. He immediately arranged for trucks to deliver the extra boxes.

Said Urban:

"It's been a long, long time since such a thing has happened. A few precincts sent for extras in 1944, but it looks as if there would be more this year—maybe 15 or 20."

Two of the first three extra boxes went to downtown polling places, at John R and Erskine and in the Clay School, 453 Stimson. The third went to the Dossin School, Glendale and Abington, in the Northwest section.

Nov 4, 1952

The South Macomb News was a weekly suburban newspaper that reported little on the news outside Macomb County. Bob and Ferne read this paper every week. It was nuclear like the nuclear families in the suburbs. Later the *Macomb Daily News* was a daily paper but still pretty nuclear. Nuclear was a word on everyone's tongue after the bombs were dropped on Japan. I remember in grade school having bomb drills, ducking down under desks and in line in the hallways. I remember being told by my parents that in case of a tornado or a bomb, I was to go into the utility room underneath the heavy oak table. The documentary *The Atomic Café* in the 1980s revealed the propaganda and fake information that was spread about the danger of nuclear war.

British Reds Rap Coronation Plans

LONDON Dec 29 (AP)—British Communist today fired a propaganda blast against plans for public celebration of Queen Elizabeth's coronation next June. The Communist Daily Worker said, " Nobody of course, has any personal objectives to the members of the royal family. They appear to be a conscientious, fairly pleasant, though not over-intelligent group of people. Dec 29 1952

1st Atom Spy Out of Jail
Physicist Served 6 Years in Britain

Dr. Alan Nunn May, 41, the first atom traitor to be convicted of passing secrets to the Russians was freed from prison today and went into seclusion. . . . [He] pleaded guilty to passing information to a man whose identity he has always refused to reveal. He peddled the information to the Russians in Montreal during World War II. . . . Also [he] gave samples of uranium to a Russian agent. He said in his confession, "I thought this was a contribution I could make for the safety of mankind." Dec 29 1952

Dwight David Eisenhower:

"The Chance for Peace," speech to the American Society of Newspaper Editors.

Every gun that is made, every warship launched, every rocket fired signifies, in the final sense, a theft from those who hunger and are not fed, those who are cold and are not clothed. This world in arms is not spending money alone. It is spending the sweat of its laborers, the genius of its scientists, the hopes of its children. The cost of one modern heavy bomber is this: a modern brick school in more than 30 cities. It is two electric power plants, each serving a town of 60,000 population. It is two fine, fully equipped hospitals. It is some fifty miles of concrete pavement. We pay for a single fighter plane with a half million bushels of wheat. We pay for a single destroyer with new homes that could have housed more than 8,000 people. This is, I repeat, the best way of life to be found on the road the world has been taking. This is not a way of life at all, in any true sense. Under the cloud of threatening war, it is humanity hanging from a cross of iron. [...] Is there no other way the world may live? Apr. 16, 1953.

Hattie and Jeane with Jeane's girls, Linda and Karen
in front and the twins, Diane and Denise in back. May 1953

In 1953, Ferne put Ginny in the stroller. Bobby held one side and I walked along on the other side dressed in a new blue dress with ruffles around the edges. When she left me with the teacher for my first day of kindergarten, I started weeping. Out the window I saw her looking back with a very sad look on her face. At noon, when she met me at the bus stop, I was soaking wet from having cried and peed. Apparently the teacher had not sent us to the bathroom before we left. I was still crying as we walked home. "It will get easier, Barbie, I can guarantee that." She didn't scold me for wetting, not this time. Like their other neighbors and most working-class parents of their time and place, my parents believed that it was important to be strict our first six years of life, but they were never cruel.

When they bought Bobby his first bicycle, Ferne called her neighbor over to the fence. "Marie," she said, "I've told Bobby that he can only ride his bike on the sidewalks and, if he rides on anyone's lawn, he will lose it for two weeks. Please tell me if he ever rides it on your lawn."

—⚬⚬⚬—

I zoom into the photo of a young Ferne who I can barely remember. She's standing by the bushes in the back of the house wearing white shorts and a white T-shirt. Surprised at the camera, she turns her head and smiles. She looks happy, her hair pulled behind her ears. If I keep hitting the zoom she gets less and less present rather than closer and closer, finally just dots and squares of white and black and shades of gray.

Me

June 1953

Sometimes we want something so badly, but when we get it, it's more than we can handle. Ferne wanted to have her children one after another so they would be close with each other. When she discovered in November that she was pregnant again, the doctor was very worried that, with her heart problem, she might not survive another pregnancy. He had a conference with her and Bob. "Mrs. Henning, I'm very worried that, with your heart condition, you might not be able to survive this pregnancy. I am recommending that you go into the hospital and terminate this pregnancy."

"There is a child already started, Dr. Singer. I couldn't possibly interfere." She started weeping.

Bob held her. "Fernie, let's talk about this at home."

"No, absolutely not, Bob. I would never interfere with another life, *our* child, that's like Barbara, Bobby and Ginny. Never. Instead I will do everything I can to stay strong."

In early December, Ferne had just recovered from pneumonia and rheumatic fever when Bobby came down with a throat infection. Because of her childhood experiences with strep and rheumatic fever, Ferne never took a chance with her children. We were lucky to be born after penicillin had been discovered, she said. Dr. Singer gave Bobby a shot of penicillin and some sulfa tablets. When he looked at Ferne's throat, he gave her a shot, too. When he listened to her heart, he told her that he wanted her to come in every week during the winter for a shot of penicillin. "You're losing weight instead of gaining. Cut down on smoking. If you can't stop, just have one after eating, no more." She didn't tell him how much trouble she was having breathing, especially when she climbed stairs.

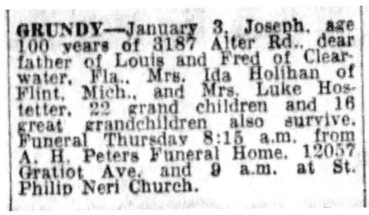

GRUNDY—January 3, Joseph, age 100 years of 3187 Alter Rd., dear father of Louis and Fred of Clearwater, Fla., Mrs. Ida Holihan of Flint, Mich., and Mrs. Luke Hostetter. 22 grand children and 16 great grandchildren also survive. Funeral Thursday 8:15 a.m. from A. H. Peters Funeral Home, 12057 Gratiot Ave. and 9 a.m. at St. Philip Neri Church.

Jan 6, 1954 DFP

Hattie's father (Grandad) died when he was one hundred years old. Now for the first time in her life, Hattie would be home with no children and with no one for her to care for. Her daughters were worried about her. Uncle John bought her a television set. She was still walking down Mack Avenue a couple of times a week to clean the pews in the church. After the funeral, the family gathered in the flat. One day Gramma took me into the sunroom. "Grandad knew how much you loved reading, Barbara, so he left you his books." I looked at the cabinet full of big books and smiled. I was only six years old and here was a set of *Harvard Classics* and a set of Mark Twain's books that would sit in my room until I left home, at eighteen.

When Ferne was about eight months pregnant, she was very weak and had a lot of trouble breathing. The doctor kept telling her and Bob that she needed help in the house. Finally Bob was able to save enough money to hire someone to come in every week. Then, when he was at work one day, he lifted the edge of a heavy airplane wing and he was taken to the emergency room with a hernia. He was off work without pay for ten days, and because he couldn't lift heavy objects after that, he couldn't continue with the same job. Instead he became the handyman on the floor and his paycheck was reduced substantially. Now he couldn't afford to hire anyone to help, so Ferne's mother and sisters made a schedule to come over during the week and help her. For three weeks, women at the church delivered baskets of food.

Ferne explained to us how everyone had to make sacrifices. "We will only have one serving at dinnertime for a while," she said. Then she asked me to give up my ballet lessons. "I don't like doing pliés anyhow," I said. "And Barb, you're old enough now to help me with the laundry. I'll teach you how to sort the clothes."

First Woman Elected to Recorder's Bench:

Judge Griffiths Wins

Heavy Vote in 21st and 22d Wards
Elect Truck Saleswoman

Blanche Parent Wise, a petite, 46-year-old truck saleswoman, unseated Councilman James H. Garlick in yesterday's election to become Detroit's second lady councilman.

It was the heavy vote of the 21st and 22d wards which turned the balance in her favor.

By Mrs. Wise's own admission, this would have been her fourth and last try if defeated.

Instead, she happily called her five children downstairs at 2:45 a.m. for an election picture with her husband, John A. Wise, vice president of Campbell Construction Co.

Overjoyed

The children needed no urging, since noises from upstairs indicated a wakefulness and celebration on par with the victory atmosphere in the living room. Mrs. Wise, normally a stickler for early-to-bed hours, had good humoredly ignored the pint-sized festivities.

Nov 4, 1953

Elizabeth Wants Husband Named:

Queen Removing Sister as Regent

By Robert A. Wiener

LONDON, Nov. 4 (INS)— Queen Elizabeth II today asked Parliament to name her "dear husband," Prince Philip, Duke of Edinburgh, as regent of the British commonwealth to replace her sister, Princess Margaret.

Nov 4, 1953

me
Barb Ginny Bobby

Easter 1954

Me Barb Ginny Ma Bob

April 30 1954

Dad Barb Ginny Gram Bob

April 30 1954

When Ferne went into labor, Bob put us in the back of the car and drove directly to the hospital. When we arrived at St. Joseph's in Mt. Clemens, Jeane and Marv were waiting in the parking lot to take us with them. The sisters embraced, and then Bob took her into the hospital in a wheelchair. Because she was so weak, the doctor kept her and the baby in a nursing wing of the hospital for a week after the birth. When she came home, we each took turns sitting on the green scratchy couch holding our new sister, Patti.

When she placed the baby on my lap, she said, "You will be a mother someday, too, dear."

Barb + Patti

27 June 1954

CHAPTER 15

1954. Ferne, Bob and Patti, Ginny, Bobby, Barbie

Ferne's health improved a little after the baby was born but, now with four children, she had a lot to do. Doctor Singer warned her that she had to rest. "Mrs. Henning, it's a miracle that you are doing as well as you are. Remember, you have scar tissue in your heart and a leaky valve. This could get worse if you don't take care of yourself. Tell Bob that he needs to help out with the children."

"But doctor, he's doing the best he can. We're strapped for money."

After Briggs Manufacturing was sold to Chrysler, Bob was transferred to the Tank Plant in Warren. It was now important that he do something to find less strenuous work and make more money. As he was reading over a list of possible positions on the bulletin board at Chrysler, he found a notice for classes to become a draftsman. He had excellent drawing skills and was mechanically minded. When he applied, he was accepted. Some of the classes were correspondence courses, but most were in classrooms at Chrysler's Institute of Engineering. This meant that Ferne was home alone with the children during the week, day and evening. But it was important that Bob get a better paying job, so she told herself that this was only temporary.

One night, Bob's sister Ginny telephoned from Brooklyn. The rooming house in Detroit where their father was staying was closing, and he needed a place to stay. He was almost eighty years old with rheumatism and a weak heart. He had only a modest social security check. Thanks to Roosevelt, he had even that. He had fathered and raised six children, but he had never saved any money. Bob's mother was given the house when she divorced him.

"Where will we put him?" Ferne asked. They were already crowded in their small house.

"We'll bring Barbara downstairs with Ginny and Patti, and we'll put him upstairs with Bobby, just for the time being until we can work something else out. I have an appointment at the bank tomorrow."

When the new mortgage was approved, Bob sat down with Marv to look at the diagrams. Marv was a carpenter who knew bricklayers and cement workers. On the weekends during the rest of the summer and fall, Bob worked alongside the others adding a bedroom and a small utility room to the back of the house.

Star of Five Careers:
Dorothy's Life Pinpointed by Papa Kilgallen

New York (INS). Written by her father James L. Kilgallen. A TV and radio personality, columnist, star reporter, magazine writer, traveler. They all add up to Dorothy Kilgallen, one of the best known and busiest young women in America. . . . the Cinderella story of the newspaper business. . . "I don't know what I'm proving, except that I'm showing it's possible to hit the typewriter and rock the cradle the same day." Dorothy's real life story would be thoroughly disbelieved behind the Iron Curtain. June 6, 1954

Public Returns Its Verdict in M'Carthy Case

By George Gallup

Director, American Institute of Public Opinion

PRINCETON, N. J., June 26—One of the interesting features of the McCarthy-army controversy was the trend as the hearing progressed, of the army's case to grow weaker in the public's mind.

Seek Quick Indo-China Aid:

French Ask U.S. Help in Airlift

WASHINGTON, June 5 (AP)—France has asked the United States for assistance in transporting reinforcements to Indo-China where the war against Communist forces is moving into a new crisis.

This was the beginning of the US's involvement in the Vietnam War. Eisenhower resisted getting involved, but his predecessors did not. The tension between Communism (the idea of shared wealth) and the West continued.

Europe to See The Pope on TV

VATICAN CITY, June 5 (AP)—Europe's major television networks will be hooked up tomorrow for a Vatican program which will conclude with a message from Pope Pius.

The program will begin at 12 noon Detroit time. It will take television viewers to St. Peter's Basilica, where some of its greatest treasures, s u c h as Michaelangelo's "Pieta," will be shown.

Viewers will then see Raphael's famous "Loggia" and finally will be shown the pontiff, seated on his throne in Consistorial Hall. They will hear him give a brief message in Italian, French, English and German.

The program will last 45 minutes. Hooked up for the broadcast will be the television networks of Italy, France, Belgium, Holland, E n g l a n d, Denmark, Germany and Switzerland.

June 6, 1954

Favorite Game:

Bingo Tops In Popularity

EDITOR'S NOTE—*This is the first of a series of three exclusive articles dealing with the controversial Bingo situation, describing how this most popular of all games of chance operates legally in New Jersey and illegally in Michigan. The second article in the series will appear in Monday's Detroit Times.*

By George Carpozi Jr.

Staff Writer New York Journal-American

Bingo, the lotto variant played regularly throughout the land by some 20 million persons—and twice as many at sporadic intervals—is the most popular game of chance in the country.

And whether it's played in a state where the game is legal or in a state where it's not, you'll find it can muster more loyal devotees than all other games of chance combined.

New Jersey, one of the few states to realize the all-embracing popularity of bingo, did something about it. It legalized bingo after all attempts to suppress it had failed.

Before the state conducted its referendum on bingo last April, New Jersey found that no number of police was able to contain the bingo habit. No law was powerful enough to stop the play.

Played in Dozens of Communities

Bingo addicts only became edged with bitterness when the law clamped down, and they openly defied the ban.

Bingo was played brashly in dozens of communities on such a lavish and broad scale that the local constabulary in many cases had to give up its efforts to enforce the law.

As a consequence, bingo became a big-time gambling operation. It was no longer in the domain of the fire house, the church hall, the ladies' aid society. The gambling syndicates took over.

June 27, 1954

18 July 1954

Robert Sr. (Bob's father), Jack and Esther, Hatti, Ferne and Ginny

One Sunday in July after church, the family gathered in the yard to celebrate Patti's baptism. The crosses are not Christian; they were put into the ground and used for stringing the clothesline. Grampa, Uncle Jack, Aunt Esther and Gramma Hattie smile into the camera and at little Ginny, who asks Ferne, "Can I have a cookie, Mama?' The sunlight bounces off Ferne's glasses.

———

I remember Ferne teaching me how to fold sheets. We were outside in the yard. The wind was flipping the laundry back and forth. She unpinned a sheet from the line. "Put the corners together, Barbara," she said. "Now walk toward me and take the other end." Smooth, crisp and folded flat. Then we started on the diapers.

In 1976, I asked my Aunt Ginny what she remembered about my mother. "After Patti was born, I flew in from New York to see your mother and my father. My dad was living in your house for a while. Your mother looked awful. She was so sick. I remember piles and piles of diapers. She was always folding diapers, smoking Pall Malls and drinking black coffee. One day I was in a tavern with Grampa when your father burst in saying that we had to get him out of the house that very day. Grampa liked to drink, and your mom did not like that happening around the children. He was not supposed to drink in the house, but she had found liquor bottles in the rafters. Another thing I remember was when I helped her rearrange the furniture. We took the split couches and set them facing each other, with the coffee table in between. Your mother said, "Look, Ginny, a cocktail lounge. She then brought in drinks, and we each had one."

"I used to play that with her, too, but we had cherry Koolaid."

Beauty After 40:
Perfume A 'Must' For Charm

By Edyth T. McLeod

THERE IS romance and mystery in every bottle of perfume! There is the glamour of far places, the charm of flowers blossoming in the sun and often coming to their full fragrance in the deep of night.

I do wish that more of you would wear perfume. It makes life pleasanter and every woman, especially those After Forty, should dramatize her personality by a touch of fragrance.

Nov 4, 1954

Lumber Dealer Held in Crash

George L. Isbell, 60 Livonia lumber dealer and former intimate of the late Huey Long is held today in Livonia for driving on the wrong side of Eight Mile road last night while drunk and hitting another car head-on.

Two women were injured in the crash.

It was the second time in less than three weeks that Isbell has been arrested for drunk driving The first was Dec. 17, when no accident was involved.

Injured in the crash near Pearl were Mrs Margaret Brehm, 40, and her mother-in-law, Mrs Emma Brehm 64 both of 20201 Westover They are in temporarily serious condition in Redford Receiving Hospital

Jan 4, 1955

U. S. Food Parcels Given to Refugees

BREMEN, Jan. 4 (AP)—More than 100,000 food parcels, a gift of the American government, will be distributed to Soviet zone refugees in West Berlin in the next few days, a U. S. relief agency said.

The 12-pound parcels contain flour, canned meat, fats and other food.

Jan 4, 1955

At the end of March, Ferne and Bob frantically pulled Bobby and me aside. They held up a newspaper pointing at a photo of a little girl with blonde hair. "This little girl has the same name as you, Barbara, and she's the same age as you, and last week she talked to a stranger. A man in a car stopped

259

her, maybe he gave her candy, and then he killed her and dumped her body in the garbage. Barbara and Bobby, never *ever* speak to any stranger, no matter what they offer you, especially someone in a car. Run home as fast as you can if someone tries to talk to you who you don't know. If someone touches you, yell and scream."

The next day, I wouldn't go outside. "Mama, I'm afraid."

When Ferne looked outside, all she could see was a group of children from the block.

"It's okay to go to the park, Barbara. Your friend Kathy is down there, and Bobby will go with you. It's just a warning. You will be safe, but don't talk to strangers."

"It's going to rain. The clouds are grey. I don't want to go out."

"Okay, stay in and read your library books, but only for today."

Bobby and I climbed into opposite corners of the couch to read. Safe at home.

3,000 SCOUTS JOIN MISSING GIRL HUNT

6 Inches of Snow Due Here

Times Offers $1,000 Reward | **2 Suspects Still Held**

By Lou Arkles and Tony Weiss

Police raced to many locations in the Detroit area this afternoon on tips phoned to two Catholic priests that the body of missing 7-year-old Barbara Gaca would be found at the base of a large gas storage tank.

Meanwhile 14 policemen and sheriffs deputies were searching a large field at 11-Mile and Groesbeck on a tip to Detroit police that a body was seen there. Officers responded from Warren Township, the State Police Post at Center Line and the Macomb County sheriff's office.

Search of one tank mentioned in the calls to the priests—at Allen and Greenfield roads—failed to show any sign of the missing girl.

All gas storage tanks in the city and suburbs were being checked.

* Other developments in the case today included The Detroit Times offer of a $1,000 reward for exclusive information leading to the whereabouts of the girl, and:

* A $500 reward posted by the common council.

* Request by the county board of auditors for legal sanction to offer a $500 reward.

* Questioning of a suspect picked up on Groesbeck Highway.

* Intensive search for two automobiles, one a green Hudson in which there was a man and a "frightened" little girl, and a station wagon. The man in the station wagon made obscene remarks to children near the school for three days before Barbara vanished.

(See Other Pictures, Pcb. 3 and 20)

The missing Barbara Gaca (at right), 7, in a recent picture with her sister Gloria. She disappeared on her way to school early yesterday morning.

Mar 25-26, 1955 DFP

260

After Ferne made Bob breakfast and he left for work, she called up the stairs, "Come on, sleepyheads, get up, come downstairs for breakfast." I remember the smell of coffee. We came down in our pajamas. "Gotta get moving. It's a school day. Brush your teeth, wash your faces and comb your hair." She laid out our clothes on the couch. Then Ginny came out of the bedroom, and the baby started crying. Ferne put a bottle on the stove to warm, and then she went into the bedroom and scooped Patti out of her crib. She sat down on the couch to feed her while directing us to eat our cereal and put our school bags together. Meanwhile Ginny started whining and pulling the tray on her highchair up and down. "Soon you will be sitting at the table, dear," she said as she laid the baby down, lifted Ginny into her chair and gave her a bowl of Cheerios.

It was no longer necessary to walk blocks and blocks to school because the city had finished construction on the school across the street. Mom took out the buggy and put Ginny in one side and the baby in the back. Away we went around the corner to the school. As she was about to return home, Bobby's teacher ran out the door.

"Mrs. Henning, I need to speak to you. I think Bobby needs glasses. Have his doctor give him an eye test. I don't think he can see what we are doing in class."

"Thanks, Mrs. Baxter. Thank you for letting us know."

As Ferne walked home with two babies, she was distraught. Where would they get the money for glasses? As much as he hated to ask, Bob would have to call his mother and ask her to pay for the glasses. That's what they would do.

At home, she washed the dishes and put a load of clothes into the washer. Then she stood in front of the bathroom mirror and combed her hair. Her face was definitely much thinner than it used to be, and she could almost see her ribs. There was too much work to be done and too little of life. She wasn't going to spend her time worrying.

She packed up a bag with bottles and diapers, took the baby and Ginny out to the car, and off they went to have coffee with Jeane, who had just finished the same routine.

After putting the twins in the playpen and Ginny in the sandbox, the two sisters sat in the kitchen watching them through the window.

"I'm worried about what's happening with my health, Jeanie."

"You look better than you did a few months ago."

"Yes, I'm not carrying a baby anymore, but the doctor gave me something to read about rheumatic heart disease. It'll probably get worse. I may die before the children grow up." She started crying.

Jeane moved close to her and hugged her and the baby. "Fernie, you've done fine so far, and you won't have any more babies. The doctors fixed that for you."

"You're right. I know you're right. That's what Ma says, too. I've been thinking about what I can do with the children now to help them, just in case I'm not here for them." She wiped her eyes.

"Maybe they will discover something to help you. Stay positive, Fernie, please."

"Bob brought a dog home, Jeane. He thought the children needed a pet, especially now. I've got to get them involved with the church, and I'm going to sign Bobby up for Cub Scouts and Barbara for Brownies. I'm not going to talk to Bob about my worries anymore. It makes him so unhappy and afraid."

"Fernie, you are *not dying*, and you don't know really what's happening."

In 1955, Bob was wearing cockeyed glasses. He had welded them together, just like he had done with Bobby's when he broke his, using a piece of metal from an old hanger. He couldn't afford to buy new frames. In the photo, Bobby is holding the stuffed animal he always carried around with him, his safety bear. I'm sitting on Ferne's lap touching Ginny's leg, her hand touching mine. Bob's holding Patti on his lap with his other arm looped around Ginny and Bobby. Worried about the future, Ferne continually emphasized our responsibilities to each other as loving caretakers of each other. It was the way her mother had raised her and her siblings.

Ginny and Jeane's daughters Denise, Diane and Linda

On summer weekends we would often go to the beaches on Lake St. Clair. Bob and Ferne didn't let her illness stop us from enjoying our life together. "Doctor Singer is researching, Fernie. He will find something. Don't worry."

"You look beautiful," he said as he snapped the photo and caught Ferne laughing, Barbie watching Patti (*Patti don't put that sand in your mouth, silly*), Bobby resting with a little sailboat while biting his lip, and Ginny burying her feet in the sand.

We were all legs, arms and sun.

Summer 1955. At Jefferson Beach. Bobby, Ferne, Barbara, Patti and Ginny in front.

Posing with missionaries at church picnic

Ginny captured and brought over to the missionaries.

Jeane at a family reunion at Ward's place in Clinton Township
Bob and Ferne at the table

"Hello, Jeanie. What are you doing? I just came back from the supermarket. Patti and Ginny are taking their nap. While I was in the store earlier, I saw a woman with children, pushing her cart and screaming at her children. Why does it have to be so difficult? Yes, you're right—What else can we do but keep it together? After I put the girls down, I laid down on the couch for fifteen minutes and when I closed my eyes, it struck me. Your spirit has this brief moment to be with the others who show up here at the same time. It's how you relate that matters. I know I sound like Ma. Anyhow I'm feeling better. Love you, Jeanie. Bye-bye."

My father's mother gave Ferne her old L.C. Smith manual typewriter and for years it sat on a typewriter table in the corner of the back bedroom. Ferne used to tell us how she had studied typing and shorthand, always emphasizing that we must finish school. One day she moved the typewriter upstairs into my bedroom. When my children were young, I kept it on the kitchen counter and wrote poems on it. When I first started teaching at Long Island University, I didn't have a typewriter, so I brought it to school with me. One morning I opened the door to my cubicle and the typewriter was gone.

On the Line:

Typewriter 'Doodlers'

By BOB CONSIDINE

LOVERS of good prose, poetry fans, psychologists, psychiatrists, collectors of Rabelaisian phrasing and bad spelling, and ordinary busy-bodies have discovered a new outdoor library at 560 Fifth avenue, New York.

This is the address of the Olivetti people, the Italian Business Machine and Typewriter Co. that has made a bold and colorful invasion of the American market.

Mounted on a graceful green marble column, outside the show-windows, is one of those light little Olivetti portables. It is exposed at waist-height to tens of thousands of daily passers-by.

An astounding number of people pause to tap out the thoughts, loves and rages possessing them at the moment.

Nov 4, 1955

It was this typewriter that Frank O'Hara mentions in his Lunch Poems. When I moved to New York City, I became an admirer of O'Hara's poems and have been deeply influenced by his work. The description on the back of the book:

Often this poet, strolling through the noisy splintered glare of a Manhattan noon, has paused at a sample Olivetti to type up thirty or forty lines of ruminations, or pondering more deeply has withdrawn into a darkened warehouse or firehouse to limn his computed misunderstandings of the eternal questions of life, co-existence and depth, while never forgetting to eat lunch his favourite meal ... (O'Hara)

"Mama, I like sitting in the rocking chair at Gramma's and watching the cars go by at night. I like the way the streetlights make long lines on the walls and the wood floor. I like the way the trolley and the buses flash their lights on the wall."

"I'm glad you like it there, Barbie, because you're going to Gramma's this Saturday with Linda. When I was young, I sat in the rocking chair watching the lights through the blinds and listening to the cars pass by. Be sure when you are with Gramma, honey, that you and Linda help her out. Don't do anything to make her worry."

"We love Gramma."

"Don't ever go off the front porch without Gramma again. Last week when you two were pretending you were hitchhiking, you scared the dickens out of her."

Gramma's birthday Sept 21,1956

On Hattie's 72nd birthday her children held a party in Marv and Jeane's basement. As Ferne danced with her mother, her polka dot chiffon skirt swished around her legs, and she remembered jitterbugging as a young woman at the Vanity with Abe. Now she was slowly circling in the arms of her mother. As they danced, Gramma turned to face the photographer. Bob was at the food table talking to Marv. Jeane must have taken the photo. My eyes move from Marv's white collar toward the dancing couple, the polka dots and the checkered tiles, 1950s style. After Ferne died, I wore that same dress to my cousin's wedding even though it didn't fit me. I was only twelve.

Nov 1956

Besides earning money by taking on sewing projects for the neighbor, Ferne made hilarious Halloween costumes for everyone in the family. One year I wanted to be the lion in the Wizard of Oz, and miraculously on Halloween morning I found on my chair in the kitchen a funny, slinky, zipped up brown flannel suit with an opening for my face and a head of yarny lion hair, along with a long tail that I swung over my shoulder when going out to beg for candy. This costume would be passed down for years, from one child to the next.

On the night before Halloween, Devil's Night in Detroit, Bob popped out of nowhere under a white sheet, scaring us and the neighborhood children too. He kept a little jewelry box in his dresser drawer with a hole in the bottom through which he would insert his finger. There was blood around the edge. He'd tell a story about how this man had his finger cut off and how he gave the finger to Bob. "Look at it," he commanded. We cautiously gathered around the box, peering at the finger. Suddenly it jumped up, and we all started screaming and running around the living room.

———— ❦ ————

On the weekends, while Bob was studying or working on the house, Ferne would take us to the library. She was determined that we love reading and do well in school. Bobby and I were already avid readers even though only seven and eight years old. We'd come home with stacks of books. The library closed at four on the weekend, so we were often in a rush to get there. Nevertheless, someone was always falling down the stairs or tripping over something on the sidewalk or getting hit with something. A regular part of her day, like other mothers, was spent consoling the children and inspiring them to get up and go on. "So you fell down the stairs when you were excited about going to the library. Get up, brush off and let's go," she said.

———— ❦ ————

As a child, when it was frigid cold, I'd put on three pairs of wool socks inside my one-size-too-big ice skates and walk a block with the skates tipping side to side. I remember one dark frigid day looking back at the house, the light on in the living room, and Ferne passing across the window. I stood still resting for a minute and then I continued. At the city pond, I forced my ankles straight, skated until my fingers were cold and tingly. Then I wobbled down the street, leaving my brother and his friends zipping around on their hockey skates. When I opened the door, our new dog—an old red and white girl named Peggy—got up off her warm spot on the floor and came over to greet me. Ferne was sitting at the kitchen table smoking Pal Mall cigarettes. "Hello, Peggy," I said. "Hi Mama." Then upstairs I went, into bed to read.

Hearst National Experts Forecast
Up and Coming -- for 1957

By Hearst National Experts.(William Randolph Hearst, Jr. et al.)

It may mark the beginning of the decline and fall of the Soviet empire. . . This coming new year is likely to show whether Russia can keep the lid from blowing off the explosive kettle of pent-up human emotions and hatred of communism in the captive states. Unlikely that West Germany could be held in check if Russian soldiers and Communist police slaughtered men women and children in eastern Germany as they did in Hungary. . . NATO powers will not go to help eastern Europe become free, they do not want to see such freedom sought at the risk of plunging the world into a nuclear conflict that might destroy civilization. . . Molotov, now minister for state control and first deputy premier, has publicly declared that atomic war would not destroy the world, but only the capitalist part of it.. . . Khrushchev . . . told the Hearst Task Force . . . that it would be madness to resort to war to settle the struggle between communism and capitalism. He expressed confidence communism would gain the upper hand eventually by measures short of war. Dec 30, 1956

Nov 4, 1956

In 1949, there were only 13 cardiologists in the country. As the 1950s progressed, the electrocardiogram became more available and there were more specialists. At the end of December, Ferne was coughing and weak, so Bob called Dr. Singer. He met them at his office and examined her throat. It was red, no white spots. He gave her a shot of penicillin just to be sure and a packet of pills. Then he told Bob that he should take her to see the new cardiologist who had an office in St. Joseph's hospital.

A week later, after listening to her heart and running an electrocardiogram, Dr. Goldman met with them. "From your past records, it appears your heart damage is a little worse.   You now have what we call an auricular flutter."

"What does that mean?"

"Your heartbeat is very fast and a little erratic, Mrs. Henning. There's definitely some leakage. The blood is supposed to flow one way. But your system is backing up. That's why you are out of breath and not thriving."

"Is there anything you can do?" Bob asked.

"Researchers and surgeons are working on a way to repair mitral valves, but the surgery has not yet been perfected. I hope for your sake, Mrs. Henning, they will be able to operate soon. What you can do for yourself is to try not to stress your body or your heart will overwork and you could have a heart attack or even a stroke. Treat your body as delicate. Be kind to yourself. Get help with the housework. I'm going to reach out to the surgeons who are working on this, and I promise that I'll contact you as soon as they are ready."

On the way home, Ferne laid her head against the window and pulled her scarf down over her face.

"Ferne, they're working on an operation. That's good news, isn't it? I wonder why Singer didn't send us to these people sooner."

"Bob, if I die, you must promise me one thing."

"You aren't going to die, Fernie. Don't say that."

"You must remarry so the children have a mother. Promise me."

"I don't want anyone else. I want you."

"Promise me, Bob."

"I promise. Next month, when I start my new job as a draftsman 3, we'll have more money to hire some help for you. I promise that I'm going to come home immediately from work and help cook dinner. We'll have Barbara and Bobby bring Ginny home from school, and they'll help you until I get home. We'll train them."

Cancel Bus Run In Montgomery

The Montgomery city commission today cancelled all night bus runs until after the New Year holiday, following the wounding of a colored mother-to-be. Rosa Jordan, 22, was wounded in both legs as she sat in the rear of a Montgomery bus last night . . . Elsewhere in the South colored followed traditional seating patterns, although legally they were free to ride in an integrated manner in Tallahassee and the bus company in Mobile had announced it would not enforce-segregated seating.. . . Meanwhile the Rev. Shuttlesworth, 34, whose home was damaged by a dynamite blast Christmas night, said he planned to preach as usual tomorrow in the Northside Negro Bethel Baptist Church. The church building also was damaged by some dynamite explosion.. . . In Baton Rouge La , colored leaders have announced they would join Birmingham and Tallahassee colored groups in going "all the way" to break the racial barrier on the city's buses.. . . In carrying out the Supreme Court's decision banning segregation in public schools, Taylor ordered the Clinton High School (Texas) to admit colored pupils. . . Racial disorders followed. Taylor then issued an injunction against anyone interfering with the "integration" of the school "either by words or acts." Dec 30, 1956

Gals Tell Why They Like Ike

attractive personality"
"he has good character"
"he is a good Christian"
"he is a family man"
"his big smile"
"his hominess"
"his sincerity"
"his complete and innate honesty
"his sincere faith in everything he
does"
"After one of his recent TV appear-
ances she talked to several factory
wives and farm women, discovered
they had the feeling Ike was talking
directly to them, personally interested in their particular problems."
Nov 4, 1956

Press Hunt For Missing 'M' Co-ed

Gone Week; Talked to Boy Friend Night of Disappearance

Police throughout Michigan Saturday in-tensified their search for Barbara Agler, 20, of Susquehanna, Pa., a blond co-ed who myste-riously disappeared from the University of Michi-gan campus more than a week ago.

She was last seen Jan. 18 and her absence reported by her landlady the following Monday, but university author-ities failed to notify her parents or police until Friday.

Jan 27, 1957

Our dog, Peggy would leap over the fence or after Bob made the fence higher, she would dig a hole. She was crazy when she was in heat. We loved her, but when Ferne became weak, the dog was too much work, so Bob gave her to a neighbor of Jeane's. All night I cried for her. My bed was next to the stairwell. While lying there, I heard them downstairs talking. "The children are going through a lot, Bob. Call Chester and ask him if we can have her back." And a few days later Peggy was returned. I remember sitting next to her on the floor in the kitchen. The pipes under the floor kept it warm, and her body was warm, too, as she stretched her head and laid it over my legs.

Even when she was weak, Ferne organized projects for us—collecting cans and bottles and scraps of material and leather from various places. We would work in the kitchen with glue and paste making pencil holders and books with waxed leaves. Then we would hold a bazaar in our backyard and sell lemonade and crafts. She made clothes for two of my dolls, a bride and a groom. The bride's dress was satin with lace trim, something Ferne never had, and neither did I. The doll had blonde hair and was about eight inches tall. The groom wore a black top hat and a tuxedo. Once Ferne organized a quilting party and invited girls from the neighborhood to sew little circles of fabric into the cover for a quilt. She made a quilt for me with butterflies. It fell apart with time, but I still have a few butterflies tucked away in a box in my closet.

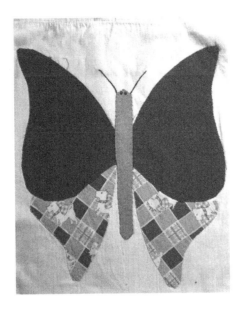

When Ferne's father and grandfather died, she was an adult. Then, at 35 years old, she was facing the possibility of her own death. She lay on the couch watching Patti and Ginny playing with blocks and dolls. Bobby and I were in our rooms reading. She hadn't talked to us yet about her condition. Dad was in the garage when the phone rang. It was Jeane. She had bad news. In the morning there had been a deadly fire in the house of their niece, my godmother, Barbara Criss. Her baby had died in the fire. Barbara's husband tried to save him, but to no avail.

"I don't want to say this, but I must, Jeane. Why would they put a baby in a crib in an attic? He had no way of escaping. I know I know, I won't say a word, except to you. I know, their hearts are broken. Where are they going to live now, the house ruined and full of grief? Poor Katie. Poor Barbara."

On Saturday, Mom dressed Bobby and me in our Easter clothes. Then we went to the funeral home. We stood in front of the coffin holding hands with Mom and Gramma Hattie. "Jesus has taken the baby's soul, children. He is living with Jesus now," Gramma said.

I whispered to Bobby, "It's not a baby, not really, it's a doll."

Father's Heroism Can't Save Baby

The heroic rescue efforts of a Warren father brought less than five hours of life to his infant son Thursday.

Ike Invites Teen Tips

WASHINGTON—(AP)—President Eisenhower told a group of teen-age "legislators" Thursday the Government might get some useful tips from them on how the country should be run.

Mr. Eisenhower spoke in the White House rose garden to the 96 delegates to the American Legion-sponsored Boys Nation, which organizes a legislative body along congressional lines during its annual week-long Washington stay.

"I sometimes think," the President said, "I would like to see the laws and resolutions you pass and some of your debates and to see whether it wouldn't help some of us oldsters a little bit."

Paul Criss, 13 months, was dragged from a burning attic bedroom by his father, Robert, 28, on the father's third attempt to break through a wall of smoke and flame.

But the baby died at 1 p.m. in Van Dyke Memorial Hospital. He had suffered second and third degree burns on half of his body.

* * *

THE FATHER also was hospitalized for treatment of burns and smoke inhalation.

"Bob tried twice to get to the crib and couldn't make it," his wife, Mrs. Barbara Criss, 26, said.

"I tried once and was driven back. The smoke was like night and the heat was terrible.

"We could hear the baby crying. It was awful. Then I soaked a blanket and threw it over Bob's head and he got through."

A neighbor, Mrs. Ida Burford, and a motorist, Philip Paul, 20, of 7520 Timken, Warren, also tried unsuccessfully to reach the blazing crib at the far end of the unfinished attic bedroom.

Paul was treated for burns of the hands and arms.

* * *

FIREMEN SAID the fire started when a hot plate, which had been stored in the attic, was plugged into a wall socket by the Criss' other children, Ann, 3 and Richard 2. The hot plate ignited some clothing.

"All the children sleep up there," Mrs. Criss said. "Ann and Dick woke us this morning crying. We found them standing at the foot of the stairs, staring up to the attic."

The fire ruined the attic of the small frame home. Criss works at the Cadillac Motor Division of General Motors.

July 26, 1957 DFP

1957

Arf!---Arf, Arf, Arf, Arf!

POCATELLO, Idaho, Nov. 4 (AP)— An Idaho radio broadcasting executive reported a signal tape-recorded from Sputnik II today "got the barking of a dog."

Tom Thompson, station manager of KBLI in nearby Blackfoot, Idaho, said:

"We have the tape on it.

"It barks once, and then there's silence, and then it barks four times in a row.

"It's a hollow-sounding bark.

"It's not a little yap-yap bark; it's a definite, heavy-type bark — like a full-grown dog barks."

Thompson, president of the Pocatello amateur radio club and a ham operator, said the tape recorder had been wired to a receiver set on Sputnik's frequency.

Nov 4, 1957

Christmas 1957

In our old red chair, Ferne in a flowery dress and high heels. Very, very Ferne. Upside down, her feet in the curtains she had made with big red flowers and darker leaves. Everything in the photo has a red or pink tint, including her hair. Whenever the name *Ferne* is mentioned, I visualize someone with red hair. When I was eighteen, I dyed my hair red.

In the first week of the new year, 1958, Ferne was running a high fever. Bob called the doctor, who sent an ambulance to take her to the hospital. When he came home, he and Hattie made a list of places where the children could stay during the week while he worked. Each of us would stay with one relative for one week, back home on the weekend and then, if necessary, with another relative the next week.

Dr. Goldman explained that Ferne had survived the infection and pneumonia, but her electrocardiogram was worse than the year before. In addition to an auricular flutter, there was more damage to the valve and that's why she was feeling so weak. "They are having success with the trials of the operation, and I think they will be ready sometime later this year, Mrs. Henning."

After ten days in the hospital, the doctor put her in a nursing home for another week so she could rest. One Sunday Bob took the children to visit her. Ferne walked out of the room wearing her bathrobe. We sat down in a visiting room. "Come here, Patti," she said. "Come and sit on my lap." For some reason three-year-old Patti was afraid. It was as if she had forgotten who her mother was. Instead, she clung to me, and Ferne started to cry.

When she came home, Bob bought a television, a dark brown cabinet with a Motorola TV inside. We were all excited. Before we could watch it, we had to do our homework. Then we sat on the floor cross-legged watching the screen-- *Leave it to Beaver*, *Father Knows Best*, *Ozzie and Harriet*.

One day, while everyone was vying for their favorite spot in the living room, Ferne called me into the back room to put pin curls in my hair. While she was combing she said, "Barbara, you know Mommy hasn't been feeling well."

"Yes, but you're better now."

"I'm a little better, honey, but still kind of weak, and the doctor isn't sure that I'll get much stronger."

"Oww. You pulled my hair."

"Sorry. There's a possibility, Barbie, that you will have to take my place soon. I want you to be ready. Starting now, honey, you have to help out in the house. Tomorrow I'm going to teach you a little bit about cooking. Every day I'll teach you something new." She patted my head as she put in the last pin curl.

"Mama, I don't want you to die." I could hear the television in the background and the others laughing.

"None of us wants to die, sweetie, but sometimes Jesus calls us." When she was in the hospital once, she told me that she had woken up in the middle of the night and she saw Jesus standing in the doorway. She reached for him and fell out of bed."

"Did a nurse come to help you? I don't want you to die, Mama. I don't want you to leave me. Tell Jesus to go away."

"I'm not dying now, sweetie. Everything is okay. Don't worry. Let's go into the living room and watch TV."

Often when we'd come home from school, the TV would be on and the drapes would be closed. Ferne would be resting on the couch or sitting at the kitchen table smoking. Then she'd get up, fold clothes, do dishes and lie down again. A shadow had anchored itself to the house. One moment, however, stays vividly in my mind. The curtains in her bedroom were pulled wide open. The white bedspread was neatly tucked in. I remember lying on her bed watching her fold towels and sheets. The sunlight fell over my body and hers. Light in the house.

Dad hired a woman to come in once a week to clean. I had never met an African American person before. I remember Mom was in the bedroom resting, and I was sitting at the kitchen table while Clarice was cleaning the cupboards.

"What grade are you in?" she asked.

"5th grade."

"You're getting to be a big girl. Your mother isn't well. Do you help her?"

"I do the laundry."

"That's good. You must help your mother."

I watched her wipe down the counters and mop the floor, then vacuum. I was curious about her life, but I didn't ask any questions. East Detroit was an all-white suburb and I had heard children saying derogatory statements about blacks, probably mimicking their parents. I came home once from the park and told my mother that a boy had called someone "a black n——." Ferne told me that we were all children of Jesus, black and white, and if someone talked like that, I should say, "*You* have a black heart."

The coffee pot was simmering and there were stacks of towels and clothes on the chairs and on the end of the table. The washer and the new dryer that Bob had bought were swishing and humming. Ferne sat at the kitchen table putting on red nail polish. The doorbell rang. It was her mother. Hattie had taken a cab over to help Ferne clean and prepare dinner. When she walked into the kitchen, she looked around. "Did Bob paint the kitchen?"

"No, I did it."

"You did it? You're not supposed to do any hard work, Fernie."

"I did a little, then I took a break, then a little more. It won't hurt anything. Bob was going to do it, and he was going to do it, and I was sick of looking at it."

"Ferne, you're not taking the doctor's warning seriously. What are these boxes doing here?"

"I am packing away some toys that the children don't use. They need to go out to the garage."

"You wait for Bob to do this. You are not supposed to exert yourself. I'm serious, Ferne."

"Ma, I am feeling better. Some days I feel normal, and then another day I feel weak."

"Well, we want you to live, Ferne. Doing what feels normal may be causing the next bad day."

—∞∞—

When we had a day off school, if she was feeling stronger, Ferne would load all four of us into her old Ford. On the way to Aunt Jeane's, the car would inevitably stall at a light and she would turn over the engine, praying. "Come on, Bessie." And so we went on, day by day, perhaps thinking that having a sick mother was a normal thing. That was pretty much all Patti and Ginny knew. Bobby and I remembered, however, when she was well, but those days were quickly slipping back into the past.

—∞∞—

After church, Ferne spoke with Pastor Johnson about finding someone to live in and help her. He put a notice in the church newsletter that one of his parishioners needed someone and there was a bedroom with meals in exchange. Shortly thereafter, Irma Manders wrote Ferne. She was living in England with one child and was interested in spending nine months in the United States. She had letters of recommendation, and one of the church women knew her well. Bob made her an offer, and she and her son David arrived in the summer of 1958. Ferne was relieved. Irma was a vigorous, healthy, optimistic and loving young woman who immediately took over the household chores.

Ferne and Irma on Halloween 1958

A "BRIGHT DIFFERENCE" CAMPAIGN was pressed in 1958 when the paper
adopted a new type of print and changed its garish red headlines to soft green
boxes. But to no avail. The paper could never live down its reputation as a
Hearst paper filled with yellow journalism and scandal. In addition the Times
circulation was hit hard by the suburban drift. The bulk of the Times distribution and circulation was in the central city, and the movement to the suburbs
meant the loss of numerous subscribers. Between 1950 and 1960, the *Times* lost
$10 million. (Ferman. *Death of a Newspaper* p. 9)

East Detroit Voters Back Water Issue

By a vote of better than 4-to-1, East Detroit voters today had backed the proposal for the city to issue general obligation bonds to build a water storage tank.

Termed an "advisory vote," the overwhelming majority served to direct the city council to pursue plans to borrow $550,000 for the erection of a tank and laying of additional water transmission mains.

Complete vote on the issue: Yes: 5,855; no 1,481.

City Manager Charles Beaubien attributed the passage of the proposition to explanatory letters mailed to householders by the city and wide publicity in newspapers.

Move for the water tank began last spring when the City of Detroit threatened to charge East Detroit $50,000 a year for water storage unless the city obtained its own storage facilities.

City officials have tentatively selected a site bounded by Hauss, Brittany and Schroeder for the tank.

• • •

Nov 4, 1958

Polio Toll In County Up to 823

The number of polio victims in Wayne County resulting from this year's epidemic climbed to 823 today following the report of four new cases.

Each of the new cases was recorded in communities outside Detroit.

IN THE CITY, there have been 623 cases, including 21 deaths, compared to 177 cases and two deaths at this time last year.

Vaccine will be available at eight city and six suburban locations tomorrow, as the county inoculation program continues in its sixth week.

Shots cost $1 or are free to persons who cannot pay.

Nov 6, 1958 SMD

Nov 4, 1958

Nov 4, 1958

In June 1959, after Irma and David returned to England and Bob's mother moved to Long Island to marry a widower, Ferne told Bob that she wanted to go on a vacation with the children. It didn't matter that she was weak and frail. Jeane was worried. "Is it wise for you to go on a long road trip, Fernie?"

"I want to be able to protect the children, but I can't," she said. "Maybe we can give them a good memory."

In August, the family headed north through Michigan to a rented cottage near Gaylord. They planned to stay for a few days, but ended up staying longer because Ferne had trouble breathing and her body hurt. Marv drove Hattie up to the cottage to help take care of her for a few days until she was strong enough to continue. When she was better, we traveled over the locks to Canada, then around to Niagara Falls, finally ending at Bob's mother's house in Copiague, Long Island where she was living with her new husband, Fred. It was a long and challenging trip. I remember we ran around like wild children. We didn't realize that on this trip we were saying goodbye to our mother.

Ginny and Ferne, August 1959

Ferne and children

Front: Patti, Ginny, Bobby; Back: Bob, Ferne, Virginia, Marie, Barbara
Copiague, LI, August 1959

In the kitchen, we posed around Marie, Fred's disabled daughter whom he had cared for ever since she was a child. Ferne looks skeletal. The look on her face says *I'm not feeling well.* Just before we left to head home, Bob and Ferne stood on the back of the station wagon for another photo. Her arm is draped around him, her other arm on his chest. Bob is holding the whole thing together, her life and the family.

At a rest stop along the turnpike

I remember watching the television show "The Millionaire" and always hoping someone would ring our doorbell and give us a million dollars.

THE "KITCHEN DEBATE" that occurred between Soviet Premier Nikita Khrushchev and US Vice-President Richard Nixon, in front of a model kitchen on display at a trade exhibition in Moscow, on 24 July 1959... . . Nixon . . . assert[ED] that the United States' global leadership was not based on its vast arsenal so much as on the fullness of daily life for the average family. He granted, for example, that the Soviet Union had better rocket engines but Americans had color television. Khrushchev, guardedly admiring the American kitchen appliances, promised in any case to surpass American consumer goods within a few years, and he indicted American industry more broadly for depleting itself on gimmicks and gizmos. The Soviet Union, he claimed, instead focused on making women more productive in their domestic work. On the defensive, Nixon countered, "What we want to do is make easier the life of our housewives." The US was an aggregate of families, he suggested, and so an easier life legitimated a national economy based on consumer goods—such as those the two leaders stood before—and validated the spread of consumer capitalism worldwide. (Sandy Isenstadt)

One morning when Bob went to pick up the children from Sunday school, there were piles of clothes to be washed and dishes in the sink. Every room in the house needed attention. Ferne lay in bed despairing. She didn't feel strong enough to do anything. A bottle of tranquilizers. *Why not get it over with?* she thought. She wanted so much to have a family and a long life, or at least long enough to raise her children, but God had given her only a drop of water instead of a full glass and so much work to do. She went into the bathroom, emptied the pills into her hand and took them all. Then she sat on the toilet and cried. Slowly she slipped onto the floor, unconscious.

The door opened and the kids came running into the house. Barbara opened the bathroom door and screamed, "Daddy, daddy, mommy fainted."

Bob lifted her up and carried her into the kitchen. She was groggy. "Drink this!" he commanded pouring cold black coffee into her mouth. "Come on, Fernie. Think about the children. Think about me. Please, honey, please."

While holding her up, he called the doctor who told him that they probably weren't strong enough to kill her. "Keep her on her feet as much as you can."

In early September, Patti was in the backyard playing with her friend Steven. Another little friend wanted a piece of their bubble gum, but Patti said no. He started crying and ran home. As he crossed the street, he was hit by a car. Steven and Patti ran into the house. Ferne was standing in the utility room, ironing. Patti was crying and couldn't speak. When Steven told her what had happened, she pushed the ironing board over, flew out the door and picked the child up off the road. His legs were smashed. A few hours later an ambulance came to the house to take Ferne to the hospital, too. She was very fragile and with all the stress she became sick again. At night Patti crawled into Bob's lap, crying. She thought it was her fault.

While Ferne was recuperating in the nursing wing of the hospital, the doctor read the report from her new electrocardiogram. "In addition to a coarse auricular fibrillation, there is now definite evidence of right ventricular hypertropy and suggestive left ventricular damage. That's the bad news, Mrs. Henning, but I have some good news, too."

"Good news?"

"Yes, I talked to the surgeon's team and they're ready to operate. They'd like to schedule the operation for mid November. He'll be coming in from the Mayo Clinic in Minnesota. They'll shave the scar tissue so the gland can close. We can't guarantee that it will work and, if it doesn't, I have to be honest: you might die on the operating table."

They had already given up hope, but now there was a chance that her life could be saved. She thought it over and decided that she wanted to be with the children for Christmas. They scheduled the operation for January 4, 1960.

Ferne parked the car in the Food Fair parking lot, and she sat for a few minutes thinking about the raw deal life had given her. Then she thought about what she was grateful for. She was grateful for her parents and especially for her mother and lifelong supporter. She had had a happy childhood. She was grateful for her sisters and brothers, especially for Jeane and Marv. She had wanted to be a mother, and she loved her children, and she was grateful for Bob. She knew that he loved her and, if she did die, he would look after the children. As she walked toward the supermarket, she looked up at the cloudy sky. How she loved the clouds and the trees too, the living beings she had shared her life with.

She'll Sell Orchids To Help Sick Vets

An orchid queen—as lovely as the exotic bloom she represents—will head a flower sales campaign Thursday through Saturday for the Roseville detachment of the Marine Corps League.

Proceeds of the sale—to be held primarily in the Eastgate Shopping Center—will be used to aid hospitalized veterans.

Connie Flaga, 18, of 30407 Clinkert, Roseville, was elected on the basis of beauty, poise and personality to reign as Orchid Queen.

She will be crowned Saturday night at the fourth annual Marine Corps Birthday Ball in Hof-Brau Hall, 16644 Fourteen Mile, Fraser.

Selected as her court were Shirley Thomas, 17, of 23008 Hoffman, St. Clair Shores, and Wallyne Ragel, 17, of 17120 Mayfield, Roseville.

More than 6,000 live baby orchids will be flown from Hawaii and sold by the girls on a donation basis. Eastgate businessmen acted as contest judges and donated several prizes for the winner.

Nov 4, 1959

On the 1st of November, Ferne became ill again. Bob was sleeping in the bedroom and Ferne was lying on the couch, running a high fever and moaning. She called out, "Bob, Bob. Oh, please help me, Bob." Over and over again. I was sleeping upstairs when I heard her call, "Barbara, Barbara, Barbara, I can't breathe."

I went downstairs, laid a cold washcloth on her forehead and combed her hair away from her face. I yelled, but still she wouldn't wake up. I watched her body alternately turn and rest on the couch. I telephoned Aunt Jeane. I was crying, I said, "Please come fast."

Within half an hour, they arrived. When they opened the door, I was sitting on the couch holding my mother's head.

Marv brought a wooden structure to help prop her up so she could breathe with more ease. She was happy to see him. "Thank you, Marv," she said. "What would I do without you? I love you."

Then she turned toward Jeane and said, "And you, I don't like you at all—you are the cause of all my problems." Then she fell asleep.

Jeane started to cry.

"She doesn't know what she's saying, Aunt Jeane. She loves you," I said.

Marv was finally able to wake my father. "We've called an ambulance for Fernie, Bob."

Ferne was delirious from the fever and hospitalized again with pneumonia. Everyone in her family was angry with Bob. After everything he had done, this single memory of one bad night left an everlasting impression on me. The truth is he always had trouble waking up and this wasn't the first time. When I was a teenager and a young adult, I treated him as if he were guilty of not having taken care of her. We never spoke of it, but I'm sure that when he looked at me, he knew I knew and he knew what I thought. It's unfortunate that he didn't have the emotional strength to discuss what was going on. He must have been very depressed. Here she was ill again. The hope of an operation was slipping further and further away. How many times had he rushed her to the hospital? How difficult it must have been to give up a dream of family life together with someone you love and watch her becoming more and more frail. What was he going to do with four children?

4 November 1959
Dearest Barb,

I am feeling as well as can be expected. Thank you all for the candy. I shared it with the lady next to me.

Dad hasn't been a mother long enough so he doesn't know that we girls learn do to things alone. Have him read over your badge work so he can see that girls of your age must learn about housekeeping early in life.

Try and do for Gramma like you did for me. Make coffee for her, and tea. Make her sit down and you wait on her. Tell her it is part of your girl scout training, then maybe she will let you.

Do your homework and if you need help, ask Dad. If he is grumpy, don't feel bad, just ask Gramma if she can help you with your problem. Always remember that Bob [Dad] is quite capable in many things that we do not give him credit for.

You may have to take mom's place sooner than you think so try and be patient and take it all in your stride.

Rev. Johnson was just here, and he explained all about confirmation so we will have a time going thru it together.

Call Mrs. Craig (Lois) and tell her who you are and ask her if she found anything about the "Bible Badge." Ask Dad what the Bible Award is for Bobby.

This is something between you and me. "Try to listen more and say less. I had the same trouble when I was young. Ask Gramma.

Well dear, I will close so hope you are doing your best to keep things going smoothly at home.

Try real hard to be mama's grown up daughter. Okay?
                              Mama

XOXOXOXOXOXOXO (In case you forgot means a hug and a kiss—plenty of these you will get in the next few years.)

[Letter from Ferne to me while she was in the hospital.]

4 November 1959

Dearest Barb,

I am feeling as well as
can be expected. Thank you all
for the candy I shared it
with the lady next to me.

Dad hasn't been a mother
long enough so he doesn't
know that we girls learn
to do things alone. Have
him read over your badge
work so he can see that girls
of your age must learn about
housekeeping early in life.

Try and do ~~you~~ for
Gramma like you did
for me. make coffee for

Ferne may have hoped that Sunday school and Girl Scouts would inspire me to be responsible and religious. Maybe she thought that religion would save me when I didn't have a mother and had to go on alone. Maybe she thought it would help me "take her place." She had said to me over and over, "Be sure Barbara that you graduate from high school." Long before I was eighteen years old, I turned away from religion. But I kept the promise about school—graduating over and over again until I had a teaching position in a university.

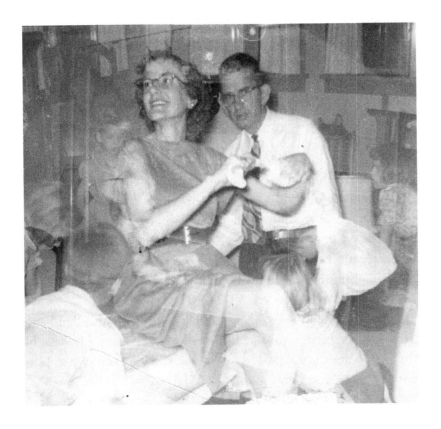

Miraculously, with the help of oxygen, antibiotics and rest in a nursing wing, she recovered and came home for Thanksgiving dinner. Everyone in her family was at Jeane's house. In the photo there are children layered over one another. I think I see myself behind her right shoulder, Ginny in the corner, Marvel Lynn in another corner. It's almost as if there are three photos layered over each other. Dad is holding her or standing behind her. She's wearing a fancy dress and holding something. He looks concerned. I remember her drinking alcohol sometimes, out of desperation, at home alone with us, but here she is happy, surrounded by her husband, children, nieces and nephews. And there was hope. The operation would take place on January 4th.

On Christmas Eve, she was back in the hospital and the doctor agreed to let us visit her. We went up the back stairs and down the hallway into her room. She was in the first bed in an oxygen tent. She asked for orange juice and reached her arm out of the oxygen tank. Ginny handed it to her. I couldn't look at her without crying. On the way home, Dad pulled over and picked up a free Christmas tree from a vendor who had abandoned his trees. We went home and decorated it.

On January 4th, Dad came home in the late morning. It was a Monday. I had a sore throat and was getting ready to go to the doctor's. He called me from downstairs. When I walked into the living room, Pastor Johnson was there. Bobby had been outside. He came through the front door and stopped in his tracks, looking at everyone. "Sit on the couch," Dad said. "The pastor wants to talk to you."

"What's wrong?" I asked.

"It's about your mother, children . . ."

Bobby leaped off the chair without giving him a chance to go on. He ran into the back room crying.

"I'm sorry to tell you, children, that your mother died today."

Ginny, Patti and I ran into the back room, crying and screaming.

I have no recollection of what happened next. Dad must have calmed us down and brought us back into the living room.

When I talked to Jeane in 1976, she said that someone had called her on the phone and told her Fernie was dead. "I couldn't believe it. She was like my right arm. Fernie was dead. I passed out on the kitchen floor. When I came to, my neighbors were there. They gave me a sedative."

On the phone, Patti, my youngest sister who is now a dean and professor of nursing, explained, "When Mom was frequently diagnosed with pneumonia, it was a sign that her heart chamber wasn't working properly. There was nothing anyone could do about it. Eventually the situation wore her down. An operation was scheduled on the day she died, but they were rarely successful back then. She would have died on the table," Patti said. "When they shaved off the scar tissue, bits and pieces would break off and often cause blood clots. Later they learned how to replace the entire valve."

PEACE IN STEEL

Auto Jobs Assured by Settlement

Top Stocks Advance Up To 2 Points

Easter Fashions Spring Into View

Jan 4, 1960

Atomic Reactor

WE'RE NOT HIGHLY concerned, one way or the other, over proposal to build an atomic reactor to supply current to the Detroit Public Lighting Commission lines.

As the proposal stands, there wouldn't be much cost for the city, beyond that of producing the same power by conventional means. The federal government would pay the rest, and write it off as the price of learning more about nuclear power plant operation.

At the same time, the city may not get the plant—just because it is not offering to shoulder much of the cost.

Detroit being as strapped as it is, financially, we can't quarrel with the administration for declining to assume more of the expense, though the result may be that we don't get the plant.

As we said, we're not very opinionated. Atomic energy certainly is coming, and it will take plants such as this, run at a loss compared to conventional plants, to learn how to get the most out of atomic furnaces.

But we in Detroit aren't in a good position to start shouldering this cost. We are confronted by more immediate needs.

Jan 4, 1960

297

Auto Plants To Speed Up

The auto industry was jubilant today about the settlement of the eight-month-long steel labor dispute. Peace removed threats of a renewed strike and layoffs for more than 300,000 auto industry employees in the Detroit area. Jan 4, 1960

Hope to MC Oscar Awards

HOLLYWOOD, Jan. 4 (AP) —Bob Hope will be master of ceremonies for the 32d annual Academy Awards show April 4. The awards will be telecast in a 90-minute program.

It will be the eighth time since 1939 that Hope has been master of ceremonies for the awards presentation.

Ex-Slave Celebrates Her 111th Birthday

Special to the Times

GRAND RAPIDS, Jan. 4— At 15, the slave girl watched from a distance as Gen. Sherman's Union troops rumbled through Georgia.

With the end of the Civil War and freedom for her family, she moved here, met and married Jordan Miller, bore his 11 children and helped him in his farm chores.

Today, Mrs. Eliza Miller, widowed for the last 20 years, has received congratulations from the President, the governor, city officials and hundreds of friends, on her 111th birthday anniversary.

Mrs. Miller lives here with a granddaughter, Mrs. Roy Johnson.

She remains in reasonably good health and spirits, although afflicted to a degree with arthritis. Yet she is able to take an occasional walk, and to do minor work about the house.

Her only living child is a son, the Rev F.A. Miller of Peoria, Ill, where the mother lived prior to coming here. She was a native of Griffin Ga. near Atlanta, born here in 1849. Jan 4, 1960

Flurries, Colder Is Forecast

HOURLY TEMPERATURES

12 mid.	24	4 a.m.	24	10 a.m.	25
1 a.m.	25	5 a.m.	24	11 a.m.	28
2 a.m.	24	6 a.m.	24	12 noon	31
3 a.m.	24	7 a.m.	24	1 p.m.	31
4 a.m.	24	8 a.m.	25	2 p.m.	32

FORECAST

Detroit: Partly cloudy and cold with a few light snow flurries today, high 24. Gently fair and colder tonight, low 12 in city, about 7 in suburbs. Tomorrow cloudy, occasional light snow and continued cold, high 25. Winds westerly 15-20 mph today becoming southwest to south 10-15 mph tonight and tomorrow.

Jan 4, 1960

Bob kept us together. He would come home from work, cook something like hamburgers and canned vegetables, and then he'd fall asleep in the recliner in the living room. We children would walk past him from the kitchen to the bedroom to the kitchen. I remember sitting across from him, watching him breathing, snoring, his chest filling with air, then the sound of his rhythmic snore. The summer after Ferne died in 1960, he drove us to New York to visit his mother and sister, and to bring his mother back to help him for the rest of the summer. While we were there, we spent a day at Jones Beach. His sister Ginny took this photo.

After school, I used to babysit for my brother and sisters while waiting for my father to come home from work. Gramma Hattie would call me on the phone to make sure I was okay. Standing at the black wall phone in the kitchen, I would be my mother talking to her mother. While my brother and sisters were chasing each other wildly around the house, Gramma and I would talk about the love affairs and deceits in the soap opera *Edge of Night*.

A year or so later, Aunt Jeane introduced my father to a woman who had been divorced and wanted a family. Perhaps Ferne made Jeane promise, too, to find a mother for her children. Bob had little to offer in terms of money, but Eugenia wanted children so she agreed and they were married. A few months later Gramma Hattie died. I used to have a reoccurring dream that I was walking by the house on Alter Road. When I recognize the house, I'd think, "I should check on Gramma to be sure she's okay. I haven't stopped by in so long." I am nervous ringing the doorbell. How did I forget her?

When she opens the door, she is very old and feeble. "Where have you been, Barbara? I haven't seen you in a long time."

In a file that my father kept, I found a receipt from Wm. D. Clyne Funeral Home for $1,259.75; casket $715.00; $100.00 for the vault; sales tax $13.75; cemetery charges: three grave lots at $100.00 each; newspaper charges $28.00; and certified copies $3.00. Dad also saved two checks cashed by the funeral home: one for $1025.25 and the other for $100.00. There was a receipt from Cadillac Memorial Gardens, 384525 Garfield, Mt. Clemens; HO3-4321; lot 675 Summit Hill, space D. All of this was locked up with the snap photo books.

The last issue of Hearst's Detroit Times *was published on November 5, 1960. Hearst bought the paper the year Ferne was born and his son sold it in the same year she died. I never knew about the* Detroit Times *when I was growing up. Yet in 1967 when I worked in downtown Detroit, I would regularly pass through Times Square and the grand building Hearst had built and later sold to* The Detroit News. *Then, like much of old Detroit, it was demolished.*

CODA

Just for fun
I put mother on my back
yet she weighed so
little. I began crying
and could not walk three steps.
Ishikawa Takuboku (1908)

———⚬⚬⚬———

Ferne was my first love. For fifty-plus years I have carried her around with me, trying to keep her alive, a bundle of emotions and memories: her love, disappointment, guilt, fear and her fragility. If she had lived until I was an adult, perhaps I would have come to know her as a particular person in the world, as Ferne Hostetter. Losing her at eleven left me with a child's adoring memory. I've done all that I could with this project to know her better by dwelling on her life and times and recreating her life inside the context in which she lived.

———⚬⚬⚬———

Ferne prepared us for her death the best she could, but after she died our lives changed radically. Bob loved us, but his love, like his emotions, was mostly held back, and our stepmother Eugenia was nothing like Ferne. For me it was as if a big machine had sucked away the love and left behind chaos, despair and discipline. At first I planned to run away to Gramma Hattie's house, but after she died I counted the days in a calendar until I could leave and, at 18, I ran away with a boyfriend; my brother briefly ran away while in high school, and then after graduation he went to Vietnam; Ginny married young; and Patti went as far away to college as she could. Still, because of the loving responsible ground Ferne and Bob had provided, we all grew up to be caring, responsible, educated adults, now with five children between us and six grandchildren.

———⚬⚬⚬———

An hour after my daughter Linnée was born in 1974, I remember carrying her through the hallway toward the living room; I was wearing an old terrycloth bathrobe just like the one my mother had worn. My hair was matted against the side of my face. Suddenly I felt my mother's presence, so strongly. It was as if I were both Ferne and the baby, and we were starting over. "Now you are a mother," I heard her say. "What's important is not the love you receive, but the love you give. That will stay with you and the one you love forever."

My sister Ginny once told me a story about a friend of hers, Jan, who used to be a barmaid at the Drop Inn Bar on Mack Avenue. In June 1986 Ginny had a party at her house; Jan was there and so was my father. Jan called Ginny aside and whispered, "I know your father. He used to come into the Drop Inn Bar where I was bartending. It was about six years ago. A couple of times a week he would stop in there and sit in the same chair at the same table. He'd have two beers and then leave. He didn't talk to anyone. Then one day I sat down next to him and asked him why he never talked to anyone. He said, 'I met the love of my life in this bar at this table. We had four children together.' He looked away. 'Then, she died.'"

LIKE A STAIRWAY

The postman pauses in front of the house—big bushy shrubs, a spindly young maple tree, white curtains half opened, peeling grey paint, a wooden screen door and then a darker solid door with a little window. He stands still, searching through his bag and shuffling a few papers and then he passes by, heading up the street. But we cross the street and slip inside the front door, making a sharp left at the foot of the stairs, passing by a Victorian style chair, covered with a dull gold cloth, bronze tacks, the wooden trim painted dark brown, and then a picture window looking out on a young maple and another grey cinderblock house. To the right, a footstool with chipped grey paint, a big brown stuffed chair and a thin man with large ears, sound asleep, his shirt unbuttoned and his armpits covered with perspiration. A checkered tie flops over the arm of the chair and half a pack of Pall Malls rests on the table. A fly buzzes around him. He reaches up and brushes it off his cheek, and then he promptly falls back asleep. Across from him a low green scratchy couch and an end table. Sit down for a moment. The ashtrays are overflowing. In the corner there is a closet with a low rod for the young children and a higher one for the adults. A TV set and a turntable in a cabinet, painted with a mahogany stain. Three ceramic ducks are flying over the archway to the stairs, first the father, then the mother, then the baby.

A sculpted beige carpet leads into a hallway and a bedroom door with yesterday's clothes on a hook and, to the right, a dresser cluttered with loose change and an ashtray. On the pale green wall, two painted girls, light skinned and blonde on a turquoise background, tiny yellow flowers laced in their hair. A low dresser with a mirror, a lace doily, hairpins, a white jewelry box and another pack of cigarettes in a brown paper bag. A wicker rocking chair piled with clothes. And a thin woman asleep in the bed, the blankets rumpled, her head falling back into the pillow like a stairway falling down, down, and then the sound of her almost non-existent breath, her young mouth open, behind her a print of Jesus with the little children. The branches of a lilac bush tap against the window, and the woman reaches up and pulls the covers over her shoulders.

Turn around and cut diagonally across the house into the kitchen, painted a deep yellow. An old oak table and four chairs. Two rows of cupboards with cans of soup and vegetables, and stacks of folded bags. A black wall phone in the corner above the milk box, a glass ashtray with cigarette butts covered with red lipstick, an address book on the counter, a white beagle curled up in a warm spot in the corner, and a child in a diaper dropping clothespins inside the furnace door, the rhythm right in tune with the dog's tail thumping and the washer splashing. Out in back, a young girl, maybe ten years old, takes clothes off the line, white sheets in the wind, and the young branches of a pear tree in the beginning stages of hibernation. A newspaper blows across the yard, resting temporarily at the base of the stairs of another grey cinderblock house.

When the dog turns over, the refrigerator starts to hum and the washer goes into spin. The golden rule is pinned above the door. Go back through the kitchen, past the sleeping man into the hallway. Follow the sound of a ball bouncing against a wall. Red plaid pajamas on the floor, a dresser with a fox hunt on top, three ceramic spaniels and a horse. In the bookshelf, fairy tales, hobby books, *Great Expectations* and the *Favorite Poems of Longfellow*. Big yellow sunflowers on the quilt, a toy fire engine in the corner, and the lone yellow ranger riding his horse across the curtains. The little boy bounces his ball at the wall, boing, back again to the bed, boing, hit a book, back again. Shut the door quietly.

In the bathroom, there's a white sink with pink tiles, water is running, a scale behind the door, four toothbrushes in a ceramic holder, and a girl sitting on the toilet, chanting, I'm three, I'm four, I'm free. Her feet are dangling over the edge. Behind her on the wall is a medicine cabinet with a shaving mug, Old Spice, a whisker brush, on the wall a razor, an extra bar of soap, Pepto Bismol, and a tube of toothpaste. A big yellow wicker hamper overflowing with clothes, a scale, a bathtub with three pink rags folded into squares and placed into each corner. The little girl pulls up the stool and climbs on top of a telephone book. Water starts to overflow.

Remember you are not the babysitter. You are not the mother. You are just passing through. Go back through the living room past the migrating ducks and up the staircase, past this and that stashed on shelves—a music box, an old doll, and a green library book. Under the rafters, a closet, crawl-through attic space, recessed dressers, half-built walls, and three beds. A little girl sits on her bed, cross-legged, carefully cutting up Dick and Jane and Sally. Their yellow hair removed, fluttering to the floor, little bits of this and that, a dog, a mother, something is starting to happen. The wind gushes into the room blowing papers all around. A comet, an eclipse, perhaps some star in the evening. A dusty cabinet full of books, an old set of rarely opened Harvard Classics and a worn collection of Mark Twain novels. An old painted dressing table with a cloudy mirror. Behind the walls, throw everything, all the scraps, throw the evidence into the darkness behind the walls. Then stand here, right here and look out the window, a panoramic daytime view of the sky and the yellow maple and oak trees, bare branches, and rows of houses, a block-by-block grid growing into the country.

Sometimes when I was a child and sound asleep, I'd climb up on the ledge, survey the horizon and then I'd jump out the window with my book under my arm—my skirt opening like a parachute, I'd land in the back seat of a black Chevy convertible. I remember looking back at the house the last time, at the lilac bush and the grey walls. My driver was wearing a black leather jacket, his hair was slicked back—he made a fast u turn at the corner, screeching and then he took me far away—never to return—into the city of dark alleys and hidden stars.

Barbara Henning, "Like a Stairway," *A Swift Passage* (2013); *Just Like That* (2018); *Jacket* (#35, 2008).

CITATIONS

Austin, Dan. "Vanity Ballroom." *HistoricDetroit.org*, 13 Aug 2017, http://historicdetroit.org/building/vanity-ballroom/. Accessed 7 Apr 2021.

Bahktin, Mikhail. "From Notes Made in 1970-71." *Speech Genres and Other Late Essays*, edited by Caryl Emerson and Michael Holquist, translated by Vern W. McGree, University of Texas Press, 1986, p. 138.

Bakke, Marvel. "World War II & Sergeant Marvel H. Bakke: A Company. 377th, 95th Infantry Division." A packet of documents and descriptions of Marvel Bakke's experience as a prisoner of war in Germany. He put this packet together and gave a copy to Barbara Henning in 2008.

Blakemore, Erin. "Why Many Women Were Banned from Working During the Great Depression: With Millions Unable to Find Unemployment, Working Wives Became Scapegoats." *History Stories*, https://www.history.com/news/great-depression-married-women-employment. Accessed 7 Apr 2021.

Bouston, Leah Platt. "Was Postwar Suburbanization 'White Flight'? Evidence from the Black Migration." *The Quarterly Journal of Economics*, vol. 125, Feb 2010, 417-443, https://doi.org/10.1162/qjec.2010.125.1.417. Accessed 7 Apr 2021.

Cohen, Adam. *Nothing to Fear: FDR's Inner Circle and the Hundred Days that Created Modern America*. Penguin, 2009, p. 31. Rpt. from Paul Dickson and Thomas B. Allen. *The Bonus Army: An American Epic*. Walker and Company, 2004, pp. 153-83, 193.

Craig, Barry. "The Case of the Protection Racket." *Barry Craig, Confidential Investigator*. NBC, Radio, Comic Web Old Time Radio. Original Airdate 24 Oct 1951, https://www.youtube.com/watch?v=gHrJxvo9FMo. Accessed 7 Apr 2021.

Detroit Free Press. Clippings from 1931, 1932, 1935, 1937, 1939, 1941, 1942, 1945, 1946, 1948, 1949, 1950, 1954 1955 and 1957. For more specifics, see particular clippings and captions.

Detroit Times. Clippings from each year, 1921-1960. For more specifics, see particular clippings and captions.

Eisenhower, Dwight David. "The Chance for Peace." Speech to the American Society of Newspaper Editors" (16 April 1953), *Social Justice Speeches*, http://www.edchange.org/multicultural/speeches/ike_chance_for_peace. html. Accessed 7 April 2021.

Ferman, Louis A. *Death of a Newspaper: The Story of the* Detroit Times: *A Study of Job Dislocation Among Newspaper Workers in a Depressed Labor Market*. The W.E. Upjohn Institute for Employment Research, 1963, pp. 9, 10.

Gordon, Colin. "The Legacy of Taft-Hartley." *Jacobin Magazine*, 19 Dec 2017, https://jacobinmag.com/2017/12/taft-hartley-unions-right-to-work. Accessed 7 April 2021.

Henning, Barbara. "Like a Stairway." *A Swift Passage*, Quale Press, 2013; *Just Like That*, Spuyten Duyvil, 2018; *Jacket*, vol. 35, 2008.

Jackson, Kenneth T. *Crabrass Frontier: The Suburbanization of the United States*. Oxford Univ. Press, 1985, pp. 244, 267.

Langevelde, Dirk. "Charles E. Bowles: Another Mayoral Klandidate." *The Downfall Dictionary: Cataloging the Past Political Scandals of the United States*, 4 Nov 2009, http://downfalldictionary.blogspot.com/2009/11/charles-e-bowles-another-mayoral.html. Accessed 7 April 2021.

Lewis, Fulton, Jr. "Mutual Network News" (April 12, 1945). *Radio Days*, http://www.otr.com/lewis.html. Accessed 7 Apr 2021.

Mintz, Steven and Susan Kellogg. *Domestic Revolutions: A Social History of American Family Life*. Free Press, 1988, pp. 153-154, 171.

Naldrett, Alan. "The Algonac Transit Company and the Fair Haven Wooden Railroad." *The Voice: Serving Northern Macomb & St. Clair Counties*, 17 Nov 2015, https://www.voicenews.com/life/the-algonac-transit-company-and-the-fair-haven-wooden-railroad/article_3 8a319c7-1575-5310-a291-55d57fa8c765.html. Accessed 7 April 2021.

O'Hara, Frank. *Lunch Poems*. City Lights, 1964.

"Progressive Party, 1948." *Encyclopedia.com*. The Gale Group, Inc., 2003, https://www.encyclopedia.com/history/dictionaries-thesauruses-pictures-and-press-releases/progressive-party-1948. Accessed 7 April 2021.

Roosevelt, Eleanor. "Pearl Harbor Radio Address" (7 Dec 1941), https://www.youtube.com/watch?v=4unsg4W0JTM. Accessed 7 April 2021.

"Sojourner Truth Housing Project." *Detroit: The History and Future of the Motor City,* http://www.detroit1701.org/Sojourner%20Truth%20Housing%20Project.html. Accessed 7 April 2021.

Smith, Paul W., Interviewer and Host. "Mayor Mike Duggan Keynote Address." *WJR NewsTalk,* 760 AM, 31 May 2017, https://www.youtube.com/watch?v=PrPAcQaYISg. Accessed 7 April 2021.

South Macomb News. Clippings from 1949, 1952, 1953 and 1958. For more specifics, see particular clippings and captions.

Stanton, Tom. *Terror in the City of Champions: Murder, Baseball and the Secret Society that Shocked Depression-Era Detroit.* Lyons Press, 2016, pp. 25, 28, 36, 95.

Stark, George W. "Joseph Grundy: Town Talk—By Stark." *Detroit News,* 1 Apr 1944.

Takuboku, Ishikawa. "Just for Fun," 1908.

"The Only Live News Report from the Attack on Pearl Harbor" (7 Dec 1941, NBC Radio Affiliate, Honolulu). *Smithsonian Magazine,* https://www.smithsonianmag.com/videos/category/history/the-only-live-news-report-from-the-attack-on_1/. Accessed 7 April 2021.

"The Truman Doctrine." "The Learning Network: Teaching & Learning." *The New York Times,* 12 Mar 2012, https://learning.blogs.nytimes.com/2012/03/12/march-12-1947-truman-doctrine-announced/. Accessed 7 April 2021.

Williams, Jeremy. *Detroit: The Black Bottom Community*. Images of America Series, Arcadia Publishing, 2009, p. 102.

"World War II GI Bill." *History.com*, https://www.history.com/topics/world-war-ii/gi-bill. Accessed 7 April 2021.

OTHER SOURCES

Bauder, Ginny. "Four Family Super 8 films," 1954-1963.

Bjorn, Lars with Jim Gallert. *Before Motown: A History of Jazz in Detroit: 1920-1960.* Univ. of Michigan Press, 2003.

Boyd, Herb. *Black Detroit; A People's History of Self-Determination*. Harper-Collins, 2017.

Cohen, Adam. *Nothing to Fear: FDR's Inner Circle and the Hundred Days That Created Modern America*. Penguin, 2009.

Cohen, Lawrence H. "Evolution of the Concept and Practice of Mitral Valve Repair." *Annals of Cardiothoracic Surgery*, vol. 4, no. 4, July 2015, http://www.annalscts.com/article/view/6447/7693. Accessed 7 Apr 2021.

"Dedicated to Documenting the Past, Present and Future of the City of Detroit." *Detroiturbex.com,* 2013, www.detroiturbex.com. Accessed 7 Apr 2021.

de Santis, Vincent P. "Eisenhower Revisionism." *The Review of Politics*, vol. 38, no. 2, Apr 1976, pp. 190-207.

Gonyeau, Rich. "From Riches to Rages: The Roaring Twenties in the Bay. *The Voice News,* Clinton Township, 2 May 2014, http://www.voicenews.com/opinion/from-riches-to-rags-the-roaring-twenties-in-the-bay/article_f090c69e-1141-543d-b35e-911dbfd56b84.html. Accessed 7 Apr 2021.

Hearst, William Randolph Jr. (With Jack Casserly). *The Hearsts: Father and Son*, Robert Rinehart, 1993.

Holmes, Sherlock. *The Hound of the Baskervilles*, 1939; *Sherlock Holmes and the Voice of Terror*, 1942.

Hyman, Sidney. "Absorbing Study of Popularity: Eisenhower's Personal Appeal." *Times Magazine*, 24 July 1960, pp. 7, 24-25.

Jouan, Jerome. "Mitral Valve Repair Over Five Decades." *Annals of Cardio-thoracic Surgery*, vol. 4, no. 4, July 2015, http://www.annalscts.com/article/view/6825/html. Accessed 7 Apr 2021.

Mirel, Jeffrey. *The Rise and Fall of an Urban School System: Detroit 1907-1981*, 2nd Edition, Univ. of Michigan Press, 1999.

Proctor, Ben. *William Randolph Hearst: The Later Years, 1911-1951*. Oxford Univ Press, 2007

Research Starters: "The Draft and WWII." The National WWII Museum. New Orleans. 16 July 2017, https://www.nationalww2museum.org/students-teachers/student-resources/research-starters/draft-and-wwii. Accessed 7 Apr 2021.

Smith, Jean Edward. *Eisenhower in War and Peace*, Random House, 2012.

United States Army, "377th Infantry Regiment." *World War Regimental Histories*, 56. 1946.

Wells, Orson. *Citizen Kane*, 1941.

"William Randolph Hearst." *Biography.com*, https://www.biography.com/media-figure/william-randolph-hearst. Accessed 7 April 2021.

Zacharias, Patricia. "When Detroit Danced to the Big Bands." *The Detroit News*, 20 Jan 2002.

PHOTOGRAPHS*

p. 18 (Ch. 2). "Lake St. Clair smugglers falling through the ice" (27822). Walter Reuther Library, Archive of Labor and Urban Affairs, Wayne State University, Detroit, http://reuther.wayne.edu/node/8241. Accessed 7 Apr 2021.

p. 35 (Ch. 3). Photo of bonus army camp. Photo by Theodor Horydczak, Library of Congress, July 1932, Underwood Archives, Zinn Education Project, https://www.zinnedproject.org/materials/bonus-army. Accessed 7 Apr 2021.

p. 36 (Ch. 3). "Unemployed, single women protesting the job placement of married women before themselves at the Emergency Relief Administration headquarters in Boston, Massachusetts." *History.com*, Bettmann Archive, https://www.history.com/news/great-depression-married-women-employment. Accessed 7 Apr 2021.

p. 42 (Ch. 3). "People milling about outside a bank that closed ca. 1933." National Archives Photo, https://www.pinterest.com/pin/503418064574725902/. Accessed 7 Apr 2021.

p. 64 (Ch 4). Cozy Corner ad. *A History of Jazz in Detroit: Before Motown, 1920-1960*. Univ of Michigan Press, 2001, p. 43. (Rpt. from *Detroit Free Press*, 23 Sept 1939).

p. 64 (Ch. 4). "It Can't Happen Here (by Lewis Sinclair)," WPA Poster, 27 Oct 1936. United States Library of Congress's Prints and Photographs division, http://loc.gov/pictures/resource/cph.3b48821/. Accessed 7 Apr 2021.

p. 88 (Ch. 6). Vanity Ballroom photo (1929). *Geocaching History Quest*, https://www.geocaching.com/geocache/GC45W7G_ghq-come-dancing-the-vanity-ballroom. Accessed 7 Apr 2021.

p. 144 (Ch. 9). "Light a Lucky and you'll never miss sweets that make you fat." Photo widely available online, http://tobacco.stanford.edu/tobacco_web/

images/tobacco_ads/keeps_you_slim/sweet/large/sweet_24.jpg. Accessed 7 Apr 2021.

p. 158 (Ch. 11). "Mr. President Please Veto." Caption: "Labor leader David Dubinsky gives a speech against the Taft-Hartley bill on May 4, 1947. Kheel Center / Flickr."

Rpt. at *https://jacobinmag.com/2017/12/taft-hartley-unions-right-to-work*. Accessed 7 Apr 2021.

p. 165 (Ch. 11). Algonac Inn postcard. The L.L Cook Co. Milwaukee, Wisc. (Postcard).

p. 222 (Ch. 14). "Presidents, Eisenhower, Miriani, Detroit, 1958 (28813)." *The Spirit of Detroit*, photo by Tony Spina, Walter Reuther Library, http://reuther.wayne.edu/node/9155. Accessed 7 Apr 2021.

p. 232 (Ch. 15). Photo of Dorothy Kilgallen. *Old Time Radio Catalog*, https://www.otrcat.com/p/dorothy-kilgallen, photo widely available online. Accessed 7 Apr 2021.

p. 241 (Ch. 15). Women at Oliveti typewriter. "What a Great Typewriter." *Print*, 31 Dec 2012, http://www.printmag.com/imprint/what-a-great-type-writer/. Accessed 7 Apr 2021.

p. 261 (Ch. 15). Nikita Kruschev and Richard Nixon. Photo by Sandy Isenstadt, 24 July 1959. Rpt. in *Cabinet Magazine,* Summer 2007, http://www.cabinetmagazine.org/issues/26/isenstadt.php. Accessed 7 Apr 2021.

p. 271 (Ch. 15). Photo of Detroit Times Building. *Detroit Times—Old Photos*, the *Detroit Free Press* Archive, http://historicdetroit.org/galleries/detroit-times-old-photos/. Accessed 7 Apr 2021.

*Most of the family snapshots were taken by Ferne, Bob or other family members.

ACKNOWLEDGMENTS

Thanks to the following people for responding to early manuscripts of *Ferne*: Suzanne Allen, Nancy Arann, Jim Feast, Johnny Hartigan, Patti Henning, Bob Henning, Jessica Holburn, Esther Hyneman, Kim Lyons, Harryette Mullen, Maureen Owen, Michah Saperstein and David Wilk. Thanks to my Aunt Jeane who for so many years told me stories about my mother; and thanks to other family members—Linda Matthew, Ginny Brzezinski, Diane Hamilton, Karen Romaine, Patricia Hostetter, Terry Hostetter, Jamie Pomante, Richard Spires, Carol Nichols and Johnny Wittenberg—for sharing photos and stories. A special thanks to my children, Linnée and Michah, for their love. And thanks to Lewis Warsh for 30 plus years of encouragement; I wish you were here to see the book, dear friend.

Thanks to my distant cousin, Wayne Till, for his help with ancestry research, and thanks to the librarians for research and help with microfilm searches: Port Huron (Janet Curtis), Mt. Clemens, Michigan State Archives in Lansing, and the Detroit Public Library (Suzanne Stocking). Thanks to the poets, HR Hegnauer for designing the book, and Esther Hyneman, Annabel Lee and Chris Tysh for proofreading. Thanks to Chris Tysh and Rebecca Mazzei for publishing "Chapter Five" in *Three Fold Detroit*. And finally, thanks to Tod Thilleman for pubishing *Ferne, A Detroit Story*.

BARBARA HENNING is the author of four novels and eight collections of poetry, as well as many chapbooks and essays. Her most recent books are a novel, *Just Like That* (Spuyten Duyvil 2018); poetry collections, *Digigram* (United Artist Books, 2020) and *A Day Like Today* (Negative Capability Press 2015); and *Prompt Book: Experiments for Writing Poetry and Fiction* (Spuyten Duyvil 2020). Barbara has taught for Wayne State University, Naropa University and Long Island University where she is Professor Emerita. Born in Detroit, she presently lives in Brooklyn. More information is available on her website www.barbarahenning.com.

Made in the USA
Middletown, DE
18 April 2022

64460443R00190